Teaching 2: Cognitive Learning and Instruction

Wesley C. Becker

Professor of Special Education   University of Oregon

Siegfried Engelmann

Professor of Special Education   University of Oregon

Don R. Thomas

Director Minnesota Learning Center   Brainerd State Hospital

A Modular Revision of
Teaching: A Course in Applied Psychology

S R A

Science Research Associates
Chicago Palo Alto Toronto Hen

A subsidiary of IBM

**To our children—
who are also teachers**

Library of Congress Cataloging in Publication Data

Becker, Wesley C   1928–
   Teaching 2: cognitive learning and instruction.

   Bibliography: p.
   Includes index.
   1. Educational psychology. I. Engelmann, Siegfried,
joint author. II. Thomas, Donald R., joint author. III.
Title. [DNLM: 1. Cognition—Programmed texts. 2.
Learning—Programmed texts. 3. Psychology,
Educational—Programmed texts. 4. Teaching-
—Programmed texts. LB1051 B396t[
LB1051.B2986   371.1'02   75-5563
ISBN 0-574-18030-3

This is a revised, three-part edition of
Teaching: A Course in Applied Psychology, © 1971.

contents

preface

New technologies of teaching are being fashioned from the growing knowledge of the events that influence learning. This course aims to teach principles underlying new teaching technologies, and at the same time to teach experienced and future teachers *what they need to do* to be better teachers. Our primary goal is to improve the practice of teaching rather than to enable the student to talk about various theories of learning.

In designing this course, we have attempted to make use of the principles we are trying to teach. Our field tests have convinced us that the student who approaches these materials with at least a modest level of diligence will come away with new skills that will be of value throughout his or her professional career. Many of you, we hope, will come away from this course as better persons because you will have learned how to help others become more capable and loving persons.

This modular edition of *Teaching* has been completely revised, updated, reorganized, and extended to cover the topic of *evaluation*. It is presented in three volumes.

Volume 1 focuses on the use of behavior principles in *classroom management*. It deals with principles and procedures underlying effective social development and the use of positive motivational methods with children and young adults.

Volume 1 is a behavior-modification primer for the teacher. Some teachers view behavior modification simply as tricks to get children to behave and make the teacher's life less troublesome. This is far from the case. Behavior modification is simply effective education. It is the systematic use of learning principles to accomplish our goals for children. From the beginning of this venture, we wish to emphasize that the primary goal of teaching is the induction of knowledge and skills that will enable a person to achieve a fuller life in our society. Even though this text at times focuses on the elimination of problem behavior, keep in mind that teaching is still the primary goal.

Volume 2 in this series shifts to an analysis of *instruction*. It concerns itself with the essential components of effective instruction, with the requirements for teaching a general case, with strategies for instructional programing, and with applications of these ideas to teaching concepts, operations, and intelligent problem-solving skills. There is also a concern with the problems of remedial and special instruction.

In volume 3, the problem of *evaluation* for and by the classroom teacher is examined with the goal of improving the teacher's skills in selection of programs and procedures, in placing and monitoring students, and in evaluating whether the instructional goals are in fact met. Basic statistical concepts helpful in evaluation are introduced and taught as needed through programed practice. Diagnostic, criterion-referenced, and norm-referenced testing are examined. The traditional concepts of aptitude and ability are re-examined. A logic for program evaluation is provided.

It is the intent of the authors to provide the teacher through these three volumes with a modern, up-to-date knowledge of, as Sidney Bijou put it, "What psychology has to offer education now."

We wish to give special thanks to Jeanne Schultz for her careful and dedicated work in preparing this revised manuscript.

to the instructor: course organization

This course is designed to operate with minimal lectures. Lectures are especially helpful preceding units 1, 2, 4, 5, and 9. The *Instructor's Manual* that accompanies this text makes it possible for the instructor to use a variety of procedures. The following suggestions represent teaching formats that have been found to be effective:

Self-Paced Progress

Each student reads a unit, does the exercises, checks his own exercises, goes over the discussion questions, and then is checked out by another student who has already passed that unit. In conducting the checkout, the examining student uses the Instructors Manual as a source of questions and criteria for acceptable responses. Tests are taken as scheduled.

Leader-Paced Progress, Students as Group Leaders

In this course format, each student reads the assigned unit, completes his exercises and checks them, and prepares for the group session, being sure he can answer each of the discussion questions. At the group session, each student is asked to write out answers to two of the questions selected by the instructor. Papers are turned in for credit. Then the instructor appoints one-fourth of the class to be group leaders for that session. Small groups of four are formed. Each group leader then uses the Instructors Manual to take the other three students through the objects of the unit. The leader asks questions from the manual and the students take turns answering. The leader and the group members help when there are mistakes or omissions.

Leader-Paced Progress, Former Students as Group Leaders

In this format there is an instructor and group leader for each ten students. The students do a lesson, complete the exercises, and check their answers prior to the group discussion session. The group leaders have the only available Instructors Manuals. At the group sessions, group members are asked in turn to respond to questions. The whole group writes answers to two questions each session, or takes a ten-minute quiz at each lecture session. Remedial assignments are made when performance is not adequate.

Each of these course organization formats attempts to provide appropriate consequences for appropriate study behavior and thereby increase the chances of each student being successful in mastering the objectives of the course. Whatever procedures are used in your course, keep in mind that *knowing* is not *doing*. Aim for changes in what students do as well as what they say.

to the student: how to use this text

Our experience suggests that you will gain the most from this text if you follow these steps.

1 Read a unit.

2 Do the self-test. If you miss 0 or 1 item, skip the programed practice exercise and do the other exercises and discussion questions. If you make more than one error, do the section called programed practice.

3 When an item gives you trouble, return to the text to study the problem in context.

4 Calculate the percentage of items correct and record it for each programed practice exercise.

5 If a score on a programed practice exercise is above 90 percent, go on to the discussion questions and other exercises. If a score is much below 90 percent, review the unit before going on to the discussion questions.

6 In answering the discussion questions, be prepared to give your answers orally or in writing. The questions serve as a basis for discussion in the group sessions.

Acknowledgments

Pp. 2–3: From *The Teacher's Guide to Open Education* by L. S. Stephens. Reprinted by permission.

P. 7: From "Computerized Instruction and the Learning Process," by R. C. Atkinson, in *American Psychologist*, vol. 23, 1968, pp. 225–39. Copyright 1968 by the American Psychological Association. Reprinted by permission.

Pp. 9–10: From "Individually Prescribed Instruction," by R. G. Scanlon, in *An Empirical Basis for Change in Education*, W. C. Becker, ed. Reprinted by permission of the author.

P. 12: From *Distar® Reading Level I* by Siegfried Engelmann and Elaine Bruner. © 1969, Science Research Associates, Inc. Used by permission of the publisher.

Pp. 98–100: From *Distar® Arithmetic III* by Siegfried Engelmann and Doug Carnine. © 1972, Science Research Associates, Inc. Used by permission of the publisher.

Pp. 101–7: From *Distar® Reading Level III* by Siegfried Engelmann and Susan Stearns. © 1973, Science Research Associates, Inc. Used by permission of the publisher.

Pp. 162, 164: From *Distar® Language Level I* by Siegfried Engelmann, Jean Osborn, and Therese Engelmann. © 1969, Science Research Associates, Inc. Used by permission of the publisher.

P. 165: From *Distar® Reading Level I, Related Skills Book* by Siegfried Engelmann and Elaine Bruner. © 1969, Science Research Associates, Inc. Used by permission of the publisher.

P. 168: From *Distar® Reading I*, Revised by Siegfried Engelmann and Elaine Bruner. © 1974, Science Research Associates, Inc. Used by permission.

Pp. 193–95: From *Stanford-Binet Intelligence Scale Form L-M*. Copyright © 1973 and 1960 by Houghton Mifflin Company. Copyright © 1937 by Lewis M. Terman and Maud A. Merrill. Reproduced by permission.

P. 203: Reprinted from *Disadvantaged Child, Vol. 3: Compensatory Education: A National Debate*, J. Hellmuth, ed., New York: Brunner/Mazel, 1970.

P. 206: From an unpublished paper by Don Bushnell. Reprinted by permission of the author.

P. 217: From *The Origins of Intelligence in Children* by J. Piaget. Reprinted by permission of International Universities Press, Inc.

P. 218: From *Judgment and Reasoning in the Child* by J. Piaget. Reprinted by permission of Humanities Press, Inc. New Jersey.

P. 222: From *The Developmental Psychology of Jean Piaget* by J. H. Flavell. Reprinted by permission of the author and Van Nostrand Co.

P. 223: From *The Child's Conception of Space* by J. Piaget and B. Inhelder. Reprinted by permission of Humanities Press, Inc., New Jersey.

unit 1

What Is Instruction?

objectives

When you complete this unit you should be able to—

1 Name the procedures essential to instruction.
2 Describe the basic characteristics of five different models of instruction and indicate the strengths and weaknesses of each.
3 Suggest which models of instruction may be more appropriate at different educational levels.

lesson

In volume 1 of this series, we developed procedures for motivating children, organizing for instruction, and teaching appropriate study and social skills. In this volume, the focus shifts to the teaching of intellectual skills. With the addition of a few new procedures, the principles developed in volume 1 can be applied to instruction in *intellectual* or *cognitive competencies*.

Instruction is a set of procedures for producing a change in behavior (learning) toward a prestated objective. Instruction can take many forms as long as it meets certain essential requirements. In a review of "Historic Exemplars of Teaching Method," Professor Broudy of the University of Illinois found the common procedures essential in instruction to be: (1) getting classroom control, (2) presentation of the learning task, (3) inducement of trial responses, (4) correction of trial responses, and (5) institution of test trials for evaluation.[1] This historic analysis of teaching identifies most of the essential procedures isolated by modern-day behavioral analysis, except the *reinforcement* of correct responses. Each of Broudy's procedures (plus reinforcement) is likely to be found in any effective teaching system. That is, an effective instructional system must provide:

1

1 Procedures for motivating the students and *securing attention* to the task being taught.
2 Procedures for presenting the tasks to be learned, presenting stimuli, and showing the response requirements of the task. That is, a *vehicle of instruction* must be present.
3 Procedures for *securing responses* from the students to see if the tasks have been learned.
4 Procedures for *reinforcing correct responses* and *correcting mistakes*.
5 Procedures for the longer-term *evaluation of mastery*, usually within the context of a *set of related tasks* that include the one just taught.

Models of Instruction

Let us examine a few widely divergent models of instruction to see how they provide for (or fail to provide for) the essential procedures of effective instruction. We will look at the open classroom, traditional large-group lecture methods, computer-controlled instruction, individually prescribed instruction, Distar*, and small-group direct instruction. Our goal is not an exhaustive coverage of models of instruction, but rather to illustrate how to analyze a model in relation to the procedures essential to instruction aimed at preset objectives.

The Open Classroom

A proponent of open education might object that the procedures for effective instruction given above are not appropriately applied to an open classroom since the objectives in open classrooms are to a large extent set by the children rather than the teacher. To be sure, there are some extreme positions in which no formal goals are stated, but in most open classrooms there are many objectives focusing, first, on the *process of learning* (teaching children how to learn) rather than on the content of a subject area. Second, there usually are definite minimal preset goals in basic skills relating to written and oral language. Lillian Stephens sees fifteen characteristics in the basic model of open classrooms as they are developing in the United States today.[2] These characteristics are:

1 A minimum of lessons for the whole class; most instruction geared to small groups or individuals.
2 A variety of activities progressing simultaneously.
3 Flexible scheduling, so that children can engage in different activities for varying periods of time.
4 An environment rich in materials, both commercial and homemade.
5 Freedom for children to move about, converse, work together, and seek help from one another.
6 Opportunities for children to make decisions about their work and to develop responsibility for setting and meeting their educational goals.

---

*Distar is the registered trademark of the Distar Instructional System, published by Science Research Associates.

7   Lack of rigid, prescribed curriculum and provision for children to investigate matters of concern to them.
8   Some integration of the curriculum, eliminating isolated teaching of each subject.
9   Emphasis on experimentation and involvement with materials.
10   Flexible learning groups formed around interests, as well as academic needs, and organized by both pupils and teachers.
11   An atmosphere of trust, acceptance of children, and respect for their diversity.
12   Attention to individual intellectual, emotional, physical, and social needs.
13   Creative activities valued as part of the curriculum.
14   A minimum of grading and marking.
15   Honest and open relationships between teacher and pupil and between pupil and pupil; teacher avoidance of exploiting authority.

In an open classroom, the space is divided into activity centers, and materials appropriate to each center are located there. The environment is planned to support learning just as carefully as a daily lesson plan might be (see figure 1.1). To manage the children in an open setting, agreements are often written on a daily or weekly basis. The agreements, which are usually written by the students, specify the tasks to be completed in the period of time specified. The teacher discusses the feasibility of the proposal and signs it if she approves. Students often decide what tasks they wish to do in the area of reading or math, but sometimes teachers make general assignments. Logistical problems can be avoided by having students sign up for activity centers that will hold only a few students. Although progress records are kept, formal

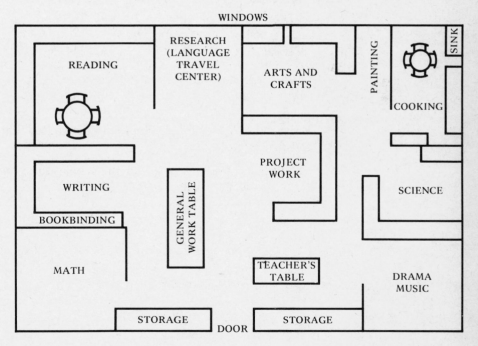

Figure 1.1   Sample room arrangement: Large room[3]

evaluations in the sense of grades are minimized in the open classroom. Individual conferences may be held to discuss progress in reading or math or some other skill area.

Properly managed, the open classroom can be a friendly, happy place for both teacher and student, but how does it stand up as a model of effective instruction?

1. *Motivation and attention.* Having choices among multiple activities, options within a focused topic area, and much material with which to interact, most children will find activities to interest them in an open classroom. The use of agreements can further aid motivation and attention by structuring what is to be done.

2. *Vehicle of instruction.* The open classroom may use many vehicles of instruction: audiovisual aids, teaching machines, projects, trips, peer tutoring, small-group teacher instruction, and individualized teacher instruction. A great burden of expertise and judgment is placed on the teacher, since she may be working with twenty-five children in eight subject areas each day, and each child might be working on separate skills. How the teacher would have the necessary feedback from each child, the knowledge of programs to know just what to do next, and the time to prepare for and react to each child is difficult to see. These factors are especially critical at beginning skills levels where the children have not yet acquired reading, language, writing, and self-study skills. Also the situation would be difficult for the slow learner, who might require ten times as much instruction as a faster learner.

3-4. *Securing responses, reinforcement, and corrections.* Work folders, project reports, self-checking systems, and teacher conferences to review progress (in a diagnostic sense) can all provide feedback to the teacher on what is being learned. Since the primary concern is often not on content *per se*, but on "learning to learn," just the fact that new learning is going on is evidence that the system works. A lack of self-directed learning for a given child would imply that correction procedures were needed. A problem for the open classroom is a lack of specification of what the "learning to learn" objectives are and therefore a lack of precise test procedures for knowing whether they have been achieved or whether it is time to work on new objectives. Another problem is the likely delay between performance and feedback.

5. *Evaluation of mastery.* This is de-emphasized for basic skills, but should be going on informally for "learning to learn" and "creative skills." Again, the lack of specific criteria makes evaluation difficult. It might be easy for the teacher to think all is going well when in fact there is little progress toward objectives.

As we have suggested in examples given in volume 1, knowledge of behavior can be used to support effective learning in an open setting. In our opinion, this is especially so after students have mastered basic skills in reading, language, and math, and have learned a variety of study skills. An open learning framework might best be seen as a set of procedures to work toward as basic skills develop.

Proponents of the open classroom often hold a number of misconceptions about children and the learning process, and use them to rationalize procedures. For example, here are some "beliefs about learning" listed by Stephens: learning is purposive; learning is self-motivated; learning requires that the child be the director, not the receiver; learning requires that material be appropriate to the child's level of development.

Although some of these statements seem to align with teacher experience, the current evidence from the experimental analysis of behavior does not support them.* Purposive explanations of behavior are logically in error because causes of behavior cannot occur *after* the behavior. Motivation has been shown to be a function of the consequences of behavior, so there is no longer a need for the mystique associated with "self-motivation." That the child *must* be the director of the learning cannot be true, since teacher-directed instruction works. The notion that "the learning material must be appropriate to a child's level of development" is part of a group of incorrect implications drawn from the work of Jean Piaget. On the basis of cross-sectional research by Piaget, stages of intellectual development are defined, then said to limit what can be taught and when. In cross-sectional research, groups of children at different age levels are studied at one point in time. No attempt is made to study different methods of teaching and their effects on later teaching. In fact, Piaget is not concerned with teaching methods. To determine what can be taught, it is necessary to use a design in which different teaching procedures are evaluated over time with the same types of children. A more careful examination of instruction shows that what can be taught is not a function of age and maturation, but a function of what has been taught previously. If we can accelerate the learning of certain preskills, we can accelerate the "readiness" for tasks (or concepts) using those preskills. The brain does not limit what can be taught as implied by some developmental theories.

Large-Group Lecture Methods

Traditional large-group instruction methods usually involve lectures (short and long), questions, textbook assignments, exercises, and tests. The students proceed in a lock-step fashion through a teacher-directed program.

1. *Motivation and attention.* Motivating a whole class is a classical problem for large-group instruction, particularly when the teacher has learned to focus on misbehavior rather than appropriate behavior and where there is a wide divergency in skills. Grades are usually used to motivate, but they may reinforce a lack of diligence in the bright child and punish hard work by a slow child. Attention to instruction is often highly variable. Good motivation and attention can be achieved for large-group instruction when: (1) all children have the assumed preskills, (2) the teacher focuses on positive goals for the class, (3) immediate reinforcers are given for using what is being taught (for example, points for passing frequent quizzes which lead to a grade), or (4) the teacher is a brilliant performer.

2. *Vehicle of instruction.* The teacher, in combination with text and exercises, provides the vehicle of instruction in this model. In most large-group instruction the teacher is the key, because the texts and teacher manuals fail to show how to teach. Suggestions may be offered, but not proven teaching methods.

----

*See *Teaching 1: Classroom Management* for a fuller explanation.

3-4. *Securing responses, reinforcement, and corrections.* This is another classical problem area for large-group instruction. It is difficult to check out twenty-five students on each task being taught and give appropriate consequences. As a result, this method usually places the responsibility for learning on the student rather than the teacher. Those who make it pass, and those who don't fail. Also characteristic of the method is for the teacher to call on one or two better students for a response and, if they give it correctly, assume the job is done. When daily exercises (homework) are assigned and corrected, individual feedback is possible, but rarely are correction procedures used. Again, this is most often a sink-or-swim method. The delay in feedback is also detrimental to learning.

5. *Evaluation of mastery.* Weekly, mid-term, and end-of-term tests are common for evaluation of mastery with the lecture method. The fact that the systems are set up so that some have to fail (or be "slipped by") often makes these procedures punitive rather than legitimately educational. Often the tests require information that has not been taught because the teacher believes the students should "generalize" even if the general case has not been taught. Also testing is too often delayed so that it comes too late to serve as a good motivator for early study, or as a diagnostic device for correction of student deficiencies.

Computer-Assisted Instruction (CAI)

Computer-assisted instruction is the most elaborate example of programed instruction and teaching machines. Less sophisticated examples are a programed reader, a language master program, a talking book, and the like. In computer-assisted instruction, the student communicates with a computer that keeps careful records of his response to each step in the program and makes decisions on what to teach next. The Stanford Tutorial System, built under the direction of Patrick Suppes in math and Richard Atkinson in reading, is an example of a quite advanced system. The initial design was intended to teach all phases of beginning reading and math skills.[4] The student station consists of a television display tube, a film projector system, a typewriter, an earphone set, and a light-sensitive pen that can be used to make responses to questions on the TV tube. The heart of the system is an IBM computer. As many as 2000 students a day in different parts of the country can use the computer for reading and math lessons through telephone line connections between student stations and the computer.

1. *Motivation and attention.* The equipment itself is motivating for most students. It responds; it is patient and supportive. The student must sign in; then the computer automatically takes him to where he left off yesterday. Arrows of light can be used to get attention to critical aspects of a lesson on the video tube, as can recorded audio messages. Since the program is individually geared to the student's responses, momentary loss of attention is not critical. The computer will wait.

2. *Vehicle of instruction.* The initial Stanford system permitted presentation of programed material through audio tapes, films, and the video screen, as noted above. In an attempt to overcome high costs, a later model used only a teletypewriter and an audio headset.[5]

3. *Securing student responses.* A signal is used in the program each time the computer wants the student to respond. For every frame of instruction, a student response is required and evaluated.

4. *Reinforcement and corrections.* When the student makes a mistake, the computer uses branching programs to correct it. Figure 1.2 illustrates such a correction. Correct responses are reinforced by words from the audio unit

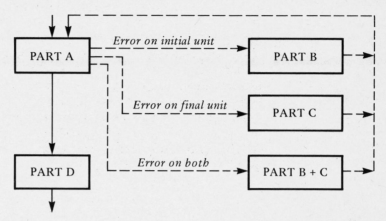

Flow chart for the construction of a cell in the matrix construction task.

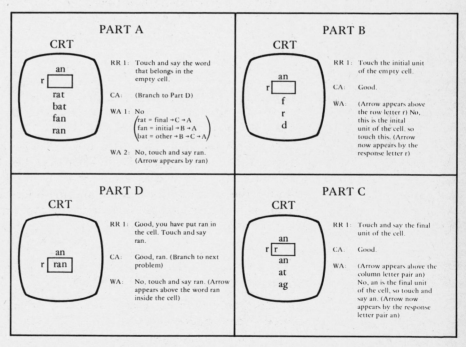

First cell of the matrix construction task.

Figure 1.2 Sample from a program for computer-assisted instruction

such as "great," "fantastic," "good." The computer's capability for providing immediate reinforcement is excellent. A fundamental problem with current computer systems for teaching beginning reading is that they cannot respond to the student's oral responses. Therefore they cannot evaluate *oral reading*. Unless the student already can say and blend sounds and say words, there is no *guarantee* that the student will learn these skills. (However, it is possible, since an audio tape can provide appropriate models for saying sounds and blending them into words.)

5. *Evaluation of mastery*.   It is easy to build periodic reviews and mastery tests into a computer program. Evaluation is an important part of such systems.

In terms of cost efficiency, there are currently some tasks that teachers can do better, such as teaching beginning skills requiring correction of oral responses (reading, language), and some skills that computers can teach better, such as practice drills and tasks that can be adequately corrected if the response is limited to a typewriter or a multiple-choice response. As an effective instructional model, the computer potentially has all of the important ingredients if lower-cost systems for evaluation of oral responses can be developed. Cost of the *revised* Stanford system for teaching reading (which places the student at grade level by the end of third grade) is about fifty-five cents per student per day, or $291 for three years of daily lessons running fifteen to thirty minutes each.

Individually Prescribed Instruction (IPI)

IPI is an instructional program using team teaching, nongraded classrooms, programed instruction, and systematic testing.[6] The curriculum material is sequentially ordered into tracks of skills (called a continuum of objectives) that build upon one another. Placement tests and pretests determine what lesson should be worked on or skipped. Curriculum-embedded tests and posttests (passed at an 85 percent criterion) indicate that it is time to move to the next unit. The children work on their own much of the time, but help is available from teachers and aides as needed.

1. *Motivation and attention*.   Since most work is individualized, attention is not a critical problem as long as there is motivation to do the work. This is initially achieved through teacher instruction and praise. Later on, the mechanics of working through a step-by-step program with lots of feedback keep most children going.

It would be easy to add a point-reward system to IPI, although the originators did not.

2. *Vehicle of instruction*.   Programed worksheets, audio-records (or tapes) at listening centers, programed readers, filmstrips combined with tape cassettes, individual teacher instruction, and small-group teacher instruction constitute the most common vehicles in IPI. How good IPI is depends to a large extent on the success of the teacher's instructional efforts because the programed materials themselves have not consistently contained an adequate instructional mechanism, particularly for the slower student. Note that this criticism is not of the model itself, only its current form.

3. *Securing responses.* The worksheets and tests connected with each objective do an excellent job of securing student responses that can be evaluated for progress through the program. However, the response form is limited.

4. *Reinforcement and corrections.* Specific feedback is given on each error and a special lesson may be set up where needed. Then, a failed unit is repeated. Reinforcement for correct responses (outside of confirmation) is not emphasized, but can easily be given. Corrective-teaching procedures (other than redoing the unit) are left up to the ingenuity of the teacher or aide.

5. *Evaluation of mastery.* IPI curriculum-embedded tests and posttests are excellent vehicles for evaluating mastery of objectives.

Figures 1.3 and 1.4 show the steps in the IPI teacher's use of time and a sample part of the continuum of objectives for mathematics.

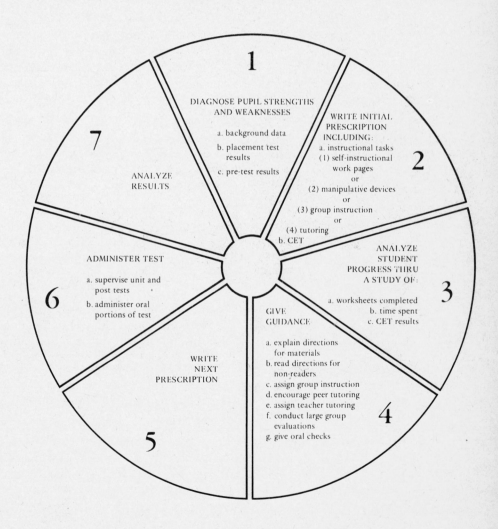

Figure 1.3 Teacher functions for individually prescribed instruction

level C	level D
Numeration	
1. Reads, writes numerals 1-200. Sequence from any starting point.	1. Reads, writes to 1,000. Any point.
2. Supplies number 1 more, or less, or in between—1 to 200.	2. Skip counts, by 3's, 4's from any point.
3. Skip counts 2's, 5's, 10's to 200.	3. (a) Identifies and reads decimal fractions to hundredths.
	(b) Converts decimal numbers to fractions and other forms.
	(c) Fills in missing single decimals.
Place Value	
1. Identifies place value of the units, 10's, 100's to 200. Indicates >, <.	1. Identifies units, 10's, 100's, 1000's. Uses >, <. Writes number before, after to 1,000.
2. Writes numbers, columns 100's, 10's, units.	2. Writes numerals, expanded notation, to 1,000. Regroups, renames.
	3. Uses number families, bridging, to work addition, subtraction problems.
	4. (a) Gives place value of decimal fractions in fractional or other form.
	(b) Makes place value chart.
Addition	
1. Use of associative principle.	1. Demonstrates mastery, sums thru 20.
2. Adds 2 numbers—sum of 20.	2. Does column addition—no carrying.
3. Sums of 2 or 3 numbers, no carrying.	3. Finds missing addends— 3 single digits.
4. Uses >, <, =. Equations, 2 step, combining add-subtract.	4. Uses words, sum, addend— labels part.
5. Works column addition—3 or more addends, sums to 20.	5. Adds, carrying to 10's using 2 digit numerals, 2 or more addends.
	6. Adds, carrying to 10's, 100's, using 3 digit numerals, 2 or more addends.
	7. Adds, carry 10's, 100's, using 3 digit numerals, 2 or more addends.
	8. Finds sums, column addition. Using 2 or more addends of 1 digit.
Subtraction	
1. Subt. problems—numbers to 18.	1. Mastery subtraction facts, numbers to 20.
2. Subt. 2 digit—no borrowing.	2. Subtraction no borrowing—3 or more digits.
3. Finds missing addend— 2 single digits.	3. Subtraction borrowing 10's place— 2 digits.
	4. Subtraction borrowing 10's, 100's —3 digits.
	5. Subtraction borrowing 10's, 100's —3 digits.

Figure 1.4 Mathematics continuum for IPI

Distar Small-Group Instruction

Distar is an acronym for Direct Instructional System for Teaching Arithmetic and Reading.[7] It provides programs for reading, arithmetic, and language at the three beginning grade levels. Combined with the methods developed by Engelmann for teaching disadvantaged children in Project Follow Through, the Distar programs provide another model for effective instruction that is especially important for teaching beginning skills and for the hard-to-teach child.

The Distar programs provide daily lessons for the teacher to follow in small-group instruction and individual work. A sample page from a reading lesson is found in figure 1.5. Where two teaching aides are available, three teaching lessons go on simultaneously. The children are placed in groups of six to nine and rotated from one subject area to another (or to self-directed seat work). The program can also be operated with one aide, but language or arithmetic would have to be taught in a large group. The children are grouped according to current skills and can be shifted from group to group according to progress shown on continuous-progress tests geared to each program.

A comparison with traditional small-group teaching. Small-group instruction has been recommended for teaching reading at beginning grade levels for some time. It has many of the advantages of individualized or one-on-one instruction with a reduced cost. Unlike current computer systems, it can respond to and correct oral responses in teaching reading and language. Several problems are common in small-group instruction, which typically uses a basal series. First, the teacher often does not have procedures effective for teaching every child. Second, a lot of time may be wasted individually correcting different errors by different children. Third, the teacher often tends to reinforce some children for inadequate performances rather than correcting them. Each of these three points will be elaborated.

The Distar programs and the procedures for using them were developed to overcome these problems. To provide constant individual corrections, the programs are prepared to remedy nearly all possible mistakes any child capable of entering the program might make. For example, it is known from empirical work that a good percentage of beginning readers will call the word *rat* "at." They make similar mistakes on various words—leaving off the beginning sound. Therefore, it is necessary to program teaching to address the problem and allow for a perfunctory correction. The children might be taught a rhyming format before they begin decoding simple words. In that format, different beginning sounds and different endings are presented. For example, the teacher writes *r* on the board. She says, "We're going to rhyme with *at*. What are we rhyming with? Rhyming with *at*." She touches the *r* and the child produces the sound "rrr." As the teacher signals, the child completes the word *rat*. After the child has worked on many similar tasks, with different endings and different beginnings, he has mastered a skill that can help in beginning reading. If the child now makes the mistake of leaving off the beginning sound when decoding the word *rat*, the correction is simple. The teacher touches the *r* in *rat* and says, "Rhymes with *at*," then signals by moving her hand under the word. "Rat," the child says. The correction requires only a few seconds. In a similar way, careful programing can guard against most possible mistakes by appropriate teaching ahead of time.

Do not tell the sounds unless the children make mistakes.

Do not point to the small letters.

Task 1
a. Read it. Point to **l**, **ā**, and **t**. Permit no pauses between sounds.
b. When **lllāāāt** is firm, say: Say it fast! What word is this? Wait. Yes. lāte.

lāte

Task 2
a. Read it. Point to **i** and then point between the **ll's** as the children hold each sound.
   Have them repeat **iiilll** until loud and firm.
b. Ask each child to read the word slowly.
   Point to each sound and permit no pauses between sounds.
   Look here. iiilll. Say it fast! Wait.

ill

Task 3
a. Read it. Point to **a**, **n**, and **d**. Permit no pauses between sounds.
b. When **aaannnd** is firm, say: Say it fast! What word is this? Wait. Yes. and.

and

Task 4
a. Read it. Point to **m**, **ā**, and **l**. Permit no pauses between sounds.
b. When **mmmāāāl** is firm, say: Say it fast! What word is this? Wait. Yes. māil.

māil

Task 5
Call on individual children to read each word. Do not present the words in fixed order.

Figure 1.5 Sample from a Distar reading lesson

Engelmann has recommended a number of procedures to be sure every child is taught. First, the teacher needs to get close to the children so that he or she can touch each child. The closer the teacher sits to the children (within limits), the better they attend. Second, the teacher needs to learn to attend to the responses of each child in the group. This skill must be practiced under supervision to be learned. A number of procedures are involved: (a) seating the children so that the lowest performers are directly in front of the teacher, (b) testing these children individually more frequently than others in the group, and (c) teaching to the lowest performer in the group with the understanding that if he has mastered a task, the others have also.

A third technique that can be introduced to insure that every child is taught is to use signals. In a one-to-one situation, the teacher or computer does not have to control the timing of the child's responses. The teacher asks a question, and the child answers it. In the small-group setting, however, a serious problem may result if the teacher merely questions the group and allows the children to respond more or less when they feel like it. Some children will initiate the response; others will merely copy them. The teacher asks, "What kind of animal is this?" Two children immediately respond, "Fish." The rest of the children come in a moment later, "Fiiiish." The teacher praises the children, "Good job." Some children in the group were not responding to the stimulus, they were responding to the answer. The teacher may therefore be teaching these children a serious error about instruction. Later, the teacher may discover that the children have "forgotten" what was "taught," and that they believe instruction involves imitating what others say, rather than responding to appropriate stimuli correctly. The solution is to require children to respond on signal. If all of the children are required to respond in this way, the teacher can quickly identify those children who copy responses. They come in late. Also, the teacher can use quick individual turns to check out any questionable responses (those that may be late). The individual turns provide children with a demonstration that they are accountable for the skills that are presented to the group.

Because error rates are high and good correction procedures are lacking in the usual small-group instruction, the teacher is likely to pass over many mistakes for lack of time and tell the children they did well when in fact they did not. This might also be done under the mistaken assumption that the teacher is shaping improvement. With a program in which the task objectives are more readily obtained by all, it is possible for the teacher to adopt a tougher criterion and to carefully reinforce only correct responses. As a consequence, children are less likely to be taught mistakes that have to be undone later.

With this background, we are now in a position to examine the Distar method as used in the Follow Through Programs, in terms of the procedures essential to effective instruction.

1. *Motivation and attention.* The teacher is close to the children, ready to provide reinforcement for attending and working. Attention signals are explicitly used to get and hold attention to the teacher presentation: "Everybody, listen." To make them even more effective, the signals are held for variable periods before the task is presented. This provides a kind of unpredictable reinforcement for attending and fosters persistent attending. If some children

do not attend, the teacher returns to the beginning of the task, gets attention, and then re-presents the task.

2. *Vehicle of instruction.* The vehicle of instruction is the daily programed lesson presented by the teacher from the *Teacher's Presentation Book.* "Take-homes" and workbooks are also provided for written practice and to encourage practice at home with parents. Because Engelmann's materials are based on programing strategies consistent with the best current knowledge of how to teach a general case, they become a powerful vehicle of instruction in the hands of a teacher trained in their use.

3. *Securing responses.* Uniquely, Distar is designed to get rapid, high-rate, oral responding from each child in the group. Teacher time is used efficiently. Through the use of aides, several groups are taught at the same time; thus, there is more responding by each child. Written responding directly geared to today's lesson is also secured on take-homes and in workbooks. Characteristically, the teacher checks each child on each new skill through in-program tests and individual responses during group instruction.

4. *Reinforcement and corrections.* The Distar programs contain teacher scripts with procedures for giving confirmation and social reinforcement at the right time. The take-homes are reinforcers for good group work. Point systems are easily added to Distar, but are not usually needed. Correction procedures are built right into the program and specified for each possible kind of error that can occur. The teacher or another child may model the correct response, the teacher may lead the child through a hard-to-say sentence, or the teacher may just give the child the answer. It all depends on the type of error. In any case, after a correction, the task is repeated to see if the child can do it before proceeding.

5. *Evaluation of mastery.* Continuous-progress tests, based on program content, are given to the children each six weeks (or more often). The continuous tests provide the teacher with information about whether the children are performing at day-in-program, ahead of day-in-program, or behind. A diagnostic key gears the test results to program tasks so that remedial action can be taken, if needed, before it is too late. Regrouping of children to maximize progress is also done on the basis of this testing.

Using these programs to teach children from poor families (defined by the Office of Economic Opportunity) in Project Follow Through, we find that poor children gain more than 1 grade level each year in spelling and arithmetic and more than 1.4 grade levels a year in reading decoding skills. A gain of 10 IQ points during the first year is also common, indicating a gain in general language and problem-solving skills.[8] (See unit 12 for details.)

summary

The various models of instruction we have discussed are compared in table 1.1. From this sampling, we can see that the various models have strengths and weaknesses. The small-group Distar model is slow in providing training in self-directed learning. Computer-assisted instruction has difficulty correcting oral responses or listening to a child read. The open classroom can be weak in teaching basic skills and evaluating its major goals. However, these models can be used in sequence for different purposes as the skill level of the child changes. Direct small-group instruction could be emphasized to get reading, language skills, and beginning arithmetic skills going; then individually programed materials and computers could take over to build skill competencies and problem-solving behaviors; and finally, one could use an open classroom to foster self-directed and creative inquiry into the many fantastic worlds of knowledge.[9] But whatever the model, if it is to be effective, it must provide the key procedures for effective instruction discussed in this unit.

TABLE 1.1 A COMPARISON OF INSTRUCTIONAL MODELS

Criteria	Open Classroom	Large-Group Lecture	CAI	IPI	Distar Small-Group
1 a. Motivation procedures	Good (self-selection)	Usually weak	Excellent potential	Relies on intrinsic	Excellent; lots of teacher praise, etc.
b. Attention to task	Variable	Highly variable	Excellent (waits for student)	Good potential, not a problem (individualized)	Explicit procedures provided
2 Vehicle of instruction: presenting tasks and showing task requirements	Equipment, materials, and heavy reliance on teacher	Depends on teacher; procedures not specific	Excellent potential	Excellent potential (current materials restricted)	Excellent; daily programed lessons given by teacher
3 Securing responses from students	Not systematic	Rare during teaching; delayed in homework, etc.	Excellent potential, except oral	Excellent potential; relies heavily on written responses	Excellent for oral responses and written responses
4 a. Reinforcement	Delayed; not systematic	Delayed; not systematic	Good potential	Confirmation provided; no emphasis on other reinforcers (but could be used)	Many excellent procedures specified
b. Correcting mistakes	Delayed or not done	Delayed or not done	Good, except for oral responses	Relies heavily on teacher	Explicit corrections provided for all possible mistakes
5 Long-term evaluation of mastery	Informal; de-emphasized	Usually done; may cover things not taught	Excellent potential	Excellent in form of curriculum embedded tests and post-tests	Excellent continuous progress tests

self-test

This section provides you with a check of your understanding of the material presented in this unit. Cover the answers on the left with a marker. Read each item and write in your answer. Then check the answer by moving your marker down one step. If you get nine or ten answers right, then we suggest you skip the section on Programed Practice and go on to the next exercise or to the Discussion Questions. If you make more than one error, do the Programed Practice, go back to the text to correct your mistakes, then go on.

1 Instruction is a set of procedures for producing a _____ in behavior toward a prestated objective.

2 Effective instruction must have:

a. Procedures for motivating the students and securing _____ to the task being taught.

b. A _____ of instruction.

c. Procedures for securing _____ from the students to see if the task requirements have been learned.

d. Procedures for _____ mistakes.

e. Procedures for the longer-term _____ of mastery.

3 In the open classroom, a great burden of expertise and judgment is placed on the _____ .

4 Because it is difficult to check out twenty-five students on each task being taught, large-group instruction usually places the responsibility for learning on the _____ .

5 Since the CAI program is individually geared to the student's responses, momentary loss of _____ is not critical. The computer will wait.

6 Unlike current computer systems, small-group instruction is highly suited for correcting _____ responses in teaching reading and language.

NUMBER RIGHT _____

Answers (left margin):

1 change

2a. attention

b. vehicle

c. responses

d. correcting

e. evaluation

3 teacher

4 student

5 attention

6 oral

exercise 1 programed practice

Cover the answers on the left with your marker. Read each item and write in your answer. Then check the answer by moving your marker down one step. Accept your answers if the meaning is the same as that given. Where you are not sure of the material covered, return to the text.

1 change	1 Instruction is a set of procedures for producing a _____ in behavior toward a prestated objective.
	2 Broudy's analysis of teaching identified most of the essential procedures isolated by modern-day behavioral analysis, except the _____ of correct responses.
	3 Effective instruction must also have:
2 reinforcement	a. Procedures for motivating the students and securing _____ to the task being taught.
3a. attention	b. A _____ of instruction.
	c. Procedures for securing _____ from the students to see if the task requirements have been learned.
b. vehicle	
c. responses	d. Procedures for _____ mistakes.
d. correcting	e. Procedures for the longer-term _____ of mastery.
	4 In an open classroom there is a minimum of lessons for the whole class; most instruction is geared to _____.
e. evaluation	
	5 Flexible scheduling is used in an open classroom so that children can engage in _____ activities for varying periods of time.
4 individuals	
	6 To manage the children in an open setting, _____ are often written on a daily or weekly basis. The agreements, which are usually written by the _____, specify the tasks to be completed in the period of time specified.
5 different	
6 agreements; students	7 In the open classroom, a great burden of expertise and judgment is placed on the _____.
	8 A problem for the open classroom is a lack of specification of _____ and therefore a lack of precise procedures for knowing whether they have been achieved.
7 teacher	
8 objectives	9 The belief that learning is purposive is logically false, since _____ must come before effects.
	10 A careful examination of the teaching process will show that what can be taught is not a function of age and maturation, but of what has been _____.
9 causes	
10 learned, taught	11 In large-group instruction, motivation and attention to instruction are often highly _____.
11 variable	

12 In most large-group instruction the _____ is the key, because the texts and teacher manuals fail to show how to teach.

13 Because it is difficult to check out twenty-five students on each task being taught, large-group instruction usually places the responsibility for learning on the _____.

14 The fact that large-group systems are set up so that some have to fail often makes testing procedures _____ rather than educational.

15 In CAI, the equipment itself is very _____ for most students. It responds, and is patient and supportive.

16 Since the program is individually geared to the student's responses, momentary loss of _____ is not critical. The computer will wait.

17 A _____ is used in the program each time the computer wants the student to respond. Each response is _____.

18 When a mistake is made, the computer uses _____ programs to correct the mistake.

19 A fundamental problem with current computer systems for teaching beginning reading is that they cannot respond to the student's _____ responses.

20 Individually prescribed instruction (IPI) uses team teaching, nongraded classrooms, _____ instruction, and systematic _____ .

21 Since most work is _____, attention is not a critical problem as long as there is motivation to do the work.

22 Specific feedback is given on each _____, and a special lesson may be set up where needed.

23 Corrective-teaching procedures (other than redoing the unit) are left up to the ingenuity of the _____.

24 Unlike current computer systems, small-group instruction is highly suited for correcting _____ responses in teaching reading and language.

25 The Distar programs and the procedures for using them were developed to overcome the common problems in _____ instruction.

26 Engelmann has recommended a number of procedures to be sure every child is taught. One of these is the use of _____ so that the children respond together.

---

12 teacher

13 student

14 punitive

15 motivating

16 attention

17 signal;
   evaluated

18 branching

19 oral

20 programed;
   testing

21 individualized

22 mistake, error

23 teacher

24 oral

25 small-group

26 signals;

27 programed
lesson

28 high-rate

29 take-homes

30 social

31 skill level

32 small-group

33 skill competencies

27 The vehicle of instruction in Distar is the daily _____ _____ presented by the teacher from the *Teacher's Presentation Book*.

28 Distar is designed to get rapid, _____, oral responding from each child in the group.

29 Written responding directly geared to today's lesson is also secured on _____ _____ and in workbooks.

30 The Distar programs contain teacher scripts with procedures for giving confirmation and _____ reinforcement at the right time.

31 These models can be used in sequence for different purposes as the _____ _____ of the child changes.

32 Direct _____ instruction could be emphasized to get reading, language skills, and beginning arithmetic skills going.

33 Individually programed materials and computers could take over to build _____ _____ and problem-solving behaviors.

discussion questions

1 What is instruction?

2 Name the procedures essential to instruction.

3 Describe the basic characteristics of an open classroom.

4 Discuss the potential strengths and weaknesses of the open classroom.

5 Why do behaviorists question the assumptions that learning is purposive, self-motivated, and must be self-directed?

6 Why would behaviorists question the assumption that what can be taught depends on the child's level of development (implying conditions related to physical maturation)?

7 Discuss the potential strengths and weaknesses of the large-group lecture method.

8 Describe the basic features of computer-assisted instruction.

9 What are the main weaknesses of CAI in its current form?

10 Describe the individually prescribed instruction model.

11 Discuss the potential strengths and weaknesses of IPI.

12 Describe the Distar small-group instruction method.

13 How does this method overcome problems common to traditional small-group instruction?

14 What are some potential weaknesses of the Distar method as a general approach to instruction? (Go beyond the text in your thinking.)

15 Suggest some ways in which the different models of instruction might be combined at various stages of education to achieve different objectives.

unit 2

A Behavioral Model of Teaching

objectives

After completing this unit you should be able to—

1 Define these terms:
   a) task
   b) task stimulus
   c) task response
   d) "do it" signal
   e) attention signal
   f) task directions
   g) prompts
2 Explain the difference between tasks and programs.
3 Specify what is required to teach a task, in addition to presenting task stimuli.
4 Explain how prompts are like directions and how they are different.
5 Analyze a task in terms of task stimulus, S-directions, R-directions, and task response.
6 Draw a diagram of a general model of teaching.

lesson

In unit 1 we examined a variety of models of instruction and their adequacy for meeting the basic requirements of instruction. It was noted that common to all instruction are procedures for securing attention, presenting tasks, securing student responses, and correcting or reinforcing responses. Also the need for longer-term evaluation of program effects was noted. In the present unit, we will analyze the teaching of tasks in terms of stimulus events controlled by the teacher and response requirements for the students. This analysis is then organized into a behavioral model of teaching.

The goal of this text is to develop the essential requirements for teaching cognitive skills. However, we must approach these requirements in steps. In this unit and the next, we will use the terms *concept* and *operation* in analyzing teaching. Since these terms are not fully developed procedurally until units 4 and 5, we need some working definitions here. Concepts have to do with *knowing* and operations with *doing*. Concepts are involved in learning a generalizable response to stimulus events. Operations are the generalized components of responses.

Tasks and Programs

Beginning instruction of necessity uses the inductive method, and therefore always involves specific examples and specific responses. That is, *specific tasks* are presented. "Put the ball on the table" is a task. It specifies stimuli (ball and table) and a response requirement under the conditions: "*Put* the ball *on* the table." "The ball is on the table" is not a task. There is no response requirement. If the teacher in the beginning can only teach with specific tasks, how can generalized responding be taught?

Some educators looking at this dilemma have concluded that "intelligent learning" can happen only when it is "self-discovered" and that teaching is useful only for specific facts, or is harmful. Actually, there is a more logical and reasonable solution to the problem. It requires a recognition of the distinctive role of a set of sequenced tasks, a *program*, in teaching concepts and operations, or more generally, intelligent behavior.

For example, a variety of tasks of the form, "Put the X on the Y" could be used to teach the operation *putting on.* This *set of tasks* could be sequenced into a program which, if coupled with relevant counterexamples (not putting on), could teach the generalized response (operation) of putting anything on anything the first time asked. (Units 9 to 11 are devoted to development of theory and procedures for programing to teach a general case.)

Components of a Task

The teacher says, "Look, Jimmy. What color is this?" (Teacher points to a yellow flower.) To respond to this task correctly, Jimmy would have to have been taught that "Look" is a signal to turn his eyes toward the teacher and what the teacher is pointing to. He would also have to know what to look at to find color cues and be able to say color names. Finally, he would have to know that "What is this?" is a signal for him to answer in a specific way.

There are ten potential functional components to a task: seven functionally different classes of preceding stimuli (discriminative stimuli),* each controlling different responses or aspects of responses; two classes of stimulus events that follow task responses, reinforcing consequences and corrections; and, of course, there is the task response. The following task illustrates each of the components of a task except corrections:

---

*Students who have not been through *Teaching 1: Classroom Management* will need to look up terms such as this in the glossary.

Task Example	Name of Component
1 "Everybody, watch me."	1 Attention signal
2 Teacher holds up a picture of an elephant.	2 Task stimulus
3 *"Look* at this *animal."* (Points.)	3 S-direction
4 "See—he has a long trunk." (Points.)	4 S-prompt
5 "This animal is an elephant."	5 R-prompt
6 *"Tell* me its *name."*	6 R-direction
7 "Johnny, say it."	7 "Do it" signal
8 "Elephant."	8 Task response
9 "Good."	9 Reinforcer

This example contains more words than an actual teaching routine would require because we have isolated each task component. Actual routines can be very brief and still present all the required stimulus components. The following routine contains all the essentials:

> Teacher: "Everybody, look. *(Teacher holds up a picture of an elephant.)* This animal is an elephant. See—he has a long trunk. *(Points.)* Johnny, what kind of animal is this?"
> Johnny: "Elephant."
> Teacher: "Good."

Definitions and Functions of Task Components

Task Stimulus and Task Response

Connecting the task stimulus to the task response is the teaching goal. When the teaching is successful the task stimulus comes to control the task response. In the example of the yellow flower, the color yellow was the task stimulus and the color name "yellow" was the task response. In the elephant example, the picture of the elephant was the task stimulus. If one were teaching the concept *larger* and presented an instance of two balls, one three inches in diameter and one five inches, the task stimulus would be the *relative size* of the two balls. If one were teaching the event concept *freezing* (of water), the task stimulus would be *changes* in the physical state of the H_2O or a representation of those changes. Getting task stimuli connected to task responses is what teaching is about.

Task Directions

Task directions tell *what to do*. Let's imagine a task without directions:
The teacher holds up a picture of an elephant and says, "Respond now." The children would not know what to do. She might teach them to say

"elephant" when she held up the picture, but if she wanted to use the same stimulus later in other tasks, she would have to undo this habit.

But by giving directions, she might hold up the picture for later tasks and ask these questions:

"How many legs does it have?"
"What color is it?"
"What can it do?"
"What can it say?"
"How much does it weigh?"
"What can you tell me about its mother?"
"Where is its trunk?"

Or she might give these instructions:

"Say its name."
"Write its name."
"Draw a picture of it."
"Point to its trunk."
"Count its legs."
"Hang its picture on the bulletin board."

For any given stimulus instance, there is an endless series of tasks that can be specified. Unless the teacher wants simple habit responses to specific stimuli, it is essential to include directions in the task statement.

There are two kinds of task directions. *S-directions* control attending to the task stimulus. This can be accomplished by specifying how to attend (for example, "Look," "Listen," "Touch," "Smell," "Taste") and usually the higher-order class containing the task stimulus (for example: "Look at this *animal* and tell me its name." "Listen to this *sound* and say it after me.") *R-directions* control the general response mode (talking, writing, drawing) and also specify a response class just above the one being taught (for example: "Tell me the name of this *animal*." "What *letter* is this?"). Thus, both S-directions and R-directions have two parallel functions: (1) they cue, generally, how to attend or how to respond; (2) they specify a higher-order class containing the task stimulus or the task response.

Table 2.1 presents an analysis of a series of tasks in order to make explicit the task components that are sometimes hidden in questions or gestures. The examples illustrate the *look and say* and *think and do* operations that are emphasized in many elementary workbooks. It should be apparent from the analyses that directions tell you *what to do* to find task stimuli and make a task response. Study table 2.1 carefully.

Task directions are essential to teaching the general case. Directions provide the cues for a variety of general operations that can be brought to bear on a specific task. Without directions, teaching becomes extremely cumbersome and can degenerate into habit teaching.

Procedures for teaching children to follow directions are discussed later in the unit on operations.

TABLE 2.1   Analysis of Task Directions

Tasks
1   The teacher holds up a picture of an elephant and asks, "What kind of animal is this?"
2   The teacher shows a movie of an elephant and asks, "What can it do?"
3   The teacher shows a movie of a dog and asks, "What does it say?"
4   The teacher holds up a picture of an elephant and says, "Write its name."
5   The teacher holds up a picture of an elephant and says, "Draw a picture of this elephant."
6   The teacher holds up a picture of an elephant and says, "Say its name."

Analysis

Task Number	Task Stimuli	S-directions	R-directions	Task Responses
		Do .... what	Do .... what	
1	Picture of elephant	Look .... at animal	Say.......... name of animal	"Elephant" (spoken)
2	Movie of elephant	Look .... at behavior	Describe ..... behavior	"Run," "Walk," "Knock down trees," "Eat"
3	Movie of dog	Listen .... to voice	Imitate....... its sounds	"Bowwow"
4	Picture of elephant	Look .... at animal	Write .... its name	Elephant (written)
5	Picture of elephant	Look .... at elephant	Draw .... elephant	The drawing
6	Picture of elephant	Look .... at animal	Say.......... its name	"Elephant" (spoken)

Signals

Signals are especially important for group instruction. *Attention signals* indicate who is to attend to the teacher when, and often indicate which sense organs should be used in attending. These are some common attention signals: "Class, listen"; "Mary, look"; "Everybody, watch me." They control the operation *attend to the teacher now*. Unless the children are attending, the teaching demonstration is wasted. *"Do it" signals* specify who is to respond when. All questions contain "do it" signals. When the words *when, what, where, why,* and *how* are followed by a voice inflection or question mark, "do it" signals are being presented. Some others include "Say it," "Now," "Tell me," "Go ahead," and "Your turn." Sometimes hand signals, head nods, or voice inflections are used. "Do it" signals control the operation *respond now*.

With both large-group and small-group instruction, several recent studies by Cowart, Carnine, and Becker have demonstrated that "do it" signals can increase attention to the teacher, frequency of responding by the children, and how much is actually learned. "Do it" signals also reduce the amount of "following" that occurs in group instruction. Following involves some children cuing on the responses of other children. This leads to a condition in which the children appear to be learning to respond to task stimuli when in fact they are only imitating the task responses of other children. On individual testing, the "followers" show that they have not learned the task. What they have learned is to imitate the responses of the leaders.

Prompts

Prompts are task stimuli that were taught in earlier tasks and can now be used to get specific responses to occur to new task stimuli (see unit 6 of *Teaching 1*). There are two kinds of prompts. *S-prompts* control attending to the essential aspects of the task stimulus. *R-prompts* control the specific form of the task response. S-prompts facilitate the *discrimination* of task stimuli. For example, in counting to a number, the task might be: "Listen to me count. Tell me what I count to. One, two, three, four, *FIVE.*" Five is said louder and held longer to help discriminate it from four, three, and so on. R-prompts teach the specifics of the required response form. For example, "This is the number five. Say five." An imitation prompt is used to get the right responses going in the presence of the symbol for five.

Directions, like prompts, help to get attention to the task stimulus and help in getting the task response going. However, directions differ from prompts in an important way. Directions can be simplified in form over time, but they are essential parts of tasks and cannot be eliminated. Prompts, on the other hand, can be eliminated once the task is learned. Prompts are helpers that are eventually faded out.

Post-Task Components

When the task response occurs, various forms of reinforcement are used to strengthen correct responding.* When the task response does not occur, correction procedures are used to teach the right response to the task. They involve essentially the use of the seven kinds of preceding stimuli just discussed. How to decide on which corrections to use for which errors is discussed in the next unit.

A Behavioral Model of Teaching

Figure 2.1 shows the interrelations of the ten components involved in teaching a task. It also suggests the task sequencing involved in a program and the branching involved in corrections.

It is necessary to study figure 2.1 for a time in order to grasp the interrelations of the various components. The reader should first discriminate between *programing* and *teaching* tasks. A program is a sequence of tasks to be taught one at a time. Teaching is always concerned with a specific task. The model in figure 2.1 shows teaching as one moves from left to right. If the response is correct, the teacher goes on to the next task in the program (presented as a third dimension). If the response is incorrect, the teacher enters branch programs designed to correct specific types of errors as outlined in unit 3. Thus in figure 2.1, the essentials of *teaching a task* are presented in the first two dimensions, and *programing* considerations are represented in a third dimension.

---

*See *Teaching 1* for details.

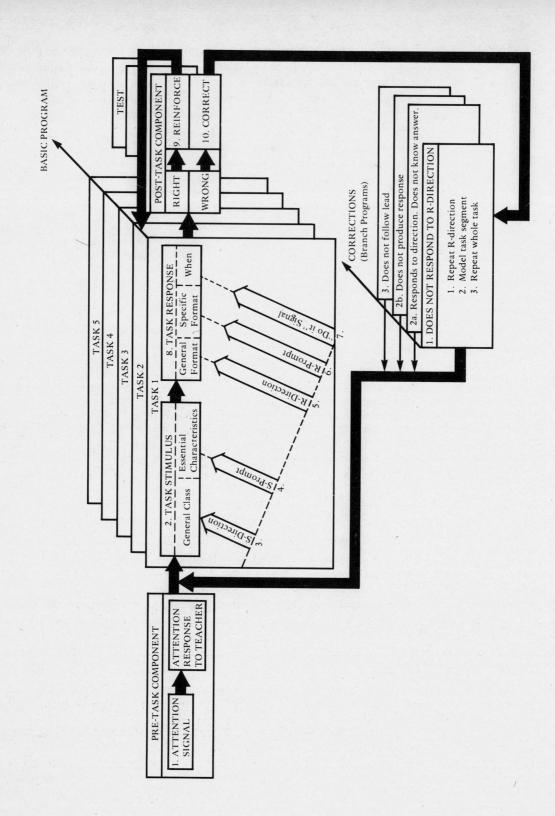

Figure 2.1 A behavioral model of teaching

The teaching of any task can be broken down into three components:

1 pre-task component
2 task component
3 post-task component

In the pre-task component, the teacher must get the children's attention. The task component is made up of a procedure designed to teach the task and one or more "do it" signals indicating when the children are to respond. The teaching procedure can be further analyzed into task stimuli, directions, and prompts. The post-task component provides for reinforcement of right responses and correction of wrong responses.

Note that signals 1, 3, and 4 control different aspects of *attending responses*. These signals help the child to zero in on the task signal. Signals 5, 6, and 7 control different aspects of the *task response*. Note also that punishment is not considered essential to teaching a task. It is rarely needed.

summary

The teacher always teaches specific tasks, although the outcome of a sequence of tasks (a program) can be the teaching of a generalized concept or operation. Tasks are instances of the more general stimulus-response relationships the teacher wishes to establish. The act of teaching involves getting the task response going in the presence of the task stimulus and using procedures to strengthen such connections.

In teaching a task, the teacher has to establish and control a variety of stimulus events to make learning happen. There are ten potential functional components of tasks. These are:

	Component	Teacher Action
1	*Attention signal*	Get the children to attend on signal.
2	*Task stimulus*	Present the task stimulus.
3	*S-directions*	Give directions for orienting to a task stimulus.
4	*S-prompts*	When needed, provide cues to aid in the discrimination of concept instances and not-instances.
5	*R-directions*	Give directions for the general form of the response.
6	*R-prompts*	Use previously taught stimulus-response connections to get a specific response to the task stimulus.
7	*"Do it" signals*	Get the children to respond on signal.
8	*Task response*	
9	*Reinforcement*	Reinforce right response.
10	*Corrections*	Use above procedures to correct wrong responses.

These components were interrelated in a behavioral model of teaching in figure 2.1. To complete the model, it is necessary only to add the sequences of tasks that constitute a basic program of instruction, or branch correction programs.

Beginning instruction should focus on those tasks that are common to the teaching of many other tasks. Especially important in this respect are directions and signals.

Directions are important in teaching the general case. Directions tell you what to do. S-directions specify what to do with task stimuli ("Look at the color") and R-directions specify what to do in making task responses ("Say the color name"). S-directions specify a sense organ and a stimulus class that is of a higher order than the one the task signal is in. R-directions specify a response mode (general operation) and a class above the one containing the task response.

Signals are especially important for group instruction. Attention signals indicate who is to attend to the teacher when. "Do it" signals specify who is to respond when.

Prompts are also important in teaching most tasks. Prompts are previously taught stimulus-response connections that can be used to get a specific response to occur in the presence of a new stimulus. Although directions cannot be eliminated, prompts are helpers that can be eventually faded out.

self-test

1 Is this a task? "Touch the blue objects." *Yes* or *No?*

1 Yes

2 A program is a _____ of tasks.

2 sequence

3 Task directions tell _____ to do.

3 what

4 "Do it" signals specify who is to respond _____ .

4 when

5 Prompts are task stimuli taught in earlier tasks that can now be used to get specific responses to occur to _____ task stimuli.

5 new

6 R-prompts indicate the specific form of the _____ _____ .

6 task responses

7 In the behavioral model of teaching, the _____ is represented as a third dimension.

7 program

8 In the behavioral model of teaching, _____ are seen as branch programs.

8 corrections

9 The teacher can also use three kinds of signals to get the right task response going in the presence of the task signal. These are R-directions, _____ , and _____ _____ _____ .

9 R-prompts;
  "do it" signals

NUMBER RIGHT _____

exercise 1 programed practice

1 tasks

2 response;
  stimulus, signal

3 Yes

4 No

5 stimulus-
  response

6 sequence

7 tasks

8 response;
  task stimulus

9 components

10 what; do

11 task stimulus

12 task response

13 who;
  when

14 who;
  when

15 responding

16 new

17 task signals

18 task responses

19 reinforce,
  strengthen

20 correct

---

1 The teacher always teaches _____.

2 A task requires a particular _____ to a particular _____.

3 Is this a task? "Touch the blue objects."

   Yes or *No*?

4 Is this a task? "The objects are blue."

   Yes or *No*?

5 Tasks are the specifications of the _____ - _____ relationships the teacher is to establish.

6 A program is a _____ of tasks.

7 When _____ are properly selected and sequenced, they can be used to teach a generalization.

8 Teaching involves getting the task _____ going in the presence of the _____ _____.

9 There are ten potential functional _____ of a task.

10 Task directions tell _____ to _____.

11 S-directions control attention to aspects of the _____ _____.

12 R-directions control the general form of the _____ _____.

13 Attention signals indicate _____ is to attend to the teacher _____.

14 "Do it" signals specify _____ is to respond _____.

15 The use of signals has been demonstrated to increase the frequency of attending and _____ by the children.

16 Prompts are task stimuli taught in earlier tasks that can now be used to get specific responses to occur to _____ task stimuli.

17 S-prompts aid in the discrimination of _____ _____.

18 R-prompts indicate the specific form of the _____ _____.

19 To teach a task, the teacher has to also _____ right responses.

20 To teach a task, the teacher has to also _____ wrong responses.

21 Read the example and fill in the answers.

Teacher: Watch me. This is tough. (*The teacher makes a row of three objects in a form board.*) See this. (*Teacher points.*) Can you make a row that looks like my row? Do it.

Children: (*They make a row with their form boards and cards.*)

Teacher: (*Points to each child's row.*) Look at Bill's row. It looks just like my row. Good.

a) What was the attention signal? _____

b) What was the "do it" signal? _____

c) What was the S-direction? _____

d) What was the R-direction? _____

e) What was the S-prompt? _____

f) What was the R-prompt? _____

g) What was the task response? _____

h) What was the task signal? _____

i) What was the consequence? _____

22 In the behavioral model of teaching, the _____ is represented as a third dimension.

23 In the behavioral model of teaching, the sequence of basic components in _____ a task is represented as a left-to-right flow chart.

24 In the behavioral model of teaching, _____ are seen as branch programs.

25 The teacher can use three kinds of stimuli to direct the child's attention to the essential characteristics of a task stimulus. These are attention signals, _____, and _____.

26 The teacher can also use three kinds of signals to get the right task response going in the presence of the task signal. These are R-directions, _____, and _____ _____ _____.

27 In the behavioral model of teaching, _____ is not included. _____ is not essential to teaching a task. It is rarely needed, if ever.

21a) "Watch me."

b) "Do it."

c) "See this."

d) "Make a row that looks like my row."

e) "See this" and pointing.

f) Teacher making the row.

g) Children making rows like the teacher's row.

h) Teacher's row of cards.

i) "Look at Bill's row. It looks just like my row. Good."

22 program

23 teaching

24 corrections

25 S-directions; S-prompts

26 R-prompts; "do it" signals

27 punishment; Punishment

discussion questions

1 Define the term *task*.
2 How is programing different from teaching a task?
3 Define *task stimulus*.
4 Define *task response*.
5 Define *"do it" signal*.
6 Define *attention signal*.
7 Define *task directions*.
8 Define *prompts*.
9 Why is it that the teacher does not actually teach concepts and operations?
10 What is required to teach a task in addition to presenting task signals?
11 Compare prompts and directions. How are they similar and how do they differ?
12 Give a task and analyze it in terms of task stimulus, S-directions, R-directions, and task response.
13 Draw the general model of teaching, excluding the program components.

unit 3

Teaching Tasks:
Skills for Direct Instruction of Groups

objectives

When you complete this unit you should be able to—

1 Describe and demonstrate procedures for teaching attention signals, "do it" signals, and directions.
2 Identify prompts of various kinds and give rules for their use.
3 Describe and demonstrate fading procedures.
4 Analyze the kinds of errors that can be made in basic instruction and demonstrate correction procedures for each.
5 Give four procedures that apply to each of the three teaching-model components (pre-task, task, and post-task).

lesson

The model of teaching presented in unit 2 implies that the teacher needs a number of specific skills. In our experience, these skills are especially important with hard-to-teach children, in beginning instruction, and in group instruction. At advanced levels, the basic components of the model of teaching are still important, but they can be provided by methods other than direct instruction. For example, a "do it" signal may be an instruction at the bottom of a page specifying that the student should take a checkout on his own and go over it with the teacher.

The skills involved comprise:

teaching and using signals
teaching directions
using prompts efficiently
using reinforcers
correcting mistakes
pacing the presentation

The use of reinforcers is covered in *Teaching 1*, especially in unit 10. The rest of these skills will be covered here. Although this unit may help some students learn the skills being discussed, actual supervised practice is usually needed.

Teaching Attention Signals

Signals tell each student when to pay attention and when to respond. They are especially important for group instruction. Attention signals should be taught before proceeding with any other group task. The steps are as follows:

1 *State a contingency.*   Tell the children what will happen if they perform the desired task: "Everybody, watch me and I'll show you a picture."
2 *Pause.*
3 *Give the signal:* "Watch me."
4 At the same time, *use a hand signal to hold the children's attention.* For example, hold up your right hand.
5 *Give a social reinforcer for good attending.* When praising the children, tell them what they are being praised for: "That's good watching."
6 *Give any other reinforcer that was promised:* Show the picture.

Correcting Inattention

If one or more of the children do not attend to the signal, use the following correction procedure.

1 Praise children who are attending. Praise them by name and tell them what they are doing well: "Sue, that's good paying attention."
2 Point out an attentive child's behavior to the child who is not attending: 'Glenda, look at Sue. She can really pay attention. See how she watches me."
3 Do not praise the child who is inattentive.
4 Say, "Once more," or "Let's do it again."
5 Pause.
6 Repeat the task, starting with the attention signal "Everybody."
7 At the end of the task, praise all the children who attended well: "Glenda, Sue, Don, and Sherrie, you were all really paying attention. You watched every second."
8 Repeat the task until all the children respond correctly.

Lengthening Attending to Include the Task Presentation

The above procedures teach children to respond to attention signals by reinforcing the behavior "Good watching," "Good listening," or "Good attending." At first, reinforce with praise or some tangible reinforcer. Once the attention response is taught, reinforcement is gradually eliminated between the attention response and task presentation. Reinforcement is given only at the end of the task. A chain is established as follows:

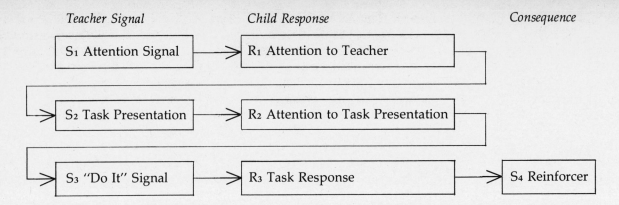

Teacher Signal	Child Response	Consequence
S₁ Attention Signal	R₁ Attention to Teacher	
S₂ Task Presentation	R₂ Attention to Task Presentation	
S₃ "Do It" Signal	R₃ Task Response	S₄ Reinforcer

The teacher first establishes the $S_1 \rightarrow R_1$ part of the chain by using direct reinforcement. Then, with a task that the teacher knows the children can do, the direct reinforcement for attending is faded out, and the chain for attending is lengthened to include the task presentation and the task response by the child. Simple motor tasks like "Everybody, stand up" or "Everybody, sit down" are fun and effective at the start in teaching attention signals.

Varying the Length of Attention Signals

The teacher should vary the length of time she holds the children's attention before presenting the task. Since the task presentation is followed by reinforcers, it will come to function as a conditioned reinforcer for responses that precede it. Varying the start of the task presentation by varying the length of the attention signals serves to place reinforcement for paying attention on a variable-intermittent schedule. The result is more persistent attending behavior.

Teaching "Do It" Signals

"Do it" signals specify *when* someone is to respond. Words like "when?" "what?" "where?" "why?" and "who?" function as "do it" signals. So can phrases like "Say it," "Do it," "Your turn," "Tell me," and "Go ahead." Hand signals, head nods, and voice inflections can also function as "do it" signals.

Where to Give Signals

"Do it" signals are given when we want the children to respond. First, examine the tasks in a program and mark the places where the children are to respond. Consider this task:

> We are going to count to 10. What are we going to do? Yes, count to 10. Get ready, count.

There are two places where the children are to respond: (1) after "What are we going to do?" and (2) after "Get ready, count." By identifying these places ahead of time, the teacher will be able to follow the first rule for using "do it" signals. The rule is *always pause before a "do it" signal*. The pause gives a general cue that a "do it" signal is coming. The children will then be prepared to respond together. The duration of the pause is determined by task difficulty. A longer pause is used with more difficult tasks (such as a new word in reading) to give the students time to get ready. The children who pay careful attention to the signals are more likely to make correct responses.

"Do It" Signals and Task Segments

A "do it" signal should be presented only with the whole task in which it occurs. This permits the task responses to be tied to task stimuli. Any time a response is required, it should be in the presence of the task stimuli (or right after it for auditory signals).

Single-Segment Tasks. In a single-segment task, there is one task stimulus followed by a task response. Consider the following single-segment task:

The teacher points to a picture of a cat, then says, "This is a cat." *(Short pause.)* "What is this?" (Teacher drops his hand as a "do it" signal.) Jimmy says "cat" two seconds after the others in the group. To teach Jimmy to respond to the signal, the teacher repeats the whole task modeling the correct response: "My turn." *(Points.)* "This is a cat." *(Short pause, hand held out palm facing students.)* "What is this?" *(Drops hand.)* "A cat. Your turn. This is a cat." *(Short pause, hand held out.)* "What is this?" *(Drops hand.)* Jimmy says, "Cat."

When the children respond to the signal correctly, the teacher goes on to other tasks of the same format to teach that the same signal is used for many similar tasks:

"This is a house." *(Short pause.)* "What is this?" *(Drops hand.)*

"This is a ball." *(Short pause.)* "What is this?" *(Drops hand.)*

"This is a tree." *(Short pause.)* "What is this?" *(Drops hand.)*

Once a "do it" signal has been taught with a particular task format, teaching is simplified for all objectives within that format.

Series Tasks. In a series task, the task response is to perform a chain of responses in sequence. The same sort of "do it" signal is used for the series, to tell the children when to move to the next segment in the chain.

In teaching spelling by sounds, the children might be required to say one sound as long as the palm of the teacher's hand is toward them, and switch to the next sound when the teacher turns the back of the hand toward them, and so forth. For example, the teacher says, "Listen. I can spell *man* by sounds." He holds up his hand in a fist and says "Listen." When he starts to spell by sounds, the palm of his hand facing the children signals "*mmmm*," the back of the hand facing the children signals "*aaaa*," and the palm again toward the children signals "*nnnn*."

As in teaching other "do it" signals, the general procedure is to demonstrate the task, the signals, and the required responses, and then take the children through a set of similar tasks to teach the "do it" signal. *A series task cannot be broken into segments to make corrections.* When there is an error, the teacher returns to the beginning of the series and starts again.

Multiple-Segment Tasks. In a multiple-segment task, there is more than one task-stimulus/task-response segment, and several different signals require several different responses. The example for "do it" signals (page 34) was a two-segment task. The first segment ended with the "do it" signal, "What are we going to do?" The task response was, "Count to 10." The second segment ended with, "Get ready, count." The task response was a chain, "One, two, three . . . ten." *Responses to "do it" signals in a multiple-segment task may be taught separately (as in a single-segment task) and then put together.*

Prompts

A prompt is a previously taught task stimulus that the teacher can use to get a specified response to a new task stimulus. It will eventually be faded out. For example, a child says "mmmm" when he hears the sound "mmmm," but not when he sees the letter *m*. To get the right sound going in the presence of visual *m*, the teacher points to the letter *m* and says, "This is mmmm. Say mmmm." As the child learns to say "mmmm" to the letter *m*, the teacher withdraws (fades out) her help. What the child already can do is used to teach him something new.

Prompts can be divided into two classes, depending on the kind of responses they are used to get. Every task requires at least two kinds of responses: an attention response to the critical aspects of the task stimulus and the prescribed task response. Prompts that aid in the discrimination of task stimuli are called S-prompts. Those that aid in getting the right task response going are called R-prompts.

S-Prompts

S-prompts help in the discrimination of task stimuli by focusing attention on essential characteristics and by making the discriminations simpler. Any stimulus that will accomplish the teacher's objective can serve as a prompt. The following are examples:

Verbal Instructions. The teacher might say: "This is an *h* and this is an *n*. See how they differ. The *h* is higher before the curved part. The *n* is not high." This instruction controls the operation of looking back and forth between the two letters to compare them.

Physical Prompting. In physical prompting the teacher physically moves the child's body through the desired motions. This might involve turning his body or head toward the demonstration. It might involve taking the child's hand and touching or tracing the critical stimuli. This latter procedure assumes that the child's eye movements will follow the hand movements.

Added Cues. To help differentiate between numbers that are likely to be confused, the teacher might say: "Listen to me count. Tell me what I count to. One, two, three, four, *five. (Five is said louder and held longer.)* What did I count to?" By emphasizing *five*, it is made less similar to one, two, three, and four. In early parts of the Distar Reading Program, silent letters are made smaller than the other letters to cue their "silentness" until context cues are learned;

then they are gradually made larger. The cue that is used as a prompt is slowly faded out.

R-Prompts

R-prompts help get the right response going in the presence of task stimuli. The following are examples:

Imitation. The most common type of R-prompt is giving a model response that the child is to imitate: "This is *m*. Say mmmmmm," or, "Watch me do it. Now, you do it." Because most children have already learned to imitate most sounds and actions by the time they come to school, imitation can be a powerful tool for getting responses to occur under the right stimulus conditions.

Verbal Instructions. Instructions are also frequently used as R-prompts. If the child has learned appropriate verbal signals for operations, the teacher can use them to get responses going. For example, "Around the tree, around the tree, makes a three" can be used to prompt the response of writing the number 3. Rules such as "*i* before *e* except after *c*" are also instructions that can be used as prompts.

Nonverbal Instructions. To prompt a place (location) response, simply point where you want the child to respond. If the task is "Put your name in the upper right-hand corner," point to the place where the response is to be made. A number of nonverbal instructions are used by choir directors to keep the group together. He paces their response and controls their loudness by arm and hand signals. The teacher can do the same when working with small groups. A foot tap may be used to keep a group counting together. As the group becomes proficient, these prompts are faded out.

Physical Prompting. Use of physical prompting to get responses going might involve taking a child's hand to help him draw a three, or closing a child's lips to get "mmmm." The child is given a demonstration using his own body rather than a model to be imitated.

Added Cues. A cue can also be added to help differentiate similar responses. If the child cannot differentiate a forward 3 from a backward 3 in writing, and he is right-handed, have him place his left thumb on the paper and write 3 so that the three points of the 3 touch his left thumb. In teaching a child to write, one could start with having him trace letters or numbers, then trace dotted lines, then copy a model, and finally write from dictation. Cues are added to help get the different writing responses going and then they are slowly faded out.

Prompts and Programing

In building a systematic teaching program for complex behavior such as multiplying, solving equations, or reading, it is often necessary first to teach the component tasks that can be used later as prompts. In fact, good programing insures that the teaching demonstrations and correction procedures are nothing more than previously programed tasks. *Once a task has been taught, it can be used as a prompt in teaching new tasks.*

In good programing, tasks are taught to cover the most general case in which they may be needed later. In arithmetic, the children may be taught to count *to* any number under 20, to count *from* any number under 20 *to* a number under 20, or to use fingers or lines while going from one number to another in order to determine how many are being added, and so forth. All these skills are then used later as prompts to solve equations of the form 5 + □ = 9. Given any equation in that form, the child has the component skills needed to find the answer. The necessary prompts have been made part of his behavior by earlier teaching. They can also be called problem-solving skills.

In teaching the blending of sounds you cannot hold such as *t*, *b*, and *c*, a rhyming prompt is often helpful. To teach the word *tan*, the teacher says, "Rhymes with *man, fan, ran* . . . So this must be . . . ?" It becomes highly probable that the child will now say "Tan" if he has been taught to rhyme earlier in the program.

A child may be taught a rule about some instances of a concept class and then be taught to apply it later to other instances. For example: "How do we know a car is a vehicle? We know because *vehicles take us places.*" Later the teacher can ask about new instances. She prompts with these questions: "Is this a vehicle? How do we know?" The child can now use the rule to test out the new instance and determine the correct response.

Using Prompts Effectively

Fading

Prompts should be faded as soon as possible. Fading involves the gradual withdrawal of prompts. A progression of intermediate steps is devised and the teacher moves step by step in the progression until the prompt is no longer required. Here are some fading progressions:

Example 1: **man**   **man**   **man**

The boldness of the arrow that cues left-to-right reading of sounds is gradually faded.

Example 2:
"Listen to me count. Tell me what I count to. One, two, three, four, FIIIIVE!"
"Listen to me count. Tell me what I count to. One, two, three, Foooour!"
"Listen to me count. Tell me what I count to. One, two, three, four, five, Siiix!"
"Listen to me count. Tell me what I count to. One, two, three, four, fiive!"
"Listen to me count. Tell me what I count to. One, two, three."

By gradually reducing the loudness and the length of the final number, the teacher fades her prompt.

Example 3: The prompt for a silent *e* is faded:

$$k\bar{\imath}t_e \qquad k\bar{\imath}te \qquad k\bar{\imath}te$$

Example 4:

In physical prompting of a written response, the teacher gradually uses less pressure in moving the child's hand as the child begins to move it more correctly by himself.

Example 5:

Fading an imitative prompt can be accomplished by giving less and less of the behavior to be imitated. The teacher might use these steps: (1) say the whole word the child is trying to read; (2) say just the first two sounds; (3) say just the first sound; and (4) just make the lip movements without the sound.

Example 6:

Prompts that involve pointing or tapping of the feet are faded by gradually reducing the action.

Example 7:

The prompts in a writing program might have the visual supports for forming letters slowly withdrawn.

Use the Weakest Possible Prompt

In choosing a prompt, consider the progression by which it will be faded and start as close to the end of the progression as you can and still get the appropriate response.

The Task Stimulus Precedes the Prompt

Never present a prompt unless the task stimulus is present or, for auditory stimuli, unless the task stimulus has just been given. Suppose the teacher says, "Here's that funny letter again" (the prompt), and then shows the letter *h*. The child doesn't have to look at *h*; he can just respond to the "funny letter" cue. If the letter *h* is shown first, then the teacher says, "Oh, this is that funny letter," the child is more likely to attend to *h* before the response is prompted. The correct response is therefore more likely to become linked to *h*, and the need for the prompt in the future is reduced.

Do Not Detract Attention from the Task Stimulus

Suppose the task is to teach color concepts. The teacher presents an instance of blue and asks, "Is this ball blue?" The teacher prompts "yes" by nodding, which calls attention away from the task stimulus. It is an ineffective prompt because it leads the children to look at the teacher instead of the blue ball. A more effective prompt would be to give the answer first: "This ball is blue. What color is this ball?"

Some prompts actually direct attention to the task stimulus. For example, a voice inflection can emphasize the critical word to be attended to, as in the following: "We're going to count to *five*. What are we going to count to?"

Examples of Ineffective Prompting

By using faulty prompts, teachers sometimes fool themselves into thinking that their students know more than they actually do. The following are some common errors:

1 A question is asked with an inflection to prompt yes or no. The children can answer yes or no correctly without knowing what was asked.
2 The teacher says, "Oh, you know that word. I just told you on the last page." The child thinks of the word he was told on the last page, instead of sounding out the word.
3 The teacher says, "I'll bet you can think of that word if I tell you it's an animal that says 'Quack, quack'." Again, the child does not have to read the word to answer.

These prompts do not insure that the child will attend to the task stimulus while making the response.

Teaching Directions

If a student does not know a task direction, the teacher can tell by the nature of the mistake. When an answer is not in the class called for by the direction, you know it is necessary to teach the direction. For example, if the task was "What's the name of this animal?" and the response was "Brown," it would be clear that the child did not know the R-direction, "Name the animal." Recall from the last unit that S-directions orient attention to the task stimulus and R-directions specify the general form of the task response.

To teach the operations involved in directions, like *looking* and *naming*, a set of tasks is required. The procedure to follow is this:

1 Identify a general task format containing the directions to be taught and specify the operations to be learned. For example:

General Format	Operations
"What *(object characteristic)* is this *(object)*?"	Look at a characteristic and say its name.
"Touch every *(object class)*."	Look and touch.
"What is this?"	Look and name.
"What did it say?"	Listen and imitate.

2 Using the general format, devise a number of related tasks:
   "What *shape* is this *ball*?"
   "What *color* is this *car*?"
   "What *pattern* is this *blouse*?"

3 Devise a number of tasks involving related operations to use as not-instances. If directions about object characteristics are being taught (as in step 2 above), include not-instances such as these:
"What do we call this object?" *(Present a ball.)*
"What is this?" *(Point to a blouse.)*
"Where is this ball?"

4 Teach the set by reinforcing correct responses. The child has learned both the direction concepts and their operations when he can perform any or all tasks in the set correctly, even if some of them have not been presented before.

The teaching of required direction concepts and operations should take place early in an educational sequence.

It is suggested that the student re-examine the teaching requirements presented in this unit after carefully studying later units on the requirements for teaching concepts and operations.

Basic Corrections

Assuming that the teacher does not start a task unless the children are attending, and assuming that the tasks are adequately programed to provide sufficient prompts and directions, we can summarize basic correction decisions in figure 3.1.

(Numbers in circles indicate points at which decisions must be made)

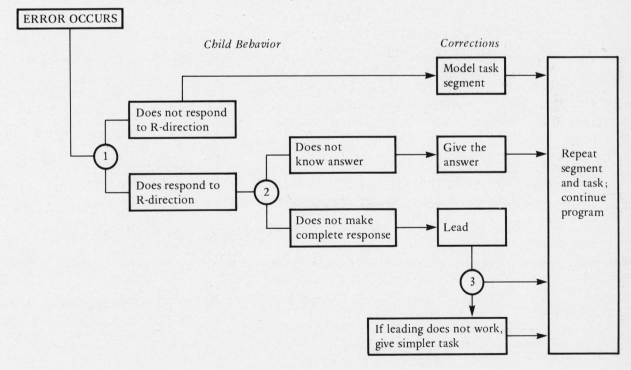

Figure 3.1 The decision process for correcting errors on basic tasks

The first task in learning to make corrections is to classify the kind of tasks being taught. A correction includes the whole task if it is a single-segment task or a series task, and includes one segment if the task is a multiple-segment task.

R-Direction Errors

When a child makes a mistake, determine whether or not he is responding to the R-direction. To decide whether the child is responding to the R-direction, see whether his response includes the general operations implied by the R-direction.

Example:	Teacher:	*(Presents a piece of chalk.)* What is this?
	Child:	What is this?
	Analysis:	The R-direction implied that the child was to look at an object and name it. The child's response shows imitation. He did *not* follow the R-direction.
Example:	Teacher:	*(Presents a piece of chalk.)* What is this?
	Child:	A crayon.
	Analysis:	In this case the child looked at and named an object, even though he named it incorrectly. He followed the R-direction.
Example:	Teacher:	*(Presents a piece of chalk.)* What is this?
	Child:	No response.
	Analysis:	No response is treated as not following the R-direction, although it may also be a failure to follow the "do it" signal. In either case, the correction is the same.
Example:	Teacher:	*(Presents a piece of chalk.)* What is this?
	Child:	I don't know.
	Analysis:	The response, "I don't know," indicates that the child probably understood the R-direction. The teacher should test to be sure. The test is to give the answer and see if the child then follows the R-direction.

If the child does not respond to the R-direction, correct by modeling the task. Follow these procedures:

1 Repeat the direction in order to call attention to the part of the task to which the child should respond.
2 Present a model. Go back to the beginning of a one-segment task or to the preceding response in a multi-segment task and present that entire segment to someone who will give the correct response or do it yourself.

3 Repeat the segment (if there is more than one) to the child, letting the child respond to the signal. (Do not answer with him.)
4 Repeat the whole task.

Example:

	Teacher:	Listen. Ham—burger. Say it fast.*
	Child:	Ham—burger.
	Correction:	1. Teacher: Say it fast. Say it fast.
		2. Teacher: Watch Henry. He can really say it fast. Henry's turn. Ham—burger. Say it fast.
	Henry:	Hamburger.
		3. Teacher: *(To the child who made the mistake.)* Your turn. See if you can say it fast. Ham—burger. Say it fast.
	Child:	Hamburger.
	Teacher:	Good. That's saying it fast.

Information Errors

If the child responds to the R-direction but gives the wrong response, determine whether he does not know the answer or whether he cannot make the response.

The child may be capable of making the required response, but not know just which response is expected. In the following tasks, the child does not know the specific task response:

Example:

	Teacher:	*(Presents egg.)* What is this?
	Child:	A ball.
	Analysis:	The child understood the R-direction. He did not know the name of the object that the teacher presented.

Example:

	Teacher:	*(Presents a picture of a rake, and points to the handle.)* What part of a rake is this?
	Child:	I don't know.
	Analysis:	The child understood the signal. He did not know the name of the part.

When the child can make the response but does not know the answer, give him the answer. Follow this procedure:

1 Give the answer.
2 Repeat the segment of the task that was missed (if there is more than one).
3 Repeat the whole task.

---

*This task involves a reading preskill. Before children learn to hook sounds together and say the word, they are taught to hook broken up words together and "say it fast."

Example: Teacher: *(Presents egg.)* What is this?
            Child: A ball.

            Correction: Teacher: It's an egg. What is it?
                           Child: An egg.

Response Form Errors

In the following tasks, the child follows the directions, shows that he knows the expected response, but does not produce the complete response called for by the task.

Example: Teacher: This is a ball. Say the whole thing.
            Child: Di a baw.

            Analysis: The child followed the direction. He simply did not produce the complete response.

Example: Teacher: Count to five. Get ready—count.
            Child: One, two, three, five.

            Analysis: The child followed the direction, but did not produce the complete response.

When the child follows the R-direction but does not make the complete response, correct first by leading him through the response. Follow this procedure:

1 Lead the child—that is, make the response with him.
2 Repeat the lead as many as eight times. Do not make the lead tedious or punishing.
3 Present the part of the task that the child missed without leading him.
4 Finally, if the child does not produce the correct response without assistance, go to a simpler task. If the child produces the response, repeat the whole task.

Example: Teacher: This is a ball. Say the whole thing.
            Child: Di a baw.

            Correction: 1. Teacher: Let's do it together. Say the whole thing. This is a ball.
                           2. Teacher: Again, the whole thing. This is a ball. Once more, the whole thing. This is a ball. That's pretty good. Let's do it again in a big voice. This is a ball. Once more. This is a ball. This is the last time. Say the whole thing. This is a ball.
                           3. Teacher: Now all by yourself. This is a ball. Say the whole thing.

	Child:	Di i a baw.
	Teacher:	Good job. You're getting it.
	4. (Teacher goes to another task.)	

Example: Teacher: We have four and we *(pause)* plus three.
          Child: *(Unable to hold up three fingers.)*
          Teacher: How many fingers do you want to hold up?
          Child: Three.

      Correction: 1. Teacher: Here, let me help you.
                      2. Teacher: *(Places child's thumb over end of little finger.)* There. You're plussing three with your fingers.
                      3. Teacher: Try it again all by yourself. Open up your fingers. Listen. We have four and we *(pause)* plus three.
                        Child: *(With some effort holds up three fingers.)*
                        Teacher: Good plussing three with your fingers.

When the child follows the R-direction but does not make the complete response, and leading does not work, give a task with a simpler response requirement. Follow this procedure:

1 Break the response into simple components and present one component at a time, beginning with the final one.
2 As one component is mastered, add the next closest component to it.
3 Continue until the full task response is mastered.
4 Repeat the whole task.

Example: Teacher: This is a ball. Say the whole thing.
          Child: Di a baw.

      Correction: 1. Teacher: Ball. Ball. Say "ball."
                        Child: Ball.
                        Teacher: Right, ball. Good.
                      2. Teacher: A ball. A ball. Say "a ball."
                        Child: A ball.
                        Teacher: Good. You're getting it.
                      3. Teacher: Say "is a ball." Say it.
                        Child: A ball.
                        Teacher: *(Repeats as necessary.)*
                      4. Teacher: This is a ball. Say the whole thing.
                        Child: This is a ball.
                        Teacher: Very good. You got it. Let's try it once more.

Procedures for correcting mistakes positively and efficiently are a very important part of teaching. Knowing when to model, when to give the answer, when to lead, and when to go to a simpler task can carry the teacher a long way in this endeavor. At more advanced levels of instruction there is another correction procedure the teacher should consider. Suppose the student reads *robe* as *rob*. The nature of the error shows a failure to discriminate the importance of the final *e* in making the *o* in *robe* long. The correction takes advantage of the kind of error made to teach an important discrimination. "The word is robe. When there is an *e* on the end of the word, the vowel says its name, *oooh.*" The teacher then takes a student through a short series of practice trials with rob, robe, robe, rob, and perhaps some other comparisons from the same family (not, note, and so on). *Discrimination practice* is very useful where highly similar concept instances are confused with each other.

Pacing a Routine

The final set of teaching skills to be mentioned is the pacing of a teaching demonstration. Every demonstration has different pacing requirements. For example, when the same operation occurs in each segment of a task (as in the plus-one series), *rhythmical* pacing and similar inflections help to prompt attention to the common operation: "We haaave twooo, and we plus one. *(Pause.)* How many do we have? We haaave threee, and we plus one. *(Pause.)* How many do we have?" Look for the pacing that is most helpful in each routine.

Another important aspect of pacing is quickness. Keep the lesson going and you will hold interest better than if it drags or there are unneeded pauses between tasks while you decide what to do next.

Finally, the change of pace should be kept in mind. Interest can be held by dramatically changing the pace from a quick routine to an unexpected holding of an attention signal, a long pause before a "do it" signal, a change in loudness, or a change in voice pitch.

summary

The skills involved in the direct instruction of groups consist of using signals, teaching directions, prompting, using reinforcers, correcting mistakes, and pacing the presentation. This unit has reviewed procedures for each of these skills except use of reinforcers. Remember that to become proficient it is important to get supervised practice in use of the skills.

In summarizing, we will look at the various skills as they are integrated in the behavioral model of teaching.

Procedures Applying to the Pre-Task Component

1   Secure attention before proceeding with the teaching demonstration.
2   State the rules for reinforcement before presenting the task.

3 Use hand signals to help hold attention.
4 Vary the duration of the attention signals unpredictably.

To teach attention signals: (1) state what will happen if the children attend (the contingency); (2) pause; (3) give the signal; (4) at the same time use a hand signal to hold attention for a variable time; (5) praise good attending; and (6) give the reinforcers that were promised.

To correct children who are not attending, praise by name (or otherwise reward) children who are attending and describe their behavior to the inattentive children. Repeat the task, and praise (or otherwise reward) the children who attend.

After attention signals have been established, use easy tasks to fade out reinforcement between the attention response and the task presentation. The goal is to give reinforcement only at the end of the task (after the child gives a task response). This builds a chain of attending behavior that includes the teaching demonstration.

Procedures Applying to the Task Component

1 Study each teaching demonstration to determine its pacing requirements.
2 For prompts not controlled by the program, be sure to: (a) use the minimum prompt necessary; (b) fade the prompts as soon as possible; (c) present the task stimulus *before* the prompt; and (d) direct attention to the task stimulus.
3 Use hand signals as "do it" signals.
4 Pause before giving a "do it" signal to provide a general "get ready" cue.

Teaching demonstrations differ. It is important to analyze tasks to find the pacing that will be most helpful. Pacing decisions should consider phrasing, tempo, pauses, and dramatic changes.

Every task requires an attention-to-task-stimulus response as well as a task response. Prompts can be used to facilitate the occurrence of both kinds of responses. Use *S-prompts* to help focus attention on task stimuli. Use *R-prompts* to get the right task response going. Prompts can be verbal and nonverbal instructions, added cues, physical prompts, and models for imitation. Any stimulus that can make desired responses occur at the right time can be used as a prompt.

Fading involves the gradual withdrawal of prompts. It can consist of reducing the intensity of a stimulus, reducing or increasing the size of a visual stimulus, presenting less and less of a response to be imitated, and so forth. Any way in which a stimulus can be made less discriminable in a given teaching context can constitute fading.

"Do it" signals specify when someone is to respond. Always pause for a variable length of time before giving a "do it" signal. This pause provides a general cue that a "do it" signal is coming and sets up a variable reinforcement schedule for good attending.

"Do it" signals are taught just like any other signal. Present several tasks using the same signal, reinforce appropriate responses, and correct inappropriate ones.

In multiple-segment tasks, a "do it" signal in one segment can be taught without going through the whole task. In a series task, the chain of responses should not be treated separately. If there is an error, the whole task is presented again.

Procedures Applying to the Post-Task Component

1 Reinforce correct responses. This is done by confirming the correct response, then giving praise, and so on.
2 As learning progresses make reinforcement more intermittent.
3 Correct all mistakes. Teach task directions where necessary.
4 When a child is having a lot of difficulty, reinforce trying.

The decision process in correcting mistakes in basic instruction is as follows. When an error occurs, determine whether or not the child responded to the R-direction. If not, repeat the direction to call his attention to it, and then model the task segment in which the error occurred. If the child responded to the R-direction, determine whether he does not know the answer or is having difficulty making the response. Do this by examining the response the child did make. If the child does not know, give him the answer and repeat the task. If the child is having difficulty making the complete response, lead him through the response several times. If this fails, try to simplify the response requirements by breaking them down into smaller units and building them up again.

To see if the correction procedure has worked, present the task segment again, giving no help. Then the whole task is presented again, and the program is continued. In advanced instruction, errors most commonly involve discriminative confusion of related concepts. By presenting a series of instances of both concepts, the teacher can improve the discrimination between them.

It is sometimes necessary to teach explicitly the operations involved in task directions ("look," "name"). To do this, design a general format containing the directions, construct a set of related tasks by following the general format, and teach the tasks using prompts, reinforcers, and corrections.

self-test

1 before

2 varying

3 pause

1 Attention signals are taught to children _____ proceeding with any other task.

2 Attention signals are given for _____ lengths of time.

3 Always _____ before presenting a "do it" signal.

4 A series task cannot be broken down into _____ when corrections are needed.

5 Task stimuli differ from prompts in that they are not eventually _____ _____ .

6 Taking a child's hand and tracing a letter is an example of _____ _____ .

7 Fading often involves decreasing the _____ of a stimulus.

8 When the child responds on signal, but does not give a response of the right class, the general correction is to teach the _____ .

9 When the teacher says "My turn," repeats the task segment, and gives the answer, the procedure is called _____ .

10 The teacher presents an arithmetic problem, points to the equal sign, and asks, "What's the rule?" The children do not respond. The teacher says, "What's the rule? As many as we count to on one side of the equal sign, we have to count to on the other side of the equal sign. Say it with me. What's the rule? As many . . . ," The children respond with the teacher as the rule is repeated several more times. This correction is an example of _____ .

NUMBER RIGHT _____

4 segments, parts

5 faded out

6 physical prompting

7 intensity

8 R-directions

9 modeling

10 leading

exercise 1 programed practice

1 Attention signals are taught to children _____ proceeding with any other task.

2 The teacher first states the _____ , then _____ .

3 Next, the teacher gives a _____ .

4 Those who attend well are given praise and _____ what they are being praised for.

5 When the child who was inattentive eventually does perform, _____ him for doing so.

6 After the attending response has been learned, reinforcement is _____ eliminated between the attention response and the task demonstration. Reinforcement comes only at the _____ of the task.

1 before

2 contingency; pauses

3 signal

4 told

5 reinforce, reward

6 gradually; end

7 varying

8 when

9 pause; cue

10 single

11 same

12 separately

13 segments, parts

14 "do it";
   point

15 general format

16 previously;
   new

17a) P (imitative
   prompt)

b) TS

c) P (physical
   prompting)

d) P (added cue)

e) TS

7   Attention signals are given for _____ lengths of time.

8   "Do it" signals specify _____ a child is to respond.

9   Always _____ before presenting a "do it" signal. This provides a _____ that a "do it" signal is coming.

10 In a _____-segment task, there is one task signal and a task response.

11 To teach a "do it" signal, several different tasks are given with the _____ format.

12 Responses to "do it" signals in the segments of a multiple-segment task can be taught _____, and then the segments can be put together.

13 A series task cannot be broken down into _____ when corrections are needed.

14 In a series task, the same sort of _____ signal is usually used for each response in the chain or series. For example, in sounding out a word, the teacher might point to a sound for as long as he wants the group to hold it, and then move to the next sound when he wants the group to move. The _____ is the "do it" signal.

15 To teach directions, construct a set of tasks using the same _____ _____ and containing the direction.

16 A prompt is a _____ taught task stimulus that the teacher can use to get a specified response to a _____ task stimulus.

17 For each of the following, circle P if the underlined words are a prompt, and TS if they are a task stimulus.

   P TS a) The teacher shows a picture of a cow and says, "Listen, I can say its name. Cow. You say it."

   P TS b) The teacher shakes her head as Billy starts to leave the room. Billy returns to his seat.

   P TS c) The teacher takes Mary's hand to help her write her name.

   P TS d) When teaching color names, all the red objects are presented by the teacher in her left hand. All the blue objects are presented in her right hand.

   P TS e) The teacher says, "Listen. Say 'Mmmmmaaaannnn'." The child says "Mmmmmaaaannnn."

P TS f) In teaching left and right, the teacher says, "You write with your <u>right hand.</u> Now which hand is your right hand?" Jacob pretends to write and then holds out his right hand.

18 Task stimuli differ from prompts in that they are not eventually _____ _____.

19 Prompts that focus attention on task stimuli are called _____.

20 Prompts that help get the right task response going are called _____.

21 Taking a child's hand and tracing a letter is an example of _____ _____.

22 Probably the most common form of prompting used by the teacher is _____.

23 Fading involves the _____ withdrawal of prompts.

24 Fading often involves decreasing the _____ of a stimulus.

25 Fading in a writing program might involve withdrawing _____ cues used to guide the formation of letters.

26 The task stimulus should come before the prompt or at the same time, so that the child will attend to the _____ _____ and not only to the _____.

27 When the child can follow the R-directions, but does not know the right response, the general correction is to _____ him the answer.

28 When the child can follow R-directions, responds on signal, but still cannot make the complete task response, the general correction is to use _____ or to present a simpler task.

29 When the teacher says, "My turn," repeats the task segment, and gives the answer, the procedure is called _____.

30 A modeling correction has four steps:
    a) Repeating the _____.
    b) Presenting a _____ of the task or segment.
    c) Repeating the _____ (if there is more than one).
    d) Repeating the _____ task.

31 A leading correction has these steps:
    a) _____ the child. The teacher produces the responses with him.

---

f) P (rule or instruction)

18 faded out

19 S-prompts

20 R-prompts

21 physical prompting

22 imitation

23 gradual

24 intensity

25 visual

26 task stimulus; prompt

27 give

28 R-prompts

29 modeling

30a) direction

b) model

c) segment

d) whole

31a) Leading

b) _____ the lead as many as eight times.

c) Presenting the part of the task that was missed _____ leading.

d) Repeating the _____ task if successful.

32 To simplify the task response, follow these steps:

a) Break the response into simple components and present one component at a time, beginning with the _____ one.

b) As one component is mastered, add the next _____ one to it.

c) Continue to _____ components until the full task response is mastered.

d) Repeat the _____ task.

33 When the teacher responds with the children, it is called _____.

34 For each of the following, circle "Yes" if the child has responded to the R-direction and "No" if he has not.

YES NO a) The teacher points to a tree next to a bush and asks, "Is the tree tall?" The child says, "No."

YES NO b) The teacher points to a red car and says, "What color is this car?" The child says, "Yellow."

YES NO c) The teacher points to a picture of a man and asks, "Is this a man?" The child says, "Blue."

35 Suppose the student reads *robe* as *rob*. The nature of the error shows a failure to _____ the importance of the final *e* in making the *o* in *robe* long.

36 To correct this kind of error, the teacher then takes a student through a short series of practice trials with *rob* and *robe*. This correction is called _____ _____.

37 In determining pacing requirements, consider _____, pauses, _____, and change of pace.

exercise 2 finding "do it" signals

For each item below, first put a check (✔) where the children are to make responses. When this is done, draw a line under that part of the statement that includes the "do it" signal. Then, indicate with a circle (O) where you would pause. Note that in most cases, the statement that includes the "do it" signal also includes the R-direction.

Example A. "Listen. We have four and we **O** <u>plus three.</u>"
(Children are to hold up three fingers.)

Example B. (Point to 5.) **O** <u>"How many are in this group?"</u> ✔
(Point to -3) "And then it tells me to minus **O** <u>how many?"</u> ✔

1 (Show letters.) "When I touch it, you say it. Keep on saying it as long as I touch it." (Touch *m*.)

2 (Point to the girl who is not standing.) "Is this girl standing?" "Why not?"

3 (Point to bicycle.) "What's this?"

4 "Yes, this is a bicycle. Say the whole thing."

5 (Point to bicycle.) "Is this a tree? Is this a truck? What is this?"

6 "We're going to count to seven. What are we going to count to?"

7 "Let's count to seven. What are we going to count to?" "Yes, count to seven. Get it going . . . Threeee." (Children say "Threeee.")

8 (Presents words *mat, rat, sat, cat.*) "Watch me read these words." (Point. Read words.) "Mmmmat, rrrrat, ssssat." (Point to *c* in *cat*.) "So this must be . . ."

9 "Listen. We haaaave four and we plus two. We haaaave four and we plus two. We haaaave four and we plus two. How many do we haaaave?"

10 (Point.) "Is this girl skinny? Is this girl smiling? Is this girl skinny and smiling? Why not? Right, because she's not skinny."

Answers to Exercise 2

1 (Show letters.) "When I touch it, you say it. Keep on saying it as long as I touch it." **O** (<u>Touch *m*. ✔</u>)

2 (Point to the girl who is not standing.) **O** <u>"Is this girl standing?"</u> ✔ **O** "Why not?" ✔

3 (Point to bicycle.) **O** <u>"What's this?"</u> ✔

4 "Yes, this is a bicycle. **O** <u>Say the whole thing."</u> ✔

5 (Point to bicycle.) **O** "Is this a tree? ✔ **O** Is this a truck? ✔ **O** What is this?" ✔

6 "We're going to count to seven. **O** What are we going to count to?" ✔

7 "Let's count to seven. **O** What are we going to count to?" ✔ "Yes, count to seven. **O** Get it going . . . Threeee." ✔ (Children say "Threeee.")

8 (Present words *mat, rat, sat, cat.*) "Watch me read these words." (Point. Read words.) "Mmmmat, rrrrat, ssssat." **O** (Point to *c* in *cat*.) "So this must be . . ." ✔

9 "Listen. We haaaave four and we plus two. We haaave four and we plus two. We haaave four and we plus two. **O** How many do we haaave?" ✔

10 (Point.) **O** "Is this girl skinny? ✔ **O** Is this girl smiling? ✔ **O** Is this girl skinny and smiling? ✔ **O** Why not? ✔ Right, because she's not skinny."

exercise 3 correction procedures

Directions: Fill in the answers and check them by referring to the key at the end of the exercise.

1 What are the steps the teacher goes through if the child does not respond to the R-direction?

a) _____

b) _____

c) _____

d) _____

2 There are two types of mistakes that a child can make if he does respond to the R-direction. What are they?

a) _____

b) _____

3 What are the steps the teacher goes through if the child does not know the answer?

a) _____

b) _____

c) _____

4 What are the steps the teacher goes through if the child is unable to make the complete response?

a) _____

b) _____

c) _____

d) _____

Answers

1   a)   Repeats the R-direction
    b)   Models the task (or task segment if there are segments).
    c)   Repeats the segment (if there are segments).
    d)   Repeats the whole task.

2   a)   He does not know the answer.
    b)   He cannot make the response.

3   a)   Gives the answer.
    b)   Repeats the segment (if there are segments).
    c)   Repeats the whole task.

4   a)   Leads the child.
    b)   Repeats the lead up to eight times.
    c)   Repeats the segment (if there are segments).
    d)   Repeats the whole task.

discussion questions

1   Demonstrate a procedure for teaching children to respond to an attention signal.

2   Demonstrate a correction procedure for failure to respond to an attention signal.

3   Describe how the teacher goes about eliminating reinforcers between the attention responses and the task presentation. Why is this done?

4   Explain why the teacher varies the length of attention signals before starting the task presentation.

5   How do you go about finding the "do it" signals in a program?

6   Why do you pause before a "do it" signal?

7   Give the basic procedure for teaching a "do it" signal.

8   State the difference between a multiple-segment task and a series task.

9   Specify how to teach the operations involved in responses to directions.

10 Give an example of an S-prompt.

11 Give an example of an R-prompt.

12 How does good programing build and use prompts?

13 What is fading?

14 Demonstrate an instance of fading.

15 Give three rules for the use of prompts in teaching.

16 Give an example of ineffective prompting where the task stimulus comes after the prompt.

17 Give an example of a prompt that detracts attention from the task stimulus.

18 Explain the difference between responding to the R-direction and not responding to it, and give an example.

19 Give the correction steps to follow when the child does not respond to the R-direction.

20 State two types of mistakes that can occur if the child does respond to the R-direction.

21 Give the correction steps used when the child does not know the answer.

22 Give the steps used when the child is unable to make the complete response.

23 Draw a diagram of the decision process for correcting errors in teaching basic skills.

Directions for items 24 through 27. For each of the following tasks and errors, classify the error and demonstrate an appropriate correction procedure.

24 Teacher: Let's hear you count to six.
    Child: One, two, three, four, five.

25 Teacher: *(Presents an egg.)* What is this?
    Child: A ball.

26 Teacher: This is a vehicle. Say the whole thing.
    Child: Vehicle.

27 Teacher: *(Points to a bush.)* This is a bush. What is it?
    Child: Green.

28 State the features to be considered in determining the pacing requirements of a task.

29 Give four procedures that apply to the pre-task component of a model of teaching.

30 Give four procedures that apply to the task component of a model of teaching.

31 Give four procedures that apply to the post-task component of a model of teaching.

unit 4

Basic Requirements
for Teaching Concepts

objectives

When you complete this unit you should be able to—

1 Define concept from a behavioral view.
2 Explain what is meant by *teach the general case*.
3 Outline the procedures most essential to teaching concepts as general cases.
4 Describe and explain the weakness of stimulus control procedures that fail to teach a general case.
5 Describe concept learning as a multiple discrimination problem.
6 Contrast the effectiveness of cumulative programing and successive-pair programing in teaching sets of concepts.
7 Define S+, S–, and Si.

lesson

The building blocks of intelligent behavior are concepts and operations. The basic requirements for building these structures will be considered in this unit and the next. A concept can be defined as the *set* of stimulus characteristics unique to a set of stimulus instances in a given group of concepts. An operation can be defined as the common effect of a set of responses under stimulus control. The goal in teaching concepts and operations is to develop competencies that extend beyond the specific tasks used in instruction. The goal is to teach a general case.

Test for a General Case

The test for teaching a general case will be illustrated with a concept example. Inspect the following diagram:

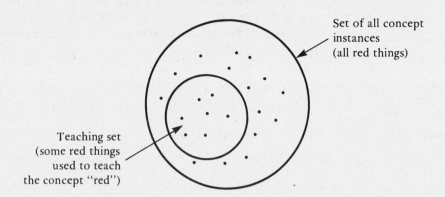

Set of all concept instances (all red things)

Teaching set (some red things used to teach the concept "red")

A general case has been taught when, after teaching *some* members (instances) of a concept class, *any* member is identified correctly (that is, responded to in the same way consistently). Furthermore, nonmembers of the concept class are responded to in a different way. Thus, the most common test for the induction of a concept is to present concept instances which were not used in the instruction and see if they are correctly identified.

Concept Learning and Operant Behavior

In the field of operant psychology, conceptual behavior is seen as a special case of the stimulus control of operant behavior; that is, the control of operant behavior by discriminative stimuli. When a child can appropriately respond one way to instances of a concept, and another way to not-instances, he is said to have learned the concept. His operant behavior is controlled explicitly by stimuli that are the essential concept characteristics. Conceptual behavior is a component of cognitive behavior, which can include a large variety of inductive and deductive problem-solving skills. For now, however, we will focus explicitly on identifying procedures by which operant behavior can be brought under the control of essential characteristics of concepts.

Operant behavior can be brought under the control of preceding stimuli through the use of differential reinforcement.* In the presence of certain stimuli, only appropriate responses are reinforced. In the absence of the certain stimuli, those responses are not reinforced. For example, to teach the

---

*See *Teaching 1*, unit 6, for more detail.

concept *longer*, we might present two toy cars, one four inches long and one two inches long, and ask, "Which car is longer?" If the child points to the four-inch car, he is told, "Right! You pointed to the *longer* car." The teacher might then present two pencils and go through the same routine. Other examples (both positive and negative) may be required to teach the general case, but the beginning discriminations have been made. Thus, the first requirement in teaching a concept is to use *differential reinforcement*—present both positive and negative concept instances and reinforce appropriate responses to them. The process is called *discrimination learning*.

A Comparison of Four Procedures for Establishing Stimulus Control

To develop a better understanding of exactly what is involved in concept learning (at least with the naive learner, where shortcuts cannot be taken), we will examine the implications of four procedures for establishing stimulus control of behavior.

Procedure 1: Use one positive instance and one negative instance that differ in several ways

The simplest stimulus control procedure uses two stimulus instances or examples. A particular response is reinforced to the positive instance and not reinforced to the negative instance.

Consider this example:

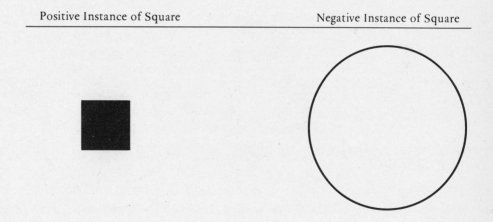

| Positive Instance of Square | Negative Instance of Square |

The square and circle are repeatedly presented until the child always responds one way to the square and another way to the circle. Has a concept been taught? How can you tell? It is not possible to look inside the child's head. Other stimuli must be presented to see how the child responds to them.

New members of the positive and negative classes are presented to test for concept induction:

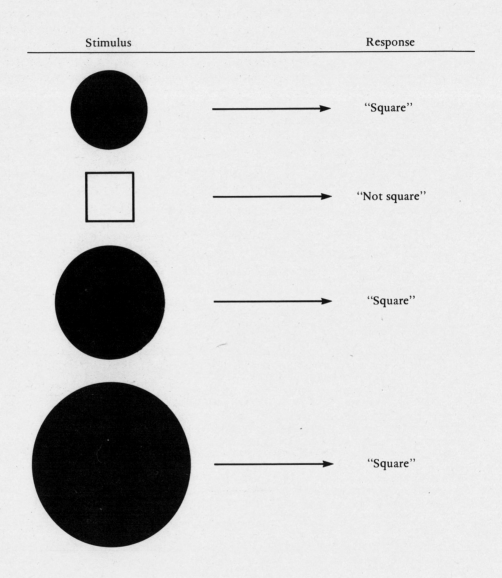

Stimulus	Response
(black circle)	"Square"
(open square)	"Not square"
(black circle)	"Square"
(black circle)	"Square"

All *black* figures were called squares. We therefore infer that the effect of our prior training was to teach a black-white discrimination rather than the concept *square*.

Implications of Procedure 1

This procedure isolates an important problem in teaching concepts. *If a discrimination between positive and negative instances can be made in terms of characteristics other than those to be taught, a discrimination may be learned in terms of those other characteristics.*[1] With the examples given above, the teacher would probably find that some children learn to respond in terms of *shape*, some *size*, some *color*, and if position was not varied, some would respond in terms of *position* also. The rule is: If several cues can be used as a basis for obtaining reinforcement, different learners will respond to different cues. In fact, some children might learn to respond in terms of several of the characteristics just mentioned.

A classroom illustration of this problem can often be found in teaching beginning reading. A group is working on beginning sounds at the board with the teacher. Four sounds are written on the board for that day's lesson. The teacher goes over them until all the children have mastered them. The next day she writes them on the board again, but *in a different order* and with slightly different form. Surprise! The children have "forgotten" them. Actually, they didn't necessarily forget what they were taught; they just learned the wrong thing. Some may have learned to call the sounds by their positions, some by irrelevant aspects of their shapes or sizes. These teaching errors can be prevented by clearly understanding the requirements for teaching concepts.

Procedure 2: One positive instance and one negative instance with control of irrelevant stimuli

Suppose we take the preceding example and control for irrelevant stimuli by making them the same for our positive and negative instances and presenting each one in the same position.

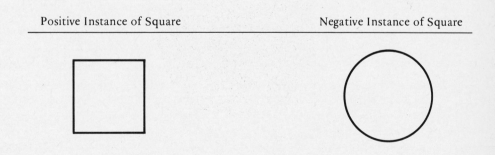

| Positive Instance of Square | Negative Instance of Square |

Our positive and negative instances of squareness now differ only in shape. Training is now continued until there is one consistent response to the positive instance ("Square") and a different response to the negative instance ("Not Square"). We again test for concept induction:

When our test began to vary irrelevant characteristics such as size, pattern, and color, the discrimination sometimes broke down.

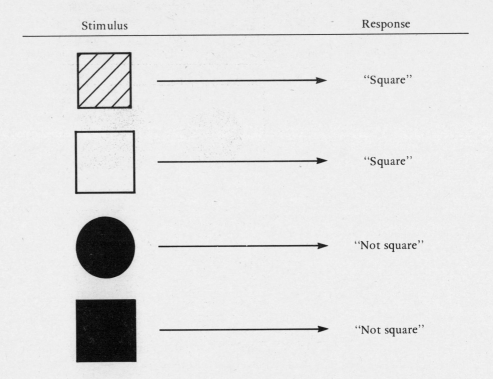

Stimulus	Response
	"Square"
	"Square"
	"Not square"
	"Not square"

Implications of Procedure 2

When irrelevant characteristics are held constant in training, the more new examples differ from the training examples in irrelevant characteristics, the more likely a breakdown in the discrimination.

Procedure 3: A series of positive and negative instances with varying irrelevant characteristics

An alternative control procedure leads to more interesting effects. Suppose that we present a series of positive and negative instances in pairs (or one at a time) and randomly vary irrelevant characteristics. The task is, "Point to the square."

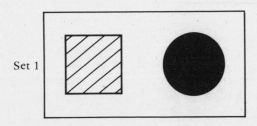

Set 1

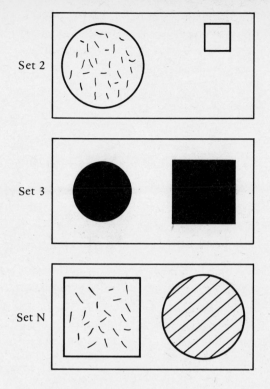

Set 2

Set 3

Set N

We then test as follows:

	Stimulus Pair	Figure Chosen
Set 1		Square
Set 2		Square
Set 3		Square

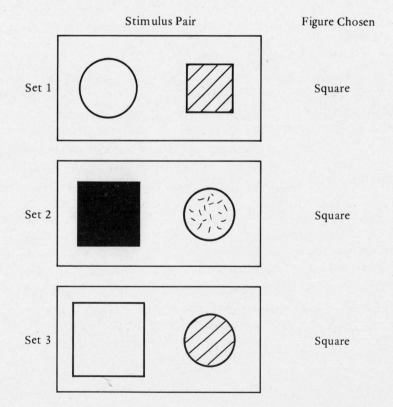

With an adequate number of training examples, learners give a perfect performance on the test trials with "new" examples.

Harlow has shown that a procedure like this can be used to teach monkeys a concept such as *oddity* ("Choose the one that is different.").[2] When irrelevant characteristics (such as, form and position) are varied, they cannot be consistently associated with reinforcement, and therefore, will not control responses. In a Harlow experiment, a monkey might be given four trials on each of a series of problems like these:

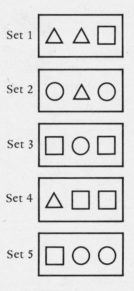

After about 250 problems, monkeys respond correctly about 90 percent of the time on first trial. For the concept *oddity*, form and position are irrelevant. When these characteristics are varied from trial to trial (or every four trials), the monkeys learn to choose the one that is not like the other two and to bypass those that are the same.

The importance of this procedure has also been demonstrated in research by Ferster and Hammer.[3] In teaching arithmetic concepts to chimpanzees, they make a strong case for varying all stimuli not related to the reinforcement contingency (all stimuli irrelevant to the concept being taught). Chimpanzees did not attend to the *number* of items in an example if responding to color, position, shape, size, or some other irrelevant cue was consistently reinforced.

Implications of Procedure 3

By presenting many positive and negative instances in which irrelevant stimulus characteristics are varied, it is possible to teach a discrimination that will be maintained when any "new" instances are presented.* A general case can be taught; but, how general is it?

---

*"New" refers to new examples involving new combinations of irrelevant characteristics, *all* of which have been taught.

Another Look at Procedure 2

Let's return to procedure 2 where we have a positive and negative instance and have controlled for irrelevant characteristics by keeping them constant. Our training instances were as follows:

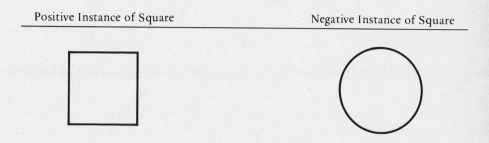

| Positive Instance of Square | Negative Instance of Square |

Now let's try another test, with *irrelevant* characteristics held constant:

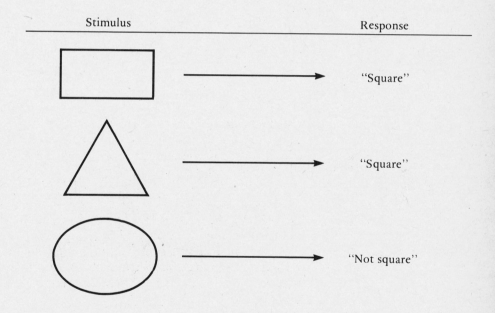

Stimulus	Response
	"Square"
	"Square"
	"Not square"

On this test, the responses imply that the child was responding to corners and/or straight sides in discriminating square from circle, but 90° angles and equal sides were missed as essential characteristics. We would infer that it is because these stimulus characteristics have not been discriminated that rectangles and triangles were called "Square."

Similarly, if Harlow's monkeys had been presented with test problems of this sort:

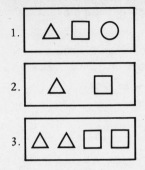

It is very likely that wrong responding would occur since they were not taught how to respond to negative instances of oddity (examples of concepts that might be confused with oddity).

It is necessary to teach the discriminations *between concepts* which might be confused with each other.

A Second Implication of Procedure 2

If two concepts differ in many ways, one can learn to discriminate between them by attending to any essential difference. But as new concepts are added to the set-to-be-discriminated-from-each-other, there is a need to teach additional essential characteristics.

Procedure 4: Teaching discriminations among a set of related concepts

Figure 4.1 shows five concepts from the set of closed geometric figures. The figure shows a set of related concepts, sets of essential concept characteristics (for example, a, b, c for *square)*, and sets of necessary discriminations between concepts (for example, f vs. a for *rectangle* vs. *square*). Study figure 4.1 carefully before going on.

Now let's explore further the notion of a-set-to-be-discriminated-from-each-other. There are two fundamentally different procedures for teaching the discrimination of a set of related concepts.

Procedure 4a. Teach successive pairs of discriminations. Square and circle are taught to a criterion of perfect performance. Then, a square and rectangle are brought to criterion. Then, rectangle and circle, and so on, until all ten pairs of discriminations have been taught.

Procedure 4b. Cumulatively build the set of concepts discriminated from each other. Teach the discrimination of square from circle. Then add equilateral triangle to the set and bring all three to criterion when presented randomly. Then, add parallelogram, and finally, rectangle to make a set of five.

Ferster and Hammer compared successive-pair and cumulative programing procedures for teaching number-symbol identification to chimpanzees.[4] They found that, after using the successive-pair programing, the chimpanzees failed to respond above a chance level to randomly presented members of the number set. When cumulative programing was used, discrimination of randomly presented numbers was very accurate.

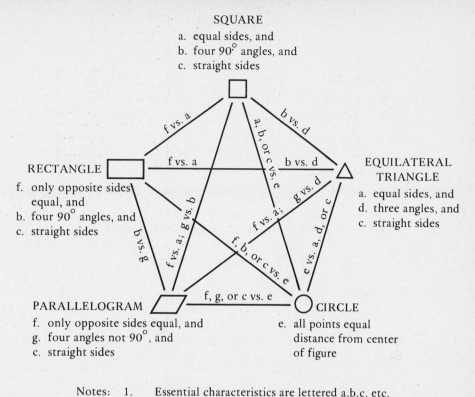

Figure 4.1 illustration labels:

SQUARE
a. equal sides, and
b. four 90° angles, and
c. straight sides

RECTANGLE
f. only opposite sides equal, and
b. four 90° angles, and
c. straight sides

EQUILATERAL TRIANGLE
a. equal sides, and
d. three angles, and
c. straight sides

PARALLELOGRAM
f. only opposite sides equal, and
g. four angles not 90°, and
c. straight sides

CIRCLE
e. all points equal distance from center of figure

Connecting line labels: f vs. a; b vs. d; a, b, or c vs. e; f vs. a; b vs. d; g vs. d; f vs. a, g vs. b; b vs. g; f vs. a; f, b, or c vs. e; e vs. a, d, or c; f, g, or c vs. e

Notes: 1. Essential characteristics are lettered a, b, c, etc.

2. Identical characteristics have the same letter.

3. Discriminations to be learned to master the set are given on the connecting lines.

Figure 4.1 Analysis of five concepts in the set of closed geometric figures

Implications of Procedures 4a and 4b

Cumulative programing is essential to teaching naive learners sets of related concepts so that they can correctly respond to randomly presented instances of the set (old or new). Cumulative programing is essential to the inductive teaching of the general case.

The ineffectiveness of successive-pairs programing can be illustrated from the analysis in figure 4.1. Suppose square and circle were brought to criterion and the characteristic of square used in the discrimination was *c* (straight sides). Next suppose we teach the discrimination of rectangle from circle. Again straight sides is the characteristic attended to. Next, we teach the discrimination of square from rectangle. The student can forget about straight sides. It won't work. So now the discrimination might focus on another single characteristic, four equal sides versus only opposite sides equal. With this procedure, there is no requirement to learn the conjunctive rule that square is *a plus b plus c* in the set of closed geometric figures. Partial rules become inadequate when new pairs are added to the set. This problem will arise with any multiple-attribute concept sharing characteristics with related concepts. Cumulative programing, in which the "current teaching set" is brought to criterion before a new member is added, overcomes this problem.

An alternative to the cumulative programing strategy might be to randomly present pairs of all possible concepts in the set. If the set is small, this might work, but the chances are that it would fail because of the "memory" requirements it imposes on the learner. This method could work with experienced concept learners, especially if accompanied by rules (deductive method) to draw attention to essential concept characteristics.

Concept Learning—A Multiple Discrimination Problem

We learn concepts because we are taught to respond one way to positive instances and another way to negative instances. The procedures for establishing stimulus control over responding, illustrated in the preceding section, point to two important sets of discriminations that are critical to learning concepts.

1 *Within positive or negative instances, it is necessary to discriminate relevant characteristics from irrelevant characteristics.* For example, a positive instance of *red* might be shaped like a truck (irrelevant), be made of wood (irrelevant), and be sitting on the table (irrelevant). Colors have to be discriminated from *shapes, materials,* and *position.* Within a negative instance of *red* (say, a blue rubber ball) there is also a need to discriminate the relevant characteristics of the negative instance (blueness) from the irrelevant characteristics (ball shape, rubber material, held in the hand).
2 *Between positive and negative instances, it is necessary to discriminate between relevant characteristics of each.* For example, to learn about red it is necessary to learn to discriminate not-red by learning to respond to blue, orange, yellow, green, and so on, as the *not-red set.*

The two aspects of this multiple discrimination problem can be illustrated as follows:

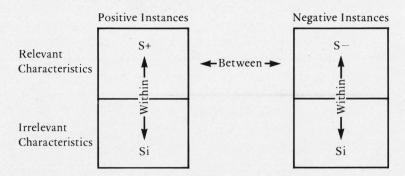

Note: S+, S−, and Si may be a single characteristic or a *set* of characteristics.

If S+ stands for the relevant characteristics of positive instances, S– stands for the relevant characteristics of negative instances, and Si refers to irrelevant characteristics of either, then the problem becomes one of learning to discriminate *within* instances S+ from Si, or S– from Si, and to discriminate *between* instances S+ from S–.*

Now what does all of this mean? Essentially it means that *a concept cannot be taught without teaching the relevant characteristics of other concepts from which the given concept is to be discriminated.* In other words, red cannot be taught without teaching not-red by presenting orange, blue, green, and so forth in the not-set. The discrimination of orange from blue does not have to be taught in order to teach red, but the discrimination of red from not-red colors must be taught. Furthermore, red cannot be taught without teaching that surface textures or patterns, or differences in shape or size of objects have nothing to do with red or any other color. In fact, for a completely developed concept of red, it would be necessary to insure that the concept of color is discriminated from the concepts of pattern, texture, size, shape, brightness, and position. Many concepts must be taught just to teach a concept as simple as red.

Basic Requirements for Teaching Concepts (Inductive Method)

Given the need for differential reinforcement of discriminations within and between instances used to teach concepts and the need to teach related concept sets as sets, an efficient teaching program must meet these requirements:

1 A *set* of positive and negative instances is required. A concept cannot be taught with a single positive and a single negative instance, because any specific instance of a concept can be an example of many concepts.
2 The set of instances should be selected so that *all* positive instances possess *all* relevant concept characteristics, and *all* negative instances possess only *some* or *none* of these characteristics. If this is not done, the teaching will provide contradictory information.
3 Irrelevant characteristics *within* positive and negative instances must be varied. Otherwise, a misrule may be taught.
4 The program must be cumulative so that the all critical discriminations in the *enlarging set* of concepts are taught. A program cannot just "teach" something once and forget it.

On Determining What Discriminations Should Be Taught

Behavioral psychologists approach the study of concepts empirically. Through the extensive study of alternative procedures, behaviorists could eventually specify the discriminations that must be taught to efficiently teach

---

*Note: S+ and S– are used as procedural concepts when planning instruction, for example, "Instances of red will be S+ in this program." S+ and S– are functional concepts when testing for the effects of instruction, "Johnny called all the red objects *red*." When used functionally, S+ is the same as SD and S– is the same as SΔ (S-delta) in the older operant literature.

specific concepts. An alternative-*logical approach* has been proposed by Engelmann which greatly simplifies empirical effort.

In his book *Conceptual Learning*,[5] Engelmann takes the position that from the point of view of the teacher, a concept can only be fully defined within a *finite set* of concepts and their instances (a teaching universe). Instances are the basic units the teacher would have to present to give examples of the concept. A concept is defined by the set of stimulus characteristics common to some instances in a finite set and not common to others. These common characteristics are the relevant or essential characteristics of a concept.

Once a concept is viewed within a finite set, it becomes possible for the programer or teacher to examine the members of that set and to *logically analyze* how concepts are the same and how they differ. Behavioral knowledge of why errors occur in discrimination learning can then be coupled with this logical analysis of concepts to produce efficient programing procedures. These ideas are so important that unit 9 is devoted entirely to them. In unit 9 we return to the problem of concept analysis within finite sets and study the hierarchical structurings among concepts.

summary

A concept can be defined as the set of stimulus characteristics unique to a set of stimulus instances in a given universe and not common to other concepts in that universe. A general case has been taught when, after teaching some members of a concept class, any member is identified correctly, and nonmembers are identified as not belonging to the concept class.

Concept learning can be viewed as bringing operant behavior under stimulus control. Basic to this learning is the principle of differential reinforcement. In the presence of instances of a concept class, one kind of response is reinforced; in their absences, other responses are reinforced. The basic teaching problem becomes one of determining which concept instances and not-instances should be presented to most efficiently teach the critical discriminations involved in concept learning.

Four procedures for establishing stimulus control over operant behavior were examined for their implications for teaching a general case. This examination indicated that a concept cannot be taught with a single positive and negative instance. A set of instances is required to isolate essential concept characteristics. In this set, all positive instances should possess all relevant concept characteristics, and negative instances only some or none of them. Within positive and negative instances, irrelevant characteristics must be varied to avoid teaching misrules and to isolate essential characteristics. When concepts fall into sets of related concepts that can easily be confused with each other, it is important to teach the set through a cumulative addition of new members to the set. Each time a new member is added, the set is brought to criterion. Through this procedure, students will learn all essential discriminations, and the members of the concept set will not be mistaken for each other.

Concept learning was thus viewed as a multiple discrimination problem where:

1   *Within* positive and negative concept instances, it is necessary to discriminate relevant from irrelevant characteristics; and,

2   *Between* positive and negative concept instances, it is necessary to discriminate between the relevant characteristics of the concept being taught and other (usually related) concepts.

Engelmann has proposed that concepts be defined only within finite sets. Once this is done, it is possible to analyze the logical properties of sets of related concepts and determine which discriminations are most important to teach.

self-test

1 new

2 discrimination

3 essential, relevant

4 vary

5 confused

6 Cumulative

7 partial

8 instances;
   responds

9 S–

1   A general case has been taught when _____ members of the concept set are identified correctly.

2   If a _____ between positive and negative instances can be made in terms of characteristics other than those to be taught, a discrimination may be learned in terms of those other characteristics.

3   Thus, in selecting concept instances and not-instances for presentation, the teacher must be sure that responding pays off consistently only in the presence of _____ concept characteristics.

4   Within the set of instances or not-instances, it is necessary to _____ stimulus characteristics that are not essential to the concept.

5   It is also necessary to teach the discriminations between concepts that might be _____ with each other.

6   _____ programing is essential to teaching naive learners sets of related concepts so that they can correctly respond to randomly presented instances of the set (old or new).

7   Without cumulative programing, only _____ rules may be learned and become inadequate when new pairs are added to the set.

8   The teacher can test for concept learning by presenting concept _____ and not-instances, and seeing if the child _____ one way to instances and another way to not-instances.

9   Stimuli that are relevant or essential to concept not-instances are given the symbol _____.

NUMBER RIGHT _____

exercise 1 programed practice

1 concepts

2 stimulus;
concepts

3 teach

4 preceding;
stimulus control

5 reinforce,
strengthen;
differential
reinforcement

6 instances;
not

7 discrimination

8 essential, relevant

9 position

10 responding,
responses

1 The building blocks of intelligent behavior are _____ and operations.

2 A concept can be defined by the set of _____ characteristics unique to a set of stimulus instances in a given universe and not common to other _____ in that universe.

3 A general case has been taught when any or all members of the concept set are responded to correctly even though some were not presented in the set of instances used to _____ the concept.

4 Concept teaching is concerned with bringing responses under the control of _____ stimuli. In behavior theory this area is called _____ _____ of behavior.

5 The basic procedure for establishing stimulus control of behavior is to _____ one response consistently in the presence of some stimuli and not in the presence of other stimuli. This procedure is called _____ _____.

6 In other words, one response is reinforced in the presence of concept _____ and some other response is reinforced in the presence of _____-instances.

7 If a _____ can be made between positive and negative instances in terms of characteristics other than those to be taught, a discrimination may be learned in terms of those other characteristics.

8 Thus, in selecting concept instances and not-instances for presentation, the teacher must be sure that responding pays off consistently only in the presence of _____ concept characteristics.

9 For example, if the teacher uses only one position on the board in teaching sounds, the children may learn to respond to the _____ cues and not the letter shapes.

10 To teach a concept it is necessary for _____ to be controlled only by the essential characteristics of the concept.

11 set, group;
   all; all

12 vary

13 reinforcement

14 reinforced

15 varied;
   "new"

16 confused

17 Cumulative

18 partial

19 relevant
   characteristics;
   irrelevant

20 instances;
   responds

11 To do this, a _____ of instances and not-instances is required. The set should be constructed so that _____ instances have _____ essential concept characteristics, and not-instances possess none of or only some of them.

12 Within the set of instances or not-instances, it is necessary to _____ stimulus characteristics that are not essential to a concept.

13 When irrelevant characteristics are varied, they can no longer be consistently associated with _____. They therefore will not control responding.

14 Ferster and Hammer have shown that chimpanzees would not attend to the number of items in an example if responding to color, position, shape, size, or some other irrelevant cue was consistently _____.

15 By presenting many positive and negative instances in which irrelevant stimulus characteristics are _____, it is possible to teach a discrimination which will be maintained when _____ instances involving the varied irrelevant characteristics are presented.

16 It is also necessary to teach the discriminations between concepts which might be _____ with each other.

17 _____ programing is essential to teaching naive learners sets of related concepts so that they can correctly respond to randomly presented instances of the set (old or new).

18 Without cumulative programing, only _____ rules may be learned and become inadequate when new pairs are added to the set.

19 Concept learning involves multiple discriminations. First, _____ _____ of instances must be discriminated from those of not-instances. Second, relevant characteristics must be discriminated from _____ characteristics within instances or not-instances.

20 The teacher can test for concept learning by presenting concept _____ and not-instances, and seeing if the child _____ one way to instances and another way to not-instances.

21 A concept has been taught when a child has learned to respond to concept instances in _____ way and to not-instances of the concept in _____ way.

22 If a concept has been taught by using some members of the concept set, then the student should be able to respond correctly to _____ _____ of the set even though he has never seen them before.

23 Stimuli relevant or essential to the concept instances are given the symbol _____.

24 Stimuli relevant or essential to concept not-instances are given the symbol _____.

25 Stimuli irrelevant to concept instances and not-instances are given the symbol _____.

26 A concept cannot be taught without teaching the relevant characteristics of other concepts from which the given concept is to be _____.

27 Engelmann believes concept should be defined only within a _____ set of concepts.

28 Once a concept is viewed within a finite set, it becomes possible for the programer or teacher to examine the members of that set and to _____ analyze how concepts are the same and how they are different.

29 Behavioral knowledge of why _____ occur in discrimination learning can then be coupled with this logical analysis of concepts to produce efficient programing procedures.

21 one;
 another

22 other members,
 all members

23 S+

24 S–

25 Si

26 discriminated

27 finite

28 logically

29 errors

discussion questions

1   Give a definition of concept and provide an illustration.

2   What is the test for a "general case" in concept teaching?

3   Explain why conceptual behavior can be considered a special case of the stimulus control of operant behavior.

4   What is the basic procedure for bringing behavior under the control of a preceding stimulus? Give an example.

5   Stimulus control procedure 1 uses one positive and one negative example that differ in several ways. What implications for teaching concepts did analysis of this procedure yield?

6   Procedure 2 uses one positive and one negative instance with control of irrelevant stimuli (they were made the same).
    a) When tested with varying irrelevant stimuli (using only squares and circles), what is the likely outcome with this procedure?
    b) When tested with additional closed-geometric figures as negative instances (keeping irrelevant characteristics constant), what is the likely outcome of this procedure?

7   Stimulus control procedure 3 uses a set of positive and negative instances with varying irrelevant characteristics. What kind of "generalized" learning does this procedure produce?

8   Procedure 4 focuses on teaching the discrimination among a set of related concepts.
    a) When the successive-pairs method of programing is used, what is the outcome?
    b) When cumulative programing to criterion is used, what is the outcome?

9   Explain why (be explicit) cumulative programing "works" and successive-pairs programing is likely to fail.

10   Define $S+$, $S-$, and Si. Give an example of each.

11   Explain the difference between S^D as used in volume 1 of this series and $S+$.

12   Draw a diagram showing concept learning as a multiple-discrimination problem. Explain the multiple discriminations involved.

13   Summarize four basic requirements for teaching a concept by the inductive method.

unit 5

Basic Requirements
for Teaching Operations

objectives

When you complete this unit you should be able to—

1 Define these terms:
   a) operation
   b) component operation
   c) formal operation
   d) thinking
2 Analyze operational behavior to show component operations.
3 Define and distinguish between habit chains and rule chains.
4 Distinguish between rule chains and creative problem-solving behavior.
5 State the basic requirements for teaching operations.
6 Design sets of tasks to teach simple operations.
7 Describe a procedure for teaching generalized imitation.
8 Describe a procedure for teaching a grammatical rule as a general case.

lesson

Operations have to do with behavior, which has a time-sequence dimension to it. In smart behavior, the sequences produce effects that we find reinforcing in some sense. In this unit we attempt to develop the concept of an operation. Working together, concepts and operations are the building blocks of intelligent behavior.

Operations

An operation is the common effect of a set of behaviors under stimulus control. We say an operation has been learned when, in the presence of a consistent cue, repeated responses occur having a common functional effect. For example, a person would be said to have learned a lock-opening operation if, in the presence of a series of locks and their keys, he uses the keys to open each of the locks even though they differ in size, shape, and location, and a different response is required in each case. Or, a person would be said to have learned agreeing and negating operations if, in the presence of any yes-no question or statement of fact, he makes responses recognized by others as agreement or disagreement.

The duration of a behavior sequence does not determine its status as an operation. The critical element is that a class (set) of responses is under stimulus control and has a common environmental effect. In behavioral development, as larger functional units are formed from the "fusion" of smaller ones, the nature of the stimulus control changes. For example, early in learning to read, sounds may be controlled by separate letters. Later, when a student becomes a word reader, he can convert written words into spoken words. He may still have the operations for reading sounds one at a time, or he may not. This can be tested by seeing if sounds are still under the control of separately presented letter stimuli.

Component Operations

Most responses can be analyzed into component operations. For example, lock opening consists of *inserting* the key and *turning* it. Behavior has a time dimension, and time can "always" be subdivided into parts. But we can only speak of component operations, if each part is under the control of a separate class of stimuli and repeated instances of the components have common effects. The separate stimulus control of an operation is important because without that you would never know when to use it.

The notion of component operations under separate stimulus control is important in programing. The programer seeks the minimum number of functional units that can be used as building blocks for the maximum number of response sequences.

There is a practical limit to breaking operations into components. For example, the letter *m* is presented and the task is to "say its sound." To break sounds into smaller functional units is conceivably possible. However, it is usually unnecessary and inefficient to do so, since the smallest unit in which speech sounds are used is the sound itself in response to single letters. The only exception to this is when a child cannot say the sound. For example, in teaching "mmmm" you might have the child say "aaaaa" and then close his lips with your fingers. The voiced part of the sound and the lip position are treated separately to teach the child to say "mmmmm."

Similarly, there is no point to breaking object names, such as *cat*, into sounds, since the name-word is the smallest unit used in naming things. However, *cat* could be broken into parts as a correction procedure if the child could not say "cat." These two examples point out that, in oral language, the smallest functional units are words. In written language (reading, writing, and spelling), the functional units may be letters and sounds (at least at some stages of learning).

Chains and Operations

Most behaviors are actually chains. One method of teaching behavior chains involves cuing each segment in the chain separately and then fading the help. "Do X, then Y, and then Z." If the same sequence is used repeatedly and reinforced, a functional unity or habit will be learned. Routines like getting dressed, eating, and brushing teeth have these characteristics. The important point to note is that most habitual behavior is initially taught through the separate cuing of each component operation. In fact, the teacher would not try to teach "counting to ten" unless the children could first say each component number on cue. The component operations are taught before the chain is built. Other examples of basic component operations are saying sounds to letters, saying names when shown objects, or following simple instructions, such as "stand," "lift," "turn," "insert," "let go," "throw," and "push."

It is useful to consider two kinds of chains. Each is built most efficiently by initially cuing the component operations separately; but after the chains are established, they differ in the nature of the controlling stimuli. These are habit chains and rule chains.

Habit Chains

In a habit chain, each response produces a stimulus which is the cue for the next response, and there are no alternative responses. Saying the letters of the alphabet forward is an example. Learning this chain will do little to help you say the alphabet backwards, or to start with a particular letter and go backwards. When a habit is learned, the stimulus for the next response is derived from the preceding response. Driving to school or work from home can become a habit chain. Taking the same route has the functional effect of getting you there each day. When a sequence of behavior is repeatedly reinforced, it tends to become a functional unit. That is what we mean by a habit chain.

Rule Chains

Rule chains are procedures used to solve sets of problems with known solutions. Each step in the chain produces information (stimuli) needed to carry out the next step. For example, to solve problems of this type, $A + B = \boxed{}$, the rules might be:

1 Place as many lines under the first number (A) as are in the set the number stands for.
2 Place as many lines under the second number (B) as the number stands for.
3 Count all the lines to find the total when the two numbers are added together.
4 Place the total in the box.

In a particular example such as $4 + 3 = \square$

Step 1 involves making 4 lines,

Step 2 involves making 3 lines,

Step 3 involves counting all the lines,

Step 4 involves putting the number 7 in the box.

After prompted practice with five or six problems using these rules, any problem of this type would likely be solved. The set of rules in the rule chain teaches a problem-solving strategy appropriate to a particular class of problems. The "habit structure" learned is the sequence of general rules, which can then control a wide variety of particular response chains producing solutions to problems not solved before.

Most problems of fact have rule-chain solutions. Some construction problems also have acceptable rule-chain solutions. An example is a recipe for making a cake or a plan for building a dog house.

Formal Operations

A limiting case of the rule-chain is the single rule. The *formal operations* of science, mathematics, and logic are usually singular rules. For example:

Density = weight ÷ volume

Rate of speed = distance ÷ time

Circumference of a circle = π times the diameter

In a two-member set (A and B), if you know it is not A, it must be B.

In a five member set (A, B, C, D, and E), if you know it is not A, it may be B, C, D, or E.

The density statement is read in this way: To find the density of an object, given its weight and volume, *divide* weight by volume. Dividing weight by volume is a general rule (operation) for determining density.

Creative Designs

There is another kind of response sequencing involved in the solution of design problems. In man's most creative work, the design of new art, new literature, new buildings, new methods of transportation, we are again dealing with response sequences. In this case, however, there are no fixed rules, and there is no clear ordering of steps. Each starting point and each step has implications for other possible steps. These implications must be traced into future steps as far as possible. Sometimes this leads to contradictory consequences and a possible sequence is discarded. Unlike rule chains, design problems lead to the consideration of multiple alternatives after each step is made. This topic is pursued further in unit 7.

Our analysis of chains and design problems indicates that operations are the key building blocks for all kinds of behavior from daily habits to the most creative acts of man.

Concepts and Operations

There is a correspondence between the structure of concepts and the structure of operations:

Concept: Red

$$S \longrightarrow R$$

A group of *stimulus instances*—

a. sharing some essential characteristics (S +):

   red ball
   red truck
   red flower

b. and varying in other ways (Si):

   shape
   location
   texture

c. are responded to in the same way:
   "red"

Operation: Throwing

$$S \longrightarrow R$$

A group of *response instances* occur—

b. having a common environmental effect (object leaves the hand, but is not dropped):

   throws the ball
   throws the spoon
   throws the rope

a. in the presence of a consistent class of cues:
   "throw the x"

c. and varying in other ways:

   direction thrown
   force of throw
   object thrown
   arm used, and so on

A concept refers to what is common to a set of stimulus instances; an operation refers to the common effect of a set of response instances. Instances of concepts and operations both have relevant and irrelevant characteristics. In the case of a concept, the response used to demonstrate learning of the concept is arbitrary (usually a convention such as the word "red"). Any consistent response will do. In the case of an operation, the cue controlling the occurrence of the operation is not critical to the operation, but arbitrary or conventional. When words are used to cue operations, they are usually called *directions*. "Throw the X," tells you what to do. But any consistent stimulus can be the cue for the appropriateness of a given operation.

Note that responses to concept instances are right or wrong. There are no approximations. However, operations can be performed well or not so well. They can get better.

Concepts About Operations

For every possible operation, there exists a possible concept about that operation. It is important to distinguish between the two. In learning an operation, the student is learning how to do something (response learning) that is part of a general case. In learning a concept, the student is learning to respond to stimulus events as members of a common class. When a student learns to add (increase the members in a group), he is learning an *operation*. However, when the student observes examples of adding and not-adding presented by the teacher, he is observing positive and negative instances of the *concept* of addition. What is an example of an operation for the *doer* is an example of a concept for the *observer*. Any verb that applies to human action can potentially refer both to an operation and a concept about that operation. *Knowing about* is different from *being able to do*.

Teaching Requirements

Basics

The operational requirements of a given task are taught by using prompts, reinforcing good responses, and not reinforcing poor responses. However, to teach an operation effectively requires a programed sequence of tasks chosen to contrast the operation with those not-operations that might be confused with it. For example, to teach a young child a throwing operation, first specify some other hand-movement operations that might be confused with throwing, such as placing, pushing, holding, and lifting. Then devise a general task format encompassing the possible tasks. A series of tasks can then be generated (assuming the object names have already been taught). Start with two operations. New ones are then added to the set, one at a time, as mastery occurs. The tasks might be of this form:

> Throw the ball to me.
> Put the ball on the table.
> Throw the ball at the wall.
> Throw the balloon to me.
> Put the spoon on the table.
> Lift the spoon up to your mouth.

Correct responses are reinforced and errors are corrected. With this approach, a basis is provided for building response systems that transcend the specific tasks used in the teaching. If a number of tasks involving the same operation are taught while the irrelevant response requirements are varied, a point will be reached where new tasks involving that operation are correctly performed on the first presentation. This means that the operation has been taught.

To teach chains of operations, component operations are taught, and then sequenced in multiple-segment tasks. There are no new teaching skills. When the chain is to be learned as a habit chain, the same ordering is used each time. When flexible sequencing of components is required in the future (as in reading words by sounds or saying sentences), systematic varying of the order of components is used to prevent wrong habits.

Note that at some point in the teaching of operations the response components are no longer important ("the skills of the trade" have been mastered). When basic operations have been mastered, faster progress can be made by teaching new operations as concepts about the operations. For example, the response skills in placing a set of objects in *serial order* by area, number, lightness-darkness, length, weight, and so on, are probably trivial to an eight-year old. Directly teaching the concept of serial order with instances and not-instances ranging across the possible sets to be seriated would lead to a more generalized operation faster.

Susie Is Taught to Imitate

Imitating the behavior of another person is one of the most important operations a child can learn. Almost all response teaching of school-age children uses imitation to get the task response going. Imagine how handicapped a child would be if he could not imitate. The development of language and gross motor operations would be greatly limited.

Susie was in a school for profoundly retarded children. She was chosen for study because she did not talk or imitate any behavior of others. She could walk, feed and dress herself, and she was toilet trained. Susie earned her meals by learning to imitate. This procedure was necessary to hold her attention.

To train imitation, the teacher would give the signal "Do this" and follow it with an action to be imitated. The first task was to raise her left arm. Susie did not respond. The teacher reached out and raised Susie's left hand, then gave her food. The teacher put Susie through the steps of the response. After doing this several times, the teacher began to fade out his help until Susie was responding on her own.

The second response to be imitated was tapping the table with the left hand. The teacher said, "Do this," and tapped the table. Susie raised her hand. "Do this" had become a signal for raising her hand, not tapping the table. Physical prompting was used once again until she could tap the table when the teacher did. The teacher then went back to saying, "Do this," while raising his left hand. Susie tapped the table. For a series of trials, the teacher went back and forth between the two responses to teach Susie that "Do this" was the signal to *look at what I do and do it*. Imitation involves the operations of looking and doing what you see someone else doing. At first, "Do this" was a signal for Susie to raise her hand. Then, "Do this" was a signal to tap the table. By going back and forth between the two tasks, she could only be right if she looked at what the teacher was doing.

The next task was to tap her chest with her left hand. She learned a little faster, but was still confused when the teacher went back to hand raising and tapping. When all of the tasks were performed on signal, a new task was introduced. Each new task was learned more quickly. By the time 50 tasks had been taught, Susie was imitating more than half of all new tasks on first presentation. She was learning the *operation*, the generalized procedure of matching her behavior to that of the teacher. By the time 130 tasks had been taught, she was imitating almost every new task on first trial. The only tasks she had trouble with were ones that were physically difficult for her, like walking while balancing a book on her head.

Part of the way through the training, she was taught to imitate whole chains of responses. The teacher would say "Do this" and then tap the table, walk across the room, and clap his hands. Then Susie would do each action in sequence.

Late in the training, when she would imitate almost anything, the teacher said "Do this" and made the sound "Ah." Susie would not do it. Imitation had been an operation controlled by "Do this" and a visual signal, not an auditory signal. The *examples* of the imitative operation had not included imitation of sounds. Susie knew what she had been taught. She had not been taught to imitate sounds. To get imitation of sounds going, the teacher put the sound in with a chain of actions. He said, "Susie, do this." He got up from his chair, walked to the center of the room, turned toward Susie, said "Ah," and returned to his seat. Susie got up, went to the center of the room, faced the teacher, and began a series of facial and vocal responses out of which eventually came something close enough to "Ah" to merit reinforcement. The basis for teaching Susie to talk (through verbal imitation) had been started.[1]

Testing

The fact that some consistent signal is required to show the presence of an operation is important in testing. Susie could not do "Say this" tasks after being taught only "Do this" tasks. Suppose that children are taught addition operations using only column formats: $\begin{array}{r} 3 \\ 4 \\ \hline \end{array}$ Then, they are given a test using only row formats: $3 + 4 = \boxed{}$. They are apt to fail. The teacher cannot infer from this that the children haven't learned the operation, but only that the student does not know that convention or format and *may* or *may not* know the operation. It is important to teach operations in the presence of the various cue conditions under which they are to be used (and tested).

It is also important for the teacher to recognize that the presence of an operation cannot be reliably inferred from looking at a single specific response. It is necessary to test for a set of responses under appropriate cue conditions to infer that an operation has been learned.

Identifying Building Blocks

Arithmetic. The importance of selecting the right set of building blocks in teaching concepts and operations can be illustrated with two examples central to the selection of educational programs. Suppose we take as our building blocks in teaching arithmetic operations the set of problems of this form:

Stimulus	Response
9 + 1 =	10
4 + 5 =	9
7 + 2 =	9
2 + 5 =	7

There are forty problems of this type with sums of 10 or less. The children could practice each of these tasks until it is learned and discriminated from the others in the set. This approach requires a lot of discrimination training, which is commonly called rote learning. When higher sums are added to the set, more learning has to go on. When the problem is changed to one of this form: $4 + \boxed{} = 7$, the learning starts over from scratch. There is no basis for transfer. Needless to say, a lot of children have been taught number facts this way and were confused (and punished) for a long time.

An alternative approach builds on the fact that each number (1 to 10) represents a set of things that can be counted and teaches a set of rules for solving problems of this type. The steps are as follows:

1 The child is taught to count to a number. This is a verbal chain.
2 He is taught to use this chain to count objects. Counting objects is an operation for determining how many are in a group.
3 Symbol identification is taught using concept teaching rules.
4 Given a numeral, the child is taught to make as many lines as the numeral stands for. This is also an operation.
5 The concepts of plus and equality are taught. Plussing is getting some more. Equality is a rule: "As many as we have on this side of the equal sign we have to have on the other side of the equal sign." The operation of counting is used to verify the equality rule. Now when a child is presented with a problem like this

$$4 + 5 = \boxed{}$$

he can solve it by putting five lines under the 5, and counting "four—five, six, seven, eight, nine." He touches each line as he counts it.
6 A little later, the lines are dropped and fingers are used in the operation. "We have four and we plus five." (The children put out five fingers on the cue "and we plus five." Then they count, "Fouuurrr, five, six, seven, eight, nine," touching each of the five fingers as they count.)
7 Still later the children are taught to count from a number to a number. They can now handle forty new problems like this:

$$4 + \boxed{} = 9$$

They just need to draw a line or stick out a finger for each number they count after four until they get to nine, and they can produce the answer. With a slight variation on counting from a number to a number, they can also do forty problems of this form:

$$9 = 4 + \boxed{}$$

While this approach may take a little more time in building the basic operations, the dividends are great, since the children can solve whole sets of new problems after going through just a few of them with the teacher. The basis has also been laid for solving algebraic equations. Note too that each example gives the child practice on the rote facts. At the end of each example he is trained to say the whole statement, "Four plus five equals nine."

Reading. Let us compare the building blocks of a hypothetical sight-reading program as compared with those in the Distar reading-by-sound program. There is no doubt that a child can be taught to give responses to ten words faster than he can be taught to give responses to ten symbols for sounds. However, by the time ten sounds have been taught (along with blending skills), the potential basis has been laid for reading-by-sound some 720 three-sound words, 4320 four-sound words, and 21,600 five-sound words. Not all of these "words" would be real words, but the number of permutations of ten sounds is illustrated. By the time forty sounds are taught, a basis has been established for reading a large percentage of the English language. Irregularities still have to be taught, but the child now has skills with which to attack any new word. He has learned the basic operations involved in decoding words.

Choice of the right building blocks in an educational program becomes an extremely important design decision.

Covert Operations

Words have meaning when they are used as the responses to appropriate sets of concept instances. "Red" has meaning when it can be used as a common response to a set of instances of red. "Under" has meaning when it can be used to denote a set of instances of the relationship. "Adding" has meaning as a concept when it can be applied appropriately to a number of examples of the operation adding. Meaning also refers to being able to specify the essential characteristics of a concept such as "squareness." When we have learned concepts and operations, and we use words or other symbols to refer to them, we can put these together into verbal chains and talk about hypothetical possibilities. We can plan. We can think. When we think to ourselves, the process is said to be covert. When we think out loud, the process is overt.

Covert thinking operations are first learned as overt operations. They are then short-circuited; that is, we learn to "talk to ourselves in our heads" and "imagine." It is our assumption that no new principles are involved when one goes from the overt to the covert level. The only change is that the process is no longer observable.

Generative Language

Linguists such as Noam Chomsky[2] have argued that S→R→S behavior theory can never account for generative language development (the use of words in new combinations following grammatical rules). Actually, the learning of generalized imitation by Susie is a problem of the same order; she learned an operation that eventually permitted successful performance on first trial. The training procedure *generated* a general skill that facilitated the new performances.

The rules of grammar are learned through repeated examples. If the rule is that the subject always precedes the verb in declarative statements, and the examples always follow this rule, then the necessary cue condition will be present to hook verbal operations (words) together into chains reflecting this requirement. For example, we might initially teach these nouns and verbs:

Nouns	Verbs
Baby	Go bye bye
Momma	Sit
Billy	Play
Doggie	Run
Dollie	Eat

We could then teach a young child (or older child who has never learned language) to make the appropriate sentences to describe actions of dolls or pictures showing the actions. For example, the statements might be: "Baby go bye bye," "Doggie run," or "Momma eat." There are twenty-five possible statements of this form which can be made with the above set of nouns and verbs. If training is given on fifteen of them, it is very likely the other ten possibilities would occur at first opportunity to use them and in the correct grammatical form.

Several experimental studies have been undertaken to demonstrate how modeling and reinforcement procedures can be used to teach grammatical rules (generative language). A ten-year-old retarded girl, Janet, who did not use plural nouns to describe objects, was the focus of one study.[3] She was shown objects, such as cups, hats, pens, and nickels, as single objects or as groups of like objects. The training sequence started with single objects, then multiple objects, then went back and forth between single and multiple objects. Before too long, a generative use of plurals and singulars was obtained. She could correctly label new objects in the singular or plural without new training.

A second study examined the conditions leading to the correct use of an unvoiced /-s/ plural versus a voiced /-z/ plural.[4] The /-s/ sound goes with words having an unvoiced ending (cup), and the /-z/ sound goes with words having a voiced ending (tree). Two retarded girls were first trained to use singular and plural endings as in the study above. One girl was trained using words with voiced endings (in their singular form) and the other was trained with words having unvoiced endings.

The results clearly showed that when the training involved the voiced plural sound /-z/ as in *bows*, this sound was used on test trials (lightz) where the unvoiced ending was the appropriate one (lights). When the training involved the unvoiced plural sound /-s/ as in *lights*, this sound was given on the test trials where the voiced ending was the appropriate one. Thus *what was learned was what was trained*, and in each case generative effects of the training were obtained.

Other studies have shown similar generative effects in training question asking,[5] in the use of comparatives and superlatives,[6] and the use of descriptive adjectives.[7]

Viewing language learning as a special case of the teaching of chains of operations, each under the control of some distinctive stimulus class, offers a powerful model to those concerned with the teaching of children with poor language skills.

summary

An operation is the common effect of a set of behaviors under stimulus control. Behavior has a temporal dimension and, therefore, usually can be broken down into smaller units. From the point of view of the teacher and programer, the critical question is "What units?" The answer is, "No smaller than the smallest functional unit required to build behavior sequences (chains)." In naming things, the functional unit is the name-word. In reading-by-sounds, the functional unit is the sound. Operations are functional units of behavior. The analysis of operations in programing seeks the minimum number of functional units that can be used as building blocks in the maximum number of response sequences when appropriately cued. With behavioral development, there is often a change in the size of the functional units under stimulus control. A whole chain of behavior may be the functional unit. The critical feature of an operation is not the size of the unit, but the existence of a class of responses, under stimulus control, that have a common effect on the environment.

Component operations can be built into habit and rule chains. They can also be used in the most creative human activities. In a habit chain, each response produces a stimulus that serves as the cue for the next response. The chain eventually becomes a functional unit. In a rule chain, each step in the chain provides the stimuli needed to carry out the next steps, but these stimuli will differ from problem to problem. They are not fixed as in a habit chain, but vary with the example. In a rule chain, the "habit structure" being learned is the general rules and their sequence of use which can then be applied to problems never solved before.

The formal operations of science, mathematics, and logic are usually singular rules, which can be used as building blocks in problem-solving behavior. For example, to find the rate of speed, given distance traveled and time taken, divide distance by time.

Concepts and operations are similar in several ways. Concepts refer to what is common to a set of stimulus instances. Operations refer to the common effect of a set of response instances. Instances of concepts and operations both have relevant and irrelevant characteristics. With concepts the response is arbitrary (a convention), with operations the controlling cue is a convention. For every operation, there is a potential concept about that operation. What is an example of an operation for the *doer* is an example of a concept for the *observer*.

Prompting and differential reinforcement are the basic procedures for teaching the operational requirements of a task. Beyond that, a sequence of tasks (a program) is required to isolate the essential requirements of the operations from nonessential characteristics and to differentiate a given operation from related operations. Cumulative programing is used to teach a set of related operations. To teach chains of operations, component operations are taught first and then put together as multiple-segment tasks. If the operations in behavior sequences are to be used in a variety of orders (as in language), then it is important to vary the order when teaching the operations. Otherwise, habit-chains will be learned. Once basic operations have been mastered, it is probably more efficient to teach new operations as concepts about the operations. The fact that some consistent signal is required to show the presence of an operation means that testing must use cues related to what has been taught. To infer that an operation has been learned, the teacher should look at a set of responses given under the appropriate cue conditions.

Programing can be smart or dumb depending on the building blocks used to teach the objectives of the program. For example, teaching reading by sounds is more efficient than the sight-word method. Operational approaches to mathematics are more efficient than rote habit approaches.

Thinking processes are assumed to involve no new principles beyond those involved in understanding overt conceptual and operational behavior. The processes are simply no longer observable.

Experimental studies in teaching language skills illustrate how a general case, such as learning the rules of grammar, can be taught through presenting a series of tasks involving operations-to-be-differentiated-from-each-other.

self-test

1 cue

2 component

3 minimum; maximum

4 operations

5 known

1 An operation has been learned when in the presence of a consistent _____ , repeated responses occur having a common functional effect.

2 Most responses, which are instances of operations, can be analyzed into _____ operations.

3 In programing the analysis of operations seeks the _____ number of functional behavior units that can be used as building blocks in the _____ number of response sequences when appropriately cued.

4 Habit chains are initially taught through the separate cuing of the component _____ .

5 Rule chains are procedures used to solve sets of problems with _____ solutions.

6 Operations are the key _____ _____ for all kinds of behavior from chained habits to the most creative acts of man.

7 What is an operation for the doer is a concept for the _____ .

8 When flexible sequencing of components is required in the future, systematic varying of the _____ of the components is used to prevent wrong habits.

9 In teaching operations, it is important to teach their use in the presence of the various _____ _____ under which they are to be used (and tested).

NUMBER RIGHT _____

6 building blocks

7 observer

8 order

9 cue conditions

exercise 1 programed practice

1 Operations refer to the _____ of behavior on the environment.

2 An operation has been learned when in the presence of a consistent _____ , repeated responses occur having a _____ functional effect.

3 The _____ of a behavior sequence is not critical to its status as an operation.

4 In behavioral development, the nature of the stimulus control changes as _____ functional units are formed from the "fusion" of smaller units.

5 Most responses can be analyzed into _____ operations. For example, lock opening consists of _____ the key and _____ the key.

6 We can only speak of component operations if each part can be demonstrated to be under the control of a separate class of _____ and there is a common effect of the components.

7 There is a practical limit to breaking operations into _____ . Do not break them into units smaller than those to be used in building _____.

8 The analysis of operations in programing seeks the _____ number of functional behavior units that can be used as building blocks in the _____ number of response sequences when appropriately cued.

1 effects

2 cue; common

3 duration

4 larger

5 component; inserting; turning

6 stimuli

7 components; chains

8 minimum; maximum

9 All behavior involves _____ if it can be divided into components.

10 In a habit chain, each response produces a _____ that is the cue for the next response.

11 Habit chains are initially taught through the separate cuing of the component _____ .

12 When a sequence of behavior is repeatedly reinforced, it tends to become a _____ unit.

13 Rule chains are procedures used to solve sets of problems with _____ solutions.

14 Each step in the chain produces information (_____) needed to carry out the next step.

15 The "habit structure" learned is the sequence of general rules, which can then control a wide variety of _____ _____ chains producing solutions to problems not solved before.

16 In man's most creative work, the design of new art, new literature, new buildings, new methods of transportation, we are again dealing with response _____ .

17 In this case, there are no _____ rules and there is no clear _____ of steps.

18 Operations are the key _____ _____ for all kinds of behavior from chained habits to the most creative acts of man.

19 For every possible operation, there exists a possible _____ about that operation.

20 What is an example of an operation for the *doer* is an example of a concept for the _____ .

21 To effectively teach an operation requires a _____ _____ of tasks having properties very similar to those required to teach concepts. A set of tasks involving the key operations and those _____ - _____ which might be confused with it are required.

22 To teach chains of operations, _____ operations are first taught and then sequenced in multiple-segment tasks.

---

9 chains

10 stimulus

11 operations

12 functional

13 known

14 stimuli

15 particular response

16 sequences

17 fixed; ordering

18 building blocks

19 concept

20 observer

21 programed sequence; not-operations

22 component

23 When flexible sequencing of components is required in the future, systematic varying of the _____ of components is used to keep wrong habits from being taught.

24 When basic operations have been mastered, faster progress can be made by teaching new operations as _____ about the operations.

25 The fact that some consistent _____ is required to show the presence of an operation is important in testing. Susie could not do "Say this" tasks after being taught only "Do this" tasks.

26 In teaching operations, it is important to teach their use in the presence of the various _____ _____ under which they are to be used (and tested).

27 Imitation involves the operation of looking and _____ what you see someone else doing. It can also involve listening and repeating what you _____ .

28 Choice of the right building _____ in an educational program becomes an extremely important design decision.

29 Covert thinking operations are first learned as _____ operations.

30 Experimental studies in teaching language skills illustrate how a _____ case, such as learning the rules of grammar, can be taught through presenting a series of tasks involving operations-to-be-differentiated-from-each-other.

23 order

24 concepts

25 signal

26 cue conditions

27 doing;
hear

28 blocks

29 overt

30 general

discussion questions

1 Define the term operation.

2 What is a component operation?

3 Consider the problem of driving a stick-shift car. Identify as many component operations and their controlling stimuli as you can.

4 Identify some of the component operations involved in cursive writing. Is writing single words a habit chain or rule chain? Does writing sentences involve habit chains or rule chains?

5 How do habit chains and rule chains differ? Give an example of each.

6 What determines the size of the functional unit of behavior used in designing a program?

7   What is a formal operation? Give examples.

8   How do creative design problems differ from problems that can be solved with rule chains?

9   Indicate two ways in which concepts and operations are alike and two ways in which they are different.

10   When is an operation a concept?

11   Summarize the basic requirements for teaching an operation.

12   What is required before chains of operations are taught?

13   Give a set of tasks you might use to teach the operation "placing on" (as in "Place the ball on the table"). Specify relevant and irrelevant characteristics, as well as the not-operations to be differentiated from placing on.

14   Give a set of tasks you might use to teach the operation of making a set equal to a sample set. Specify relevant and irrelevant characteristics of responses showing the operation, as well as the not-operations.

15   What operations are involved in generalized imitation?

16   Give an example of teaching an operation as a concept.

17   Why must testing be geared to the teaching formats or vice versa?

18   What is thinking?

19   Give an example to show how a rule of grammar can be taught as a general case through repeated examples that follow the rule.

20   Compare the advantages and disadvantages of teaching spelling with letter names as the component unit versus letter sounds.

unit 6

Teaching Experienced Learners

objectives

When you complete this unit you should be able—

1 Explain the logic of an equivalency rule.
2 Describe procedures for teaching by rules.
3 Tell how to avoid teaching verbalisms.
4 Explain how examples used in teaching with rules differ from examples used to test for rule learning.
5 Explain what function rules are and when they are used.
6 Explain the basic logic of rules.
7 Give examples of forward and backward items in teaching or testing for rules.

lesson

The basic requirements for teaching concepts and operations to naive learners involve an inductive teaching method. Examples are used to teach the general case. The movement is from concrete instances with many irrelevant characteristics to the abstract rule with no irrelevancies. However, there comes a point in acquisition of knowledge when the student has learned the language of instruction, understands a broad set of directions, and has a variety of intellectual skills (operations) for figuring out what someone else is trying to teach. At such a time (perhaps as early as the end of first grade for some children), it becomes possible to teach concepts, operations, strategies, rules, and principles through a deductive teaching method.

Rule Learning

One simple kind of teaching involves giving an alternative name for a concept that has already been taught. The teacher simply gives the equivalency rule: *"Middle* means *between," "Adding* is *plussing," "Of* in a word problem means *times."* The logic of an equivalency rule is: All x's are called between. Between is called middle. Therefore all x's are called middle. Prior concept learning is used in teaching an alternative label for the concept. The learning can be very fast, and there is little need to give a lot of examples, to vary irrelevant characteristics, or to provide negative instances.

A more complex form of the equivalency rule is the code. For example, the teacher writes:

nu	= pick up		t	= ball
be	= sit on		c	= chair
si	= kick		m	= horse

Then these examples are given:

nut = pick up the ball
nuc = pick up the chair

How would you say these:

sim

bet

sic

Most advanced learners could perform these tasks at first encounter. They need to infer from the examples that they should all be commands, that actions come before the objects, and that the rule being used is a general rule.

Gagné describes a common deductive method for teaching by rules.[1] In this method, the student is given the rule or definition for the concept. The student then must use this rule to identify examples. For example, an *uncle* is defined as "the brother of a parent." Then, a set of relationships might be described such as this: "Jimmy is the son of Julie. Julie's brother's name is Alan. Is Alan Jimmy's uncle?" Positive and negative examples are presented to test for understanding of the rule for *uncle.* In some cases, of course, the examples may actually help teach the rule inductively.

Causal principles, such as "solids melt into liquids when heated," can be taught in a similar way. The general rule is given; then, examples are used to test for learning of the rule. The student might be asked to use the rule to *predict* what would happen if ice (or wax or iron) were heated. The student might also be asked to *explain* why the ice melted when placed in the sun.

Learning through the presentation of general rules is a time-honored method of instruction for advanced students. It is basic to textbook instruction and the lecture method.

Rule Versus Discovery Learning

The following example illustrates a common finding—namely, that rule learning is often more effective than discovery learning. Carnine recently compared two methods for teaching fraction skills.[2] The skills were decoding fractions (filling in circles to illustrate the fraction), generating fractions equal to one, and identifying fractions as being greater, equal, or less than one. The two programs were prescribed in detail to the teachers. In the opportunity-to-discover program, examples were given but the rule was not stated. In the rule-learning program, the rule was given along with the examples. The examples were the same in each program. On a transfer test involving the skills as taught, but using new examples, the rule group had 86 percent correct and the opportunity-to-discover group only 48 percent correct. On a transfer test to new skills (writing fractions, making up fractions equal to one, and making up fractions which were more, equal, or less than one) the rule group had 46 percent correct and the opportunity-to-discover group had 31 percent. Both differences were significant.

With a group of high-ability second graders, the rule group scored 94 percent correct on the first transfer task and the opportunity-to-discover group scored 83 percent. On the second test, the means were 67 percent and 57 percent, respectively. Again the differences were very significant. Thus, in each case the rule group learned better than the discovery group. This should not be taken to mean that discovery learning may not be important in teaching many skills, such as problem analysis (discussed in the next unit). However, it does show that rule learning can be very efficient.

Avoiding Verbalisms

Anderson and Kulhavy have shown that college students can learn such concepts as *atavistic* and *diluvial* to a 90 percent accuracy rate when provided with one-sentence definitions.[3] Performance was at a chance level for students not given the definitions. These and similar findings indicate that learning by rules can be very efficient, given the prerequisite skills. The primary danger is that the student may learn only the verbal chain that is the rule (a verbalism), and not know how to discriminate positive and negative examples (not show "understanding"). The teacher can guard against this problem in two ways: (1) by ensuring that the prerequisite skills are present before the rule method is used; and (2) by specifically testing comprehension of the critical components of the rule.

The prerequisite skills for learning by rules are knowledge of the component concepts being hooked together by a rule. Before the relationship *uncle* can be taught by a rule, it is necessary to test for the concepts *parent* and *brother*. Before the principle about melting is taught, the teacher should test for the concepts *solid*, *liquid*, and *heat*.

Specific testing for rule acquisition involves the presentation of positive and negative examples to see if they are correctly identified. Not just any examples will do. As Markle and Tiemann,[4] and Engelmann[5] have pointed out, there is a set of logical conditions that can define the characteristics of a good test for a concept or rule. First, there is the need for a careful analysis of the concepts involved in the rule to specify relevant (S+) and irrelevant (Si) characteristics. Positive examples should broadly sample variation in irrelevant characteristics. For the concept *uncle*, irrelevant characteristics might include age, physical characteristics, sex of parent, and sex of child. Second, negative examples should focus on examples that differ from positive examples in only one essential characteristic. In the case of *uncle*, an *aunt* example would differ in one way as would a *brother of a nonparent.*

In testing for the principle about melting (solid + heat = liquid), important irrelevant characteristics include the material being melted (and its melting temperature) and the source of the heat. Negative examples would first focus on the change of state. When you go from a solid to a liquid, that is *melting*. The reverse procedure is *freezing*. Verbal examples could be used, such as:

> "Tell me if this is an example of melting. We put gasoline in a freezer and it turns solid."

> "Is this melting? We put a piece of ice on a hot sidewalk and it turns to water."

> "We heat some ice and it stays hard. Is that melting?"

It might also be important to use negative examples involving *burning* and *boiling*, since these changes of state also involve heat.

> "We burn a piece of coal. Is that melting?"

> "We heat water until it boils. Is that melting?"

The Role of Examples in Testing and Teaching

Markle and Tiemann have proposed that the kinds of examples used to explicate a rule may be very important. They studied this question with the linguistic concept *morpheme*. "A morpheme is a linguistic unit which

1 carries a stable meaning from one construction to another, and
2 contributes that meaning to the construction in which it appears, and
3 cannot be further subdivided into units having meanings related to that construction."[6]

Markle and Tiemann first showed that presenting the rules with examples illustrating the range of irrelevant characteristics (bawd's, dog-tired, incontrovertible, elephant—the morpheme is underlined) led to more correct responding to new examples than presenting no examples. In a subsequent study by Jobling and Secrest, the effects of three positive examples (bawd's, dog-tired, elephant) and three negative examples (breathe, thing, pale-face) were compared.[7] The testing used a rational set of positive and negative examples. The positive examples systematically varied the irrelevant characteristics as determined by concept analysis, and the negative examples each lacked only one of the three essential characteristics listed above. Four groups were compared: (1) rule only, (2) rule plus positive examples, (3) rule plus negative examples, and (4) rule plus positive and negative examples. The results showed that use of positive examples led to fewer errors on *new* positive examples, and use of negative examples led to fewer errors on *new* negative examples.

This result illustrates the double discrimination problem involved in all concept learning. Positive examples are important in illustrating the range of irrelevant characteristics that can vary and not change the concept, that is, in discriminating relevant (S+) from irrelevant (Si) characteristics. Negative examples are important in illustrating the boundary between essential characteristics of positive and negative instances, that is, in discriminating S+ from S– characteristics. However, the procedures used in this study fail to discriminate between good *teaching* examples and good *testing* examples. It was assumed that they were the same. This is probably a poor assumption. Very likely with the advanced learner, a focus on teaching the discrimination of S+ from S– would lead to the greatest performance gain. This can best be accomplished by changing only one thing when going from a positive to a negative example, and by selecting pairs of examples so that each pair isolates a critical characteristic of the rule or concept. Successive pairs of positive and negative examples are chosen to provide variation in irrelevant characteristics. For example:

	Positive Examples	*Negative Examples*	*Rule Violated by Negative Examples*
Pair 1	sam's	sam's	1,2
Pair 2	eat	breathe	2
Pair 3	pale-face	pale-face	3

Function Rules

Most concepts can be identified by rules dealing with essential *stimulus* characteristics. However, for many concepts, common stimulus characteristics are not obvious or easily described. Very often the teacher or programer can get around this problem by resorting to a function or use definition. When we talk of *work* animals or *hunting* dogs, the focus is on how man uses them. Most concepts concerning man-made objects are most easily defined in terms of how man uses them. These are examples of definition in terms of function: "It's a *vehicle* if it can take you places," "It's a *tool* if it helps man to do work." "It's *food* if you can eat it." In each of these cases, the visual stimulus properties of the concept instances vary considerably. It is not an easy task to show the common stimulus properties of food. It is easier to give a rule concerning use or to show that people eat celery, soda crackers, and hot dogs, but not chalk, erasers, and books.

Teaching Arithmetic Operations

The Distar arithmetic programs by Engelmann and Carnine provide many explicit examples of the use of rules to teach arithmetic operations.[8] The following example, from Level III, is on factoring.* The first task is teaching the definition of factors, "The factors of X are numbers which multiplied together produce X."

*In the Distar programs, both the teacher's questions and the student's responses are specified. What the teacher says is printed in color, and it appears here as the lighter-weight type. What the teacher does is in black, which appears as the darker-weight type. The student's response is in italics.

    a. Write $1^02 =$ on the board.

    b. Let's find some factors of 12. What are we going to find?
Some factors of 12. Repeat until the response is firm.

    c. What are factors? Factors are numbers that are multiplied together. What are factors?
Numbers that are multiplied together. Repeat until the response is firm.

    d. Here's how we find factors of 12. If we can count by a number to get to 12, the number is a factor.

    e. Can we count by 5 to get to 12? **If there is no response, ask:** If we count by 5, do we hit 12? *No.* So 5 is not a factor of 12.

    f. Can we count by 1 to get to 12? **If there is no response, ask:** If we count by 1, do we hit 12? *Yes.* So 1 is a factor of 12.

    g. Can we count by 10 to get to 12? **If there is no response, ask:** If we count by 10, do we hit 12? *No.* So 10 is not a factor of 12.

    h. Can we count by 6 to get to 12? *Yes.*
So is 6 a factor of 12? *Yes.*

    i. Can we count by 4 to get to 12? *Yes.*
So is 4 a factor of 12? *Yes.*

    j. Write $1^02 = 4(\;)$ on the board.

    k. Now let's find the factor of 12 that goes with 4. If we can count by 4 to get to 12, how many times do we count? *Three.*
Yes—if 4 is a factor of 12, the other factor is 3. **Write the complete equation, $1^02 = 4(3)$, on the board.**

    l. We found two factors that equal 12. 12 equals 4 times 3.
So 4 and 3 are factors of 12.

    m. Everybody, what are two factors of 12? *4 and 3.*

    n. Write $1^08 = 3(\;)$ on the board.

    o. Let's find the factor of 18 that goes with 3. If we count by 3 to get to 18, how many times do we count? *Six.*
Yes—if 3 is a factor of 18, the other factor is 6. **Write the complete equation, $1^08 = 3(6)$, on the board.**

    p. We found two factors that equal 18. 18 equals 3 times 6.
So 3 and 6 are factors of 18.

    q. Everybody, what are two factors of 18? *3 and 6.*

After practicing finding the factors of a number with many examples, the factoring operation is used to work familiar problems, "To factor we have to pull the same factor from each term."

Task 2   Factoring

Emphasize the words in **boldface**.

a. Write these problems on the board.

$$3(4) + 3(2) = \boxed{} \qquad\qquad 3(4) + 3(2) = \boxed{}$$

b. Let's draw a box around each simple term in the first problem. Draw the boxes.

$$\boxed{3(4)} \; + \; \boxed{3(2)} \; = \; \boxed{}$$

c. Point left. Let's see how many we have on this side of the equation.

d. Point to the first term. How many are in this term? *12.* Write 1º2 above the first term.

e. Point to the second term. How many are in this term? *6.* Write 6 above the second term.

f. Point left. Figure out how many we have on this side of the equation. *18.* Write 1º8 in the answer box.

g. Let's work the problem another way and see if we get the same answer.

h. Draw boxes around the simple terms in the second problem. We're going to factor. What are we going to do? *Factor.* To factor, we have to pull the same factor from each term. **Point left in the second problem.** Can you find the same factor in each term on this side of the equation? *Yes.*

i. Point to 3(4). What are the factors in this term? *3 and 4.* Is either 3 or 4 a factor in the other term? *Yes.* Which factor? *3.*

j. Listen. To factor, we have to pull the same factor from each term. What factor is the same in the terms on this side of the equation? *3.* What do we do with it? *Pull it from each term and carry it below.* Write 3(   ) below the equation.

k. We pulled out the factor 3 from each term, so we can cross out that factor in each term. **Cross out the 3 in each term.**

$$\boxed{\cancel{3}(4)} \; + \; \boxed{\cancel{3}(2)} \; = \; \boxed{}$$
$$3() =$$

l. Read what's left when we cross out the threes. *4 plus 2.* **That's the other factor.** So I can carry it below. Write 4 + 2 within the parentheses.

$$3(4 + 2) = \boxed{}$$

m. What are the factors in this problem? *3 and 4 plus 2.*

n. Let's see if our answer is right. **Point to the bottom equation.**
How many do we have inside the parentheses? *6.*
We're counting six times. 3 times 6. What does that equal? *18.*
Complete the bottom equation.

$$3(4 + 2) = \boxed{1^08}$$

o. Did we pull the same factor out of each term? *Yes.* What
factor? *3.* Did we revalue the equation? *No.*
How do you know? *We ended up with 18.*
**We ended up with 18 when we worked the problem the first
time.**

p. Here's the rule: When we pull the same factor out of each
term, we don't revalue the equation; we just rewrite it. Say
that with me. *When we pull the same factor out of each term,
we don't revalue the equation; we just rewrite it.*
Have the children repeat the rule until firm.

q. Repeat the entire task until every child is firm on every
response.

After practice in solving problems by factoring, the next step is to learn to express terms as factors before factoring. Later in the program, factoring is used as a method for dividing. The addition and subtraction of fractions is also accomplished by factoring the denominator.

Reading to Learn

When the experienced student has a command of basic language concepts, has mastery of decoding skills in reading, and knows how to zero in on the essentials of the material, he is ready for training in learning from books. In most school systems, fourth-grade children are expected to learn from textbooks, although most are poorly prepared for this task. Many have a hard time understanding statements such as this: "A mixture is a combination of two or more substances. When substances are combined in a mixture, each retains its original characteristics."

A good example of advanced instructional methods involving rules can be found in the *Distar Reading III Program, Reading to Learn*, by Engelmann and Stearns.[9] This program provides step-by-step training in the skills required to learn from a textbook. These skills include: (1) learning to identify key rules in a text; (2) staying with a new rule until it is understood (and getting help when needed); and (3) rehearsing and remembering rules so they will be available in the future. Productive thinking cannot occur unless there are rules to think with.

To teach these skills, the program uses stories built upon important principles from physics, biology, history, and social studies. At the beginning of the program, the key rules come early in a selection and are underlined. Later they are buried and must be found by the student. The teacher helps the students learn to use the rules and remember them. The students get practice in stating rules, explaining what they mean, and applying them to specific examples. A workbook is used to help teach applications to new examples that go beyond those covered in the reading selection. The workbook is structured to provide periodic review of rules, so that the student finds out that what he learns today will be needed in the future. The goal of the instruction is not to teach just specific contents from science, history, and social science, but also to teach a generalized approach to reading to learn—a generalized understanding of how to find and use key rules.

Read Story 120 and identify the rules. Also, do the exercises to get a better idea of how higher cognitive processes can be systematically programed and taught.

STRAIGHT T'S AND LIGHT

Do you remember about rolling a ball toward a wall? If the path of the ball forms a straight T with the wall, the ball will roll back down the T.

If the T slants this way 𝖳, the ball will roll back this way ↘. And if the T slants this way ⊤ the ball will go this way ↙.

The rule about the straight T works for mirrors. A mirror bounces light back in the same way that a wall bounces a ball back.

Let's say that you take a flashlight and shine it into a mirror. The light leaving the flashlight goes in a straight line. It hits the mirror, but it cannot go through the mirror, so it bounces back. Look at the picture below. We are looking down at a girl. The girl is shining a flashlight into a mirror.

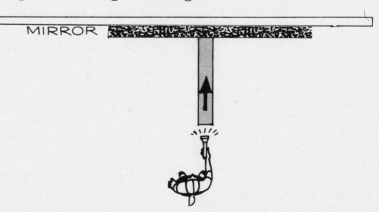

The path of light and the mirror form a straight T. So the light will come back down the same path it took when it went toward the mirror. The light will bounce back from the mirror and hit the girl.

Look at the picture below.

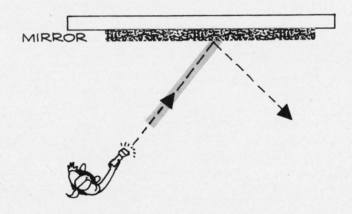

MIRROR

The girl is standing off to one side of the mirror. She shines the light into the mirror. But look at the path of light from the flashlight. It does not form a straight T with the mirror. It forms a T that slants this way 𝖳. So in which direction does the light go when it leaves the mirror? It will go in this direction ↘. The light from the flashlight will not hit the girl.

Look at the next picture.

The girl is standing off to the other side of the mirror. She shines the light into the mirror. But look at the path of light from the flashlight. It does not form a straight T with the mirror.

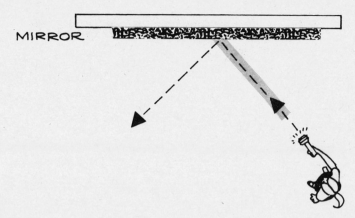

It forms a T that slants this way ⊤. So in which direction does the light bounce back from the mirror? It does in this direction ∠.

Here is a problem:

MIRROR

Look at this picture. The boy is standing in a room. There is a mirror in the room. A girl wants to see this boy in the mirror. Where would she have to stand?

Here's how to figure out the answer:

Light is going from the boy just like the light goes from the flashlight. Some of that light is making a path toward the mirror.

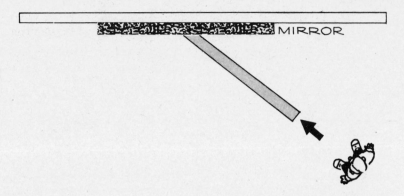

The path of light and the mirror form a T that slants this way ⊤. So the light leaving the mirror would go this way ⟋. The girl would have to stand so that her eyes were in the path of light leaving the mirror.

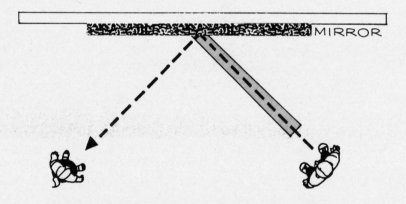

Here's another problem: Look at the next picture. The dog is sitting in the room. The mirror is on the front wall of the room. Where would a boy have to stand to see the dog in the mirror? Figure it out. Remember—some light from the dog is going toward the mirror.

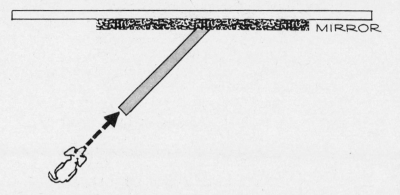

The light going from the dog forms a ⊤ that slants this way ⌐ . So the light leaving the mirror goes this way ↘ .

Look at the picture below. The boy is standing in the path of light that is leaving the mirror, so the boy can see the dog in the mirror.

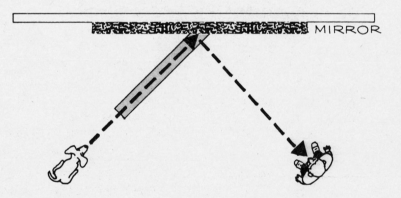

Remember the rule about the straight ⊤ . This rule is very important. Take a flashlight and shine it into a mirror. Look at the path of the light that goes into the mirror. Look at the path of the light that leaves the mirror.

Part A

3. Can light go right through a mirror? _____

4. What happens to light when it hits a mirror? _____

_____

5. **Look at the pictures below.** Each picture shows light from a flashlight shining into a mirror.
    a. In each picture draw an arrow to show where the light will go after it hits the mirror.
    b. Put a **T** under the picture that shows light forming a straight T with the mirror.

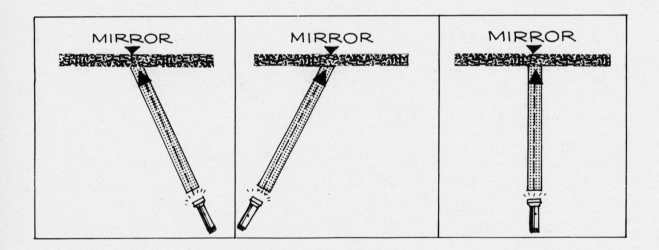

6. **Look at the pictures below.** Each picture shows a rabbit sitting in a room with a mirror.
    a. In each picture put an **X** to show where you would have to stand to see the rabbit in the mirror.
    b. Put a **T** under the picture that shows light forming a straight T with the mirror.

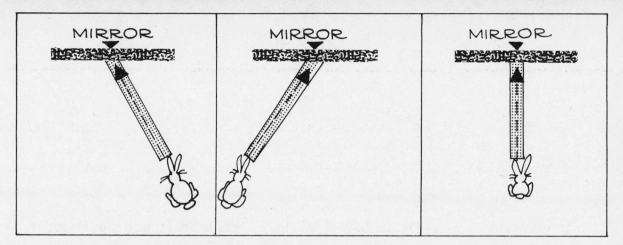

7. **Look at the pictures below.** Each picture shows a ball rolling from a wall. Draw the path that each ball took to reach the wall. Start each path from a dot.

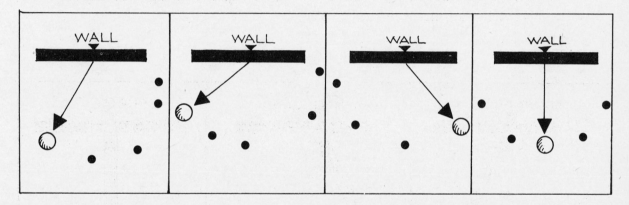

8. **Look at each of the T's.** Draw a circle around every T that is a straight T.

T ⊤ T Ⱶ Ⱶ ⋏ ⋏ T ⊤ ⊤ ⊤

A primary problem for the teacher is learning to identify examples consistent with a rule. This can be overcome by knowledge of the logic of rules and by knowing about forward and backward examples. The logic of rules is: "If A, then B; if B, then infer A." For example, "The more you eat (A), the fatter you get (B)." Given this rule, we can present forward examples and backward examples. In a forward example, an A-related statement is made and a question is asked about B. In a backward example, a B statement is made and a question is asked about A.

Forward example:

1   "This boy ate more. Did he get fatter?" (Answer: "yes")
2   "This boy did not eat more. Did he get fatter?" (Answer: "no")

Backward example:

"These boys ate. Some got fatter." (Show picture of boys.)
1   "Did this boy eat more?" (Show picture of fatter boy.) "How do you know?" (Answer: "Because he got fatter.")
2   "Did this boy eat more?" (Show picture of boy who did not get fatter.) "How do you know?" (Answer: "Because he didn't get fatter.")

Some teachers encountering this rule will not operate in terms of the logic of the rule, but rather in terms of their general experience. Since some people who eat a lot do not get fatter, the teacher might accept a "maybe" answer to some examples. But the only legitimate "maybe" answers are to backward examples where a "cause" other than *A* might be operating.

summary

Beginning instruction must usually teach by example, since the concepts and operations necessary for teaching by rules are lacking. When basics have been mastered, rule learning is possible. Some rule learning simply involves the logic of an equivalency rule. New names are given to old concepts or operations. A code is an advanced form of an equivalency rule. In most instruction by rules, a rule or principle is given and then some positive and negative examples are used to teach the details of the rule and to test for acquisition. Markle and Tiemann have empirically shown that using examples along with a rule facilitates learning the rule. Carnine and many others have shown that teaching with rules and examples is often superior to teaching only with examples and letting the students discover the rules.

A danger in teaching with rules is that the student may learn only the verbal chain that is the rule (a verbalism) and not know how to use it to identify new examples. This problem can be avoided by ensuring that component concepts are taught before being used in a rule and using specific testing procedures for each critical aspect of the rule. There are different requirements for selecting examples in testing rules and teaching rules. In *testing*, positive examples should broadly sample irrelevant characteristics, and negative examples should be designed to isolate one critical feature at a time. In *teaching* rules to experienced learners, it is probably more important to focus on discriminating S+ from S– than on discriminating S+ from Si. This can best be accomplished by changing only one element when going from a positive to a negative example and by selecting pairs of examples so that each pair isolates a critical characteristic of the rule or concept.

When the visual stimulus properties of a concept are not obvious, rules specifying function or use can be helpful in teaching: "It's a vehicle if it can take you places." "It's food if you can eat it."

Teachers need to learn how to identify examples consistent with rules. This requires an understanding of the logic of rules. A rule has the form, "If A, then B; and if B, then infer A." Forward examples of a rule give A and ask about B. Backward examples give B and ask about A. It is important to understand the logic of rules in evaluating examples.

self-test

1 name

2 examples

3 verbalism;
examples

4 concepts

5 irrelevant

6 one

7 S¡

8 uses

9 rules

1 One simple kind of teaching involves giving an alternative _____ for a concept that has already been taught.

2 In rule learning, according to Gagné, the student is given the rule or definition for the concept. The student then must use this rule to identify _____ .

3 A danger with rule learning is that the student may learn only the verbal chain that is the rule (a _____), and not how to discriminate _____ of the rule.

4 Learning by rules assumes knowledge of the component _____ being hooked together by a rule.

5 In testing, positive examples should broadly sample variation in _____ characteristics.

6 Negative examples should focus on examples that differ from positive examples in only _____ essential characteristic.

7 In teaching rules to experienced learners, it is probably more important to focus on discriminating S+ from S– than on discriminating S+ from _____ .

8 In a function definition, a concept is defined in terms of how man _____ certain objects.

9 Productive thinking cannot occur unless there are _____ to think with.

NUMBER RIGHT _____

exercise 1 programed practice

1 name

2 middle

3 rule;
  rule

4 discovery;
  efficient

5 rule

6 examples

7 prerequisite

8 chain; verbalism

9 concepts;
  brother

10 irrelevant

11 age;
  sex

12 one

13 teaching

1　One simple kind of teaching involves giving an alternative _____ for a concept which has already been taught.

2　The logic of an equivalency rule is: "All x's are called between. Between is called middle. Therefore all x's are called _____."

3　Carnine recently compared two methods for teaching three fraction skills. In the opportunity-do-discover program, examples were given but the _____ not stated. In the rule-learning program, the _____ was given.

4　In each case the rule group learned better than the _____ group. Rule learning can be very _____.

5　Gagné describes the most common deductive method for the teaching of concepts and principles, which he calls _____ learning.

6　In this method, the student is given the rule or definition for the concept. The student then must use this rule to identify _____.

7　Learning by rules can be very efficient when certain _____ skills are present.

8　A danger with rule learning is that the student may learn only the verbal _____ that is the rule (a _____).

9　Learning by rules assumes knowledge of the component _____ being hooked together by a rule. Before *uncle* can be taught by a rule, it is necessary to test for the concepts *parent* and _____.

10　In testing, positive examples should broadly sample variation in _____ characteristics.

11　For the concept of *uncle*, irrelevant characteristics might include _____, physical characteristics, _____ of parent, and sex of child of parent.

12　Negative examples should focus on examples that differ from positive examples in only _____ essential characteristic.

13　There is a difference in the requirements for selecting examples in testing rules and _____ rules.

14 In teaching rules to experienced learners, it is probably more important to focus on discriminating S+ from _____ than on discriminating S+ from _____ .

15 This can best be accomplished by changing only _____ thing when going from a positive to a negative example, and by selecting pairs of examples so that each pair _____ a critical characteristic of the rule or concept.

16 In a function definition, a concept is defined in terms of how man _____ certain objects.

17 The *Reading to Learn* program provides systematic step-by-step training in the skills required to learn from a _____ .

18 These skills include: (1) learning to identify key _____ in a text; (2) staying with a new rule until it is _____ (and getting help when needed); and (3) _____ and remembering rules so they will be available in the future.

19 To teach these skills, the program uses stories built upon important _____ from physics, biology, history, and social studies.

20 The logic of rules is: "If A, then B; if B, then infer _____ ."

21 In a forward example, an A-related statement is made and a question is asked about _____ . In a _____ example, a B statement is made and a question is asked about *A*.

14 S–;
   Si

15 one;
   isolates

16 uses

17 textbook

18 rules;
   understood;
   rehearsing

19 principles

20 A

21 B; backward

discussion questions

1 Suppose your students have been taught to call all examples where sets are combined into larger sets *plussing*. Now, you want them to also call these examples *adding*. Demonstrate a way to teach this. Explain the logic of an equivalency rule.

2 Present a simple code to your discussion group and test for its learning with some critical examples. Did you teach a general case?

3 Illustrate the basic procedures involved in teaching by rules by presenting a rule, presenting examples, and testing for acquisition.

4 Define a verbalism. How can the teacher avoid teaching verbalisms?

5 In *testing* for rule learning how are positive and negative examples selected?

6 In *teaching* with rules how should positive and negative examples be selected?

7 Suppose you are to teach the concept of *conservation of weight* using a rule method. The rule is: "If you have neither added any matter nor taken any away, it must still weigh the same." Specify the preskills necessary to teach this rule. Specify your teaching examples (three instances and three not-instances). Specify your test examples, both positive and negative.

8 What are function rules? Give an example.

9 What are the three major skills taught in *Distar III, Reading to Learn*?

10 State the basic logic of rules or principles.

11 Give a rule. Then give two forward test examples of the rule and two backward test examples of the rule.

12 Identify the rules about reflections in Story 120.

unit 7

Problem-Solving Behavior

objectives

When you complete this unit you should be able to—

1 Define problem-solving behavior in terms of component concepts and operations.
2 Distinguish between problem-analysis strategies and problem-solution strategies.
3 State why it is important to identify classes of problems requiring common solution strategies.
4 Give examples of a variety of classes of problems and their solution strategies.

lesson

In this unit, the analysis of concepts and operations is extended to show its potential relevance for analyzing and teaching problem-solving skills and creative behavior.

Some years ago a psychologist named Wolfgang Kohler gave this problem to an ape named Sultan: if he could join two bamboo sticks together to make a longer stick, he could use the sticks to reach a banana and pull it into his cage.

At first Sultan just sat. Then he picked up the two bamboo sticks and began playing with them. He happened to get them into the right position for joining them. He pushed the thinner stick into the opening of the thicker one. He then jumped up, ran to the side of the cage and drew the banana to him with the double stick. Kohler considered this an example of *insight* (a typical aspect of problem solving).[1]

Years later, Birch showed that unless apes had prior experience using sticks as extensions of their arms in poking, raking, prying, and similar operations, they did not solve the problem.[2] The solution to the problem involved two sequential operations: (1) putting two sticks together; (2) reaching with the stick to draw in the banana. The problem took some time to solve, because the apes had to learn by trial and error to join the sticks. This had not been previously taught. If training in the joining operation had been given, the problem would have been simply a combination of previously taught operations. The teaching for this problem involves (1) training in joining sticks to make them longer, and (2) training in reaching with sticks (in one piece) to pull in objects.

What Are Problems?

A mystique surrounds the field of problem solving, such as Kohler's belief that "insight" is a typical characteristic of problem solving. Insight supposedly involves a sudden mental restructuring of a problem. Actually, insight turns out to be one of those pseudo-explanations for events—an example of circular reasoning as discussed in *Teaching 1*. "Sultan put two sticks together and immediately solved the problem. He had insight." "How do you know he had insight?" "See how quickly he solved the problem after he got the sticks together." The word *insight* is a label for problem-solving behavior and not an explanation of it. When problem solving is placed in a framework of teachable concepts and operations, there is no need for a mystique of this sort.

Problems are tasks that are taught by identifying sets of tasks embodying essential characteristics of the concepts and operations to be taught. Problem-solving skills are tested by presenting "new instances" of the class. Problems often require several operations for a solution. A series of concepts and operations are chained together in a problem solution. But, in contrast to a habit-chain, the S→R links (or more correctly, the concept-operation links) in the chain are detachable units that can be recombined into many different chains (such as the rule chains and creative design sequences discussed in unit 5). Operations under the control of specific cues have the independence from one another that characterizes intelligent behavior. Piaget talks about this independence in terms of reversibility and freedom from specific contents. The tasks found on intelligence tests illustrate some of the operations involved in problem solving: comparing, searching, counting, eliminating alternatives, orienting in space, transforming, and so forth.

As noted in unit 6, the operations involved in problem-solving behavior are the *intellectual skills* that Gagné has described as the components of a learning hierarchy.[3] Gagné likens these skills to the subroutines in a computer program which, when called up (signaled), can be used to operate on a variety of information inputs and can be recombined into a variety of problem solutions. The essence of problem-solving behavior is the use of operations in new combinations to solve problems that have not been seen before. This flexibility results from each component operation being under the control of a separate signal (concept) and from the signals being present and "detected" during problem solution. It is this latter requirement that has been most neglected in the analysis of how to teach problem-solving skills.

Analysis Strategies and Solution Strategies

It is conceivable that one could have a variety of problem-solving operations in one's repertoire and not know when to use them. Detecting when particular solution strategies are likely to work involves skills in *problem analysis.* What kind of a problem is it? Is it a fact problem or a judgment problem? What is known and not known? Training in analyzing the nature of problems is the key to teaching problem-solving behavior. Without problem-analysis skills, solution strategies are useless. You would not know when to do what. Analysis strategies lead to the *task directions* (cues, stimuli, signals) that indicate which solution strategies will be more fruitful.

It is at this point in instruction that the so-called "discovery method" becomes useful. A problem example is presented and the student makes some guesses (hypotheses) as to the nature of the problem. He is gaining practice in problem analysis. A series of examples may eventually lead to the conclusion that this is an X-type problem and the answer is such and such. Now a new class of problems is introduced through new examples. A different analysis is required, a different solution is implied. After experience with multiple sets of different kinds of problems, the student may have sufficient inductive experience to begin instruction in rules for problem analysis. The process becomes one that Shulman has called "guided discovery."[4] The discovery process is programed to provide the needed inductive experience with problem classes. Then, more formal rule learning about such classes and related solution strategies can be provided.

The logic of the approach we are proposing can be best communicated through demonstration and example. We will first look at the notion of classes of problems and then see how this analysis can relate to possible solution strategies.

Classes of Problems

Problems can be analyzed into classes according to whether the solution is a *fact* or a *judgment,* and in terms of what is *given* and *not given*.

Fact versus Judgment

A fact problem has a specific answer. Criteria are available for specifying a solution or a class of equivalent solutions. "What is the diameter of the moon?" is a fact problem. "How much is 4 times 6?" is a fact problem. Judgment problems have many solutions that differ in value. For example, most problems in engineering, architecture, or creative writing involve some fixed criteria (minimum standards), but they also involve judgments about which criteria are more important (relative weighing of criteria) and about characteristics that are not specifiable in criterion terms, such as beauty. With judgment problems, people may disagree as to the value of different solutions.

Givens

Problems differ in what is given and what is not given (required for solution).
The following groupings cover the majority of tasks used to define intelligent
behavior. Most of the examples are adaptations of the Stanford-Binet (Form
LM) items. This test is discussed in more detail in unit 12.

1 *Concept words are given. The task is to identify or compare characteristics.*

Problem Class	Example
Vocabulary	"What is a lemon?"
Analogies	"Equity is an asset, a mortgage is a *(liability)*."
Essential differences	"What is the difference between concepts and operations?"
Essential similarities	"How are a tree and a rosebush alike?"
Abstract words	"What is status?"

2 *The concept is not given. The task is to find the concept.*

a) *Instances are given (induction):*

Problem Class	Example
Problem situation	"Jim saw an animal in the woods and he tried to take it home, but it got away. His parents burned his clothes when he got home. Why?"
Induction	A paper is folded once and a hole cut. Then a paper is folded twice and a hole cut. Then three times, and so on. "Give me a rule so I can know how many holes there will be?"
Proverbs	"What does this mean? 'Great oaks from little acorns grow'."
Finding causes	"What is characteristic of things that burn and characteristic of things that do not burn?"
	"Why do some plants of the same variety grow bigger than others?"

b) *Instances are not given (deduction).*

Problem Class	Example
Finding reasons	"Give three reasons why people should drink milk."
Twenty questions	"By asking questions that can be answered yes or no find out what I am thinking of."

3. *The goal response is given. The task is to identify the route to the goal.*

Problem Class	Example
Directions	"Which direction would you have to face so that your left hand is toward the south?"

Ingenuity	"Use a 4-pint can and a 7-pint can to bring back exactly 3 pints of water."
Mazes	"Show me how to take the boy to school the shortest way."

4 *The goal response is not given. The task is to use your knowledge of concepts and operations to produce the answer.*

Problem Class	Example
Reasoning	"A tree was 5 inches tall the first year, 10 inches tall the second year, and 20 inches tall the third year. How tall will it be the fourth year?"
Arithmetic problems	"If a man earns $100 a month and spends $75, how long will it take him to save $400?"
Paper cutting	"Draw how a paper that has been folded and cut will look when it is unfolded."
Comprehension	"What should you do if you find a lost child?"

5 *The criteria for goal response are given. The task is to use your knowledge of operations to construct an acceptable product.*

Problem Class	Example
Picture completion	A schematic man is given, without some features. The task is to "make all the rest of him."
Paper folding	"Watch what I do and make a triangle like mine."
Draw a diamond	"Make one just like this."
Planning a search	"Something has been lost in this given area. Show how you would search to find it."
Sentence building	"Make up a sentence that has in it the words *sled*, *snow* and *cold*."

Problem-Solving Strategies

Rules for problem solving specify possible strategies for different classes of problems. The first step is to classify the problem. Is it a fact problem or a judgment problem? What is given and what is not given? The next step is to identify possible solution strategies.

Fact Problems

Fact problems require finding the answer. There are many, many classes of fact problems where different information is given and different solution strategies are required. The following examples illustrate some major classes of fact problems.

Concept identification. Instances are given. Consider the following concept-identification task. The set of possible concepts is restricted to groups of three geometric figures, each of which is a circle, triangle, or square. Concept instances and not-instances can vary in the type of figure found in any of the three positions. The problem is to find out, from as few instances as possible, what concept this is an example of:

Select instances one at a time from the following list. After each selection, check the key below to find out if you have picked an instance or not-instance of this concept. Try to figure out the concept as you go along.

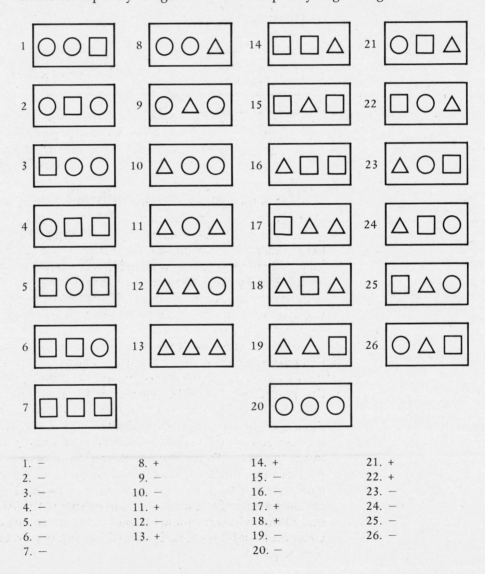

1. –	8. +	14. +	21. +
2. –	9. –	15. –	22. +
3. –	10. –	16. –	23. –
4. –	11. +	17. +	24. –
5. –	12. –	18. +	25. –
6. –	13. +	19. –	26. –
7. –		20. –	

The smart way to go about it is to select instances that change only one characteristic at a time.[5] This will tell you what is essential to instances and not-instances of the concept. For example:

Instances Selected

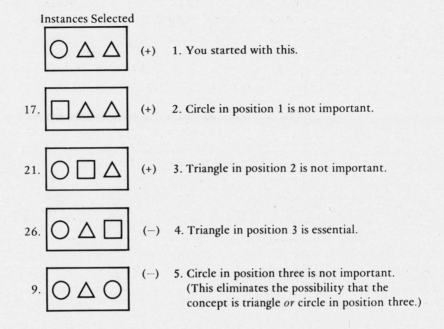

(+) 1. You started with this.

17. (+) 2. Circle in position 1 is not important.

21. (+) 3. Triangle in position 2 is not important.

26. (−) 4. Triangle in position 3 is essential.

9. (−) 5. Circle in position three is not important.
     (This eliminates the possibility that the
     concept is triangle *or* circle in position three.)

Since nothing else is common to all three instances, the concept must be "triangle (only) in position three."

Note carefully the problem-solving strategy: change only one thing at a time to identify the critical elements and to eliminate alternatives systematically. When concept instances are given, identification is most quickly accomplished by the systematic testing of alternatives. This can be done experimentally by changing things one at a time, or observationally by examining a series of instances and not-instances to see what characteristics are shared by the instances.

Concept identification. Instances are given, but there are many possibilities. If there are a large number of possibilities and only a few essential characteristics in a given concept instance, then a combination of deductive and inductive procedures should be considered. Suppose the problem is to find the cause of polio (infantile paralysis). Causes are antecedent events. Polio is a disease of the nervous system. Deductively all events that do not influence the nervous system can be eliminated. The causal events must take place inside the body. All food substances regularly used that are not followed by polio can be eliminated. There remains the weak possibility that a given food substance could act in combination with some other causal factor. Microorganisms whose effects are known can be eliminated. At this point, it is necessary to find what remaining events are common to instances of polio and not common to not-instances. Systematic testing of possibilities one at a time is now required.

Concept identification. No instances are given. The problem is the game Twenty Questions: I am thinking of something. You have to determine what I am thinking about by asking twenty questions or less that can be answered yes or no. Let's analyze the problem. It is a concept-identification problem. The answer is not given. It is known that there is a specific answer and that the answer is the name of a thing. It is necessary to search to find the answer. Because there are so many things in the world, there is no point to just guessing "Is it a baseball?" or "Is it an orange?" The characteristics of this thing must be determined. A *zeroing-in* strategy is used. Questions are asked that start at the top of the hierarchy of things and work down. Deduction is used when no instances are given.

"Is it living?" "No."

"Is it man-made?" "Yes."

"Is it larger than a breadbox?" "No."

"Is it found in the home?" "Yes."

"Would most people have one?" "Yes."

Each question eliminates about half of the alternatives until the object is identified.

Even when the question involves the identification of a concept or a stimulus within a small group, the strategy is the same: "I am thinking of a number between 1 and 10."

"Is it greater than 6?" "No."

"Is it greater than 3?" "Yes."

"Is it 4?" "Yes."

The size of the set is not critical. What is critical for this strategy is *the lack of instances and knowledge only of a higher-order set of which the concept is a member.*

Concept-characteristic problems. To teach children to handle analogies, essential similarities and differences, and other problems involving identification of concept characteristics, practice in *comparing, relating,* and *contrasting* is given after teaching the basic concepts. Without knowledge of the basic concepts, these problems cannot be solved. Without the operations of comparing, relating, and contrasting, new problems involving these problems cannot be solved.

Route-to-the-goal problems. Goal response is given. If the goal response is given, consider starting from the goal and working the problem backward. Consider this maze:

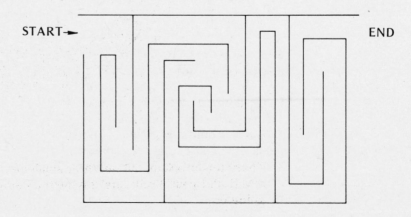

By starting at the end, the solution is readily found with no errors. Even if the task requires drawing a line from the "Start" to the "End," going through the tracing operation mentally from "End" to "Start" will allow most people to solve the maze quickly with no errors.

Similarly, people faced with Sultan's problem could start by defining the solution: "I need something long enough to reach the banana so I can pull it in." Then the search involves how to get or make something long enough.

Consider this problem: The task is to move the coal car on the right to the position of the coal car on the left and the coal car on the left to the position of the coal car on the right, and end up with the engine where it is now.

Rule 1. Only the engine can go through the tunnel.

Rule 2. The engine can hook on to cars from either end. It can move forward or backward on the tracks.

Rule 3. The sidetrack holds two cars.

E = Engine
R = Right Coal Car
L = Left Coal Car

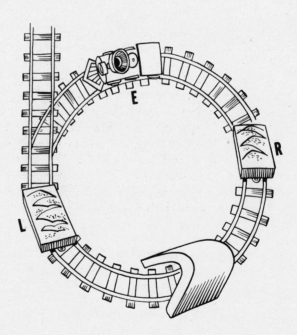

To try this problem, cut out three small pieces of paper and label them E, L, and R. Put your "train cars" on the track and try to solve the problem before going on.

BEFORE LOOKING AT THE SOLUTION, READ THIS.

If you did not solve the problem, take this information and try again. At solution, the cars will be in this order:

R		E		L

To get into this order, the step before the solution must look like this:

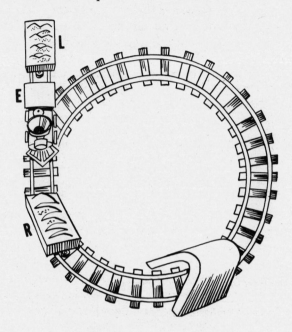

NOW TRY AGAIN!

Codes: *R position* is the starting position of R as drawn in the original problem.
L position is the starting position of L.
E position is the starting position of E.
E, L, and R stand for the cars you are moving.

Solution Steps:

 1   E puts R in sidetrack.
 2   E puts L in E position.
 3   E goes through tunnel to R.
 4   E takes R to L position.
 5   E goes through tunnel to L and takes L to R.
 6   E returns through tunnel to R.
 7   E moves R and L to sidetrack.
 8   E returns R to L position.
 9   E goes through tunnel to R and up to L in sidetrack.
10   E takes L out of sidetrack and over to R position.
11   E returns to E position.

This train problem illustrates the importance of looking at the final step (answer) in planning a solution. The final order is R, E, L, and the only way it can get that way is for some step before the final one to show this order also. When the solution is defined as getting the L car into the sidetrack ahead of the engine, the rest of the steps fall into place.

Puzzles are often difficult because the situation is structured to elicit habitual responses that are wrong. Consider this problem: The task is to draw through all nine dots with four straight lines without taking your pencil off the paper and without retracing a line.

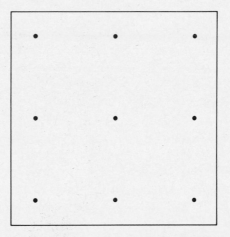

Most people will use old habits in trying to connect the dots. They will try going around the square and then play with the diagonals. Then they are stuck. Here's a hint. The solution involves drawing lines beyond the square containing the nine dots. When stuck with old habits, consider the various ways in which the problem can be transformed. Restate the question. Look at the definition of the problem implicit in your wrong responses, and ask yourself if there is a broader definition. Logically, what alternative responses can be made in this situation?

When the problem is to find something that is lost, what to look for is given, but where to look is not. Because learned associations are established forward in time rather than backward, it is best to start the search at the place where the lost item was last known to be and work forward in time, systematically eliminating alternatives.

Goal response is not given. Produce the answer. Many problems test the ability to use a variety of concepts and operations to produce an answer. Many problems of arithmetic or logical reasoning are of this form. Once the rule-chains for their solutions have been taught, they can be used in new examples. If the student does not know the solution rules, he cannot do problems of this sort. Strategies involving defining the solution, finding the question, or searching for response alternatives are not helpful. What is needed most is direct teaching of sets of prototype problems.

Criteria for goal response are given. Produce the answer. Construction problems involve producing an answer to fixed criteria. Specific concepts and operations must be taught and sequenced, as in learning to write, copy figures, make cookies from a recipe, or construct grammatically correct sentences. Construction problems with fixed criteria are taught directly as rule chains; complex strategies are not required.

Creative Judgment Problems

Judgment problems require strategies for designing creative solutions that might work. An example might be to design a vehicle for landing on the moon. Analysis of this problem would first require a statement of the functions of the vehicle and other fixed requirements. How many persons must it hold? In what kind of terrain must it land? From where must it descend? Where must it go afterward? What kind of communications system is required? What life-support systems are required? Is there a weight limit? What characteristics must the propulsion and control system have? What is the cost limit? Next, a series of trial designs are made. What incompatibilities among priorities are encountered? How can they be solved? How can weight be saved? How can cost be reduced? All initial decisions are kept tentative. Alternatives are sought by systematic review of the possibilities. Finally, alternatives are evaluated according to how well they meet specifications, and a working model is built for further evaluation. After testing, a production model is designed.

Teaching children to analyze a construction problem is quite complex and will not be dealt with here. The point to be made is that this is an important class of problems. The complex skills involved can be taught by systematic assignment of construction tasks along with the teaching of the component concepts and operations. After a large number of tasks have been mastered, the student can be taught more formal steps for analyzing construction problems.

The teaching of the many skills involved in creative designs has not yet been sufficiently analyzed into its component behaviors to permit exposition here. Very likely the component concepts and operations required will vary markedly from one area of activity to another. The component skills required by the design engineer will be quite different from those of the science fiction writer or the composer. One difference between creative design problems and fact or construction problems (which can be solved with rule chains) is that, at any point in the solution, the alternative possibilities have to be kept in mind. This implies that learning to think of unusual or different alternatives at any point in a problem solution is an important aspect of the creative solutions to design problems. Several studies have looked experimentally at what it takes to produce behavior judged to be more creative in this sense.

In a study with preschool children, Goetz and Baer[6] gave descriptive social reinforcement for producing different forms in block building. The teacher would show delight and say something like "Oh, that's nice. It's different." The findings demonstrated that when production of different forms was reinforced, the children produced many more "creative" constructions than when no reinforcement was given, or when "same" forms were reinforced.

In a study with fourth, fifth, and sixth graders, Maloney and Hopkins[7] gave points and back-up reinforcers to promote creative writing. Each day the students were given a key word that they were to work into a ten-sentence story. After five days without reinforcement for diversity, the class was divided into two teams to play the "good writing game." On various days the teams earned points by writing stories with more different adjectives, or action verbs, or both of these along with different sentence beginnings. Both teams could win the game if they made enough points. The points could be exchanged for extra recess time and a piece of candy. There were marked increases in the production of different words. Also, independent judges rated the stories more creative when diversity was reinforced.

While we are not, at this point, able to lay out a curriculum to teach creative behaviors, there should be little question that systematic work in this area will be very productive for the future and that the behavioral approach can encompass such human complexities.

summary

The components of problem-solving behaviors are operations that can be chained together in a variety of ways to solve different kinds of problems. The "recombinability" of operations into new sequences results from each operation being under the control of a separate concept class. Additionally, problem-solving behavior involves problem-analysis skills. The guided discovery method is useful in teaching problem-analysis skills.

To illustrate what is involved in problem-analysis and problem-solution skills, a variety of problems were examined. With a fact problem, the problem is to find the answer. By contrast, judgment problems most often involve the design of creative solutions where there are multiple criteria for a good product. In judgment problems, it is necessary to continuously consider the alternative possibilities and operate tentatively until a variety of possible solutions have been produced and evaluated. Curricula to systematically teach problem-solving skills are needed.

self-test

1 Saying that insight is a typical characteristic of problem solving is using _____ reasoning.

2 Often in problem solving, operations that have been taught are used in new _____ . All that is required is that each operation be under the control of a separate _____ .

1 circular, tautological

2 combinations; cue, stimulus, concept class

3 Detecting when particular solution strategies are likely to work involves skills in problem _____ .

4 A good strategy in solving a concept-identification problem in which instances are given is to change only _____ _____ at a time to identify critical elements and to eliminate alternatives.

5 Problems differ in whether the solution is a fact or a _____ .

6 It is a fact problem if there is a _____ answer.

7 If the problem is to identify a concept and no instances are given, the solution involves deduction to _____ _____ on the answer.

8 When stuck with old habits, consider the various ways in which problems can be _____

9 Judgment problems require complex strategies for designing and evaluating _____ solutions.

NUMBER RIGHT _____

3 analysis

4 one thing, one characteristic

5 judgment

6 right, definite, specific

7 zero in

8 transformed

9 new, creative

exercise 1 programed practice

1 tasks

2 circular, tautological

3 label, name

4 operations

5 intelligence

6 combinations; cue, stimulus, concept class

7 analysis

1 Problems are _____ .

2 Saying that insight is a typical characteristic of problem solving is using _____ reasoning.

3 Insight is just a _____ for problem-solving behavior and not an explanation of it.

4 When problem solving is placed in a framework of teachable concepts and _____ , there is no need for a mystique.

5 The tasks found on _____ tests illustrate some of the operations involved in problem solving.

6 Often in problem solving, operations that have been taught are used in new _____ . All that is required is that each operation be under the control of a separate _____ .

7 Detecting when particular solution strategies are likely to work involves skills in problem _____ .

8 solution

9 discovery

10 one thing,
   one characteristic

11 judgment

12 finding;
   answer

13 new, creative

14 right, definite,
   specific

15 disagree, differ

16 given

17 not given

18 zero in

19 one characteristic

20 backward

21 transformed

22 last known

23 new, creative

8 Without problem-analysis skills, _____ strategies are useless. You would not know when to do what.

9 It is at this point in instruction that the so-called _____ method becomes useful.

10 A good strategy in solving a concept-identification problem in which instances are given is to change only _____ _____ at a time to identify critical elements and to eliminate alternatives.

11 Problems differ in whether the solution is a fact or a _____ .

12 Fact problems require _____ the _____ .

13 Judgment problems require strategies for considering _____ solutions that might work.

14 It is a fact problem if there is a _____ answer.

15 It is a judgment problem if people can _____ as to the value of the solutions.

16 In various classes of problems, different information is _____ and not given.

17 Identifying what is _____ _____ establishes what the problem is.

18 If the problem is to identify a concept and no instances are given, the solution involves deduction to _____ _____ on the answer.

19 In concept-identification problems where instances are given, the solution is found most readily by testing for _____ _____ at a time.

20 If the problem involves finding a route to a goal, and the goal response is given, consider starting at the goal and working _____ .

21 When stuck with old habits, consider the various ways in which problems can be _____ .

22 When something is lost, it is best to start searching where the object was _____ _____ to be and work forward in time.

23 Judgment problems require complex strategies for designing and evaluating _____ solutions.

24 One thing about the solution of creative design problems that is different from fact problems or construction problems is that at any point in the solution, _____ possibilities have to be kept in mind.

25 This implies that learning to think of unusual or _____ alternatives at any point in a problem solution is an important aspect of the creative solutions to design problems.

26 Several studies have shown that _____ for creative productions can be effective.

27 There should be little question that the _____ approach can encompass the complexities of human problem-solving behavior.

24 alternative

25 different

26 reinforcement

27 behavioral

discussion questions

1 Why is *insight* not a good explanation of problem-solving behavior?

2 What did Birch contribute to the understanding of the stick-joining problem first studied by Kohler?

3 What are the components of problem-solving behavior?

4 What kinds of problems can be solved with rule chains?

5 What is a problem-solving strategy?

6 Give examples of problem analysis strategies and problem solution strategies.

Questions 7, 8, and 9 are examples of problems. For each one, specify whether it is a fact or a judgment problem, and tell what is given and what is not given.

7 The problem is: "What is a lemon?"

8 The problem is: "What does this mean: 'Great oaks from little acorns grow'?"

9 The problem is: "Use a 4-pint can and a 7-pint can to bring back exactly 3 pints of water."

10 If you were given a concept-identification problem and no instances of the concept, what kind of search strategy would you use to solve the problem?

11 If you were given a concept-identification problem with some instances of the concept, describe the kind of search operation you would use to identify the essential characteristics of the concept.

12 Suggest some procedures that could be used to overcome habits.

13 How do creative design problems differ from "cookbook" construction problems?

14 Suggest some procedures for teaching creative behaviors.

unit 8

Review

objectives

This review unit is designed to remind you of some of the material covered earlier in the course. It is not designed to teach you new material. If any terms or concepts are mentioned that you do not understand, you should go back to the original material and study it carefully. In addition, you should go back through the exercises you did for each unit and make sure that you know the correct answer for each item.

review

UNIT 1. What Is Instruction?

The various models of instruction we have been discussing are compared in table 1.1 (page 15). From this sampling, we can see that the various models have both strengths and weaknesses. The small-group Distar model is slow in providing training in self-directed learning. Computer-assisted instruction has difficulty correcting oral responses or listening to a child read. The open classroom can be weak in teaching basic skills and in evaluating its major goals. It should be noted that these models can be used in sequence for different purposes as the skill level of the child changes. Direct small-group instruction could be emphasized to get reading, language skills, and beginning arithmetic skills going; then individually programed materials and computers could take over to build skill competencies and problem-solving behaviors; and finally, one could use an open classroom to foster self-directed and creative inquiry into the many fantastic worlds of knowledge. But whatever the model, if it is to be effective, it must contain provisions for the key procedures for effective instruction discussed in this unit.

UNIT 2.   A Behavioral Model of Teaching

The teacher always teaches specific tasks, although the outcome of a sequence of tasks (a program) can be the teaching of a generalized concept or operation. Tasks are instances of the more general stimulus-response relationships the teacher wishes to establish. The act of teaching involves getting the task response going in the presence of the task stimulus and using procedures to strengthen such connections.

In teaching a task, the teacher has to establish and control a variety of stimulus events to make learning happen. Ten potential functional components of tasks were identified. These are:

	Component	Teacher Action
1	*Attention signal*	Get the children to attend on signal.
2	*Task stimulus*	Present the task stimulus.
3	*S-directions*	Give directions for orienting to a task stimulus.
4	*S-prompts*	When needed, provide cues to aid in the discrimination of concept instances and not-instances.
5	*R-directions*	Give directions for the general form of the response.
6	*R-prompts*	Use previously taught stimulus-response connections to get a specific response to the task stimulus.
7	*"Do it" signals*	Get the children to respond on signal.
8	*Task response*	
9	*Reinforcement*	Reinforce right response.
10	*Corrections*	Use above procedures to correct wrong responses.

These components were interrelated in a behavior model of teaching in figure 2.1. To complete the model, it is necessary only to add the sequences of tasks that constitute a basic program of instruction, or branch correction programs.

Beginning instruction should focus on those tasks that are common to the teaching of many other tasks. Especially important in this respect are directions and signals.

Directions are important in teaching the general case. Directions tell you what to do. S-directions specify what to do with task stimuli ("Look at the color") and R-directions specify what to do in making task responses ("Say the color name"). S-directions specify a sensory modality and a stimulus class that is of a higher order than the one the task signal is in. R-directions specify a response mode (general operation) and a class above the one containing the task response.

Signals are especially important for group instruction. Attention signals indicate who is to attend to the teacher when. "Do it" signals specify who is to respond when.

Prompts are also important in teaching most tasks. Prompts are previously taught stimulus-response connections that can be used to get a specific response to occur in the presence of a new stimulus. Directions cannot be eliminated; prompts can be eventually faded out.

UNIT 3. Teaching Tasks—Skills for Direct Instruction of Groups

The skills involved in the direct instruction of groups consist of using signals, teaching directions, prompting, using reinforcers, correcting mistakes, and pacing the presentation. This unit has reviewed procedures for each of these skills except use of reinforcers. Remember that to become proficient it is important to get supervised practice in use of the skills.

In summarizing, we will look at the various skills as they are integrated in the behavioral model of teaching.

Procedures Applying to the Pre-Task Component

1 Secure attention before proceeding with the teaching demonstration.
2 State the rules for reinforcement before presenting the task.
3 Use hand signals to help hold attention.
4 Vary the duration of the attention signals unpredictably.

To teach attention signals: (1) state what will happen if the children attend (the contingency); (2) pause; (3) give the signal; (4) at the same time use a hand signal to hold attention for a variable time; (5) praise good attending; and (6) give the reinforcers that were promised.

To correct children who are not attending, praise by name (or otherwise reward) children who are attending and point out their behavior to the inattentive children. Repeat the task, and praise (or otherwise reward) the children who attend.

After attention signals have been established, use easy tasks to fade out reinforcement between the attention response and the task presentation. The goal is to give reinforcement only at the end of the task (after the child gives a task response). This builds a chain of attending behavior that includes the teaching demonstration.

Procedures Applying to the Task Component

1 Study each teaching demonstration to find its pacing requirements.
2 For prompts not controlled by the program, be sure to: (a) use minimum prompt necessary; (b) fade the prompts as soon as possible; (c) present the task stimulus *before* the prompt; and (d) direct attention to the task stimulus.
3 Use hand signals as "do it" signals.
4 Pause before giving a "do it" signal to provide a general "get ready" cue.

Teaching demonstrations differ. It is important to analyze tasks for the pacing that will be most helpful. Pacing decisions should consider phrasing, tempo, pauses, and dramatic changes.

Every task requires an attention response as well as a task response. Prompts can be used to facilitate the occurrence of both kinds of responses. Use S-prompts to help focus attention on task stimuli. Use R-prompts to get the right task response going. Prompts can be verbal and nonverbal instructions, added cues, physical prompts, and models for imitation. Any stimulus that can make desired responses occur at the right time can be used as a prompt.

Fading involves the gradual withdrawal of prompts. A progression of steps between the presence of the prompt and its absence is devised and the teacher moves step by step in the progression. Fading can consist of reducing the intensity of a stimulus, reducing or increasing the size of a visual stimulus, presenting less and less of a response to be imitated, and so forth. Any way in which a stimulus can be made less discriminable in a given teaching context can constitute fading.

"Do it" signals specify when someone is to respond. Always pause for a variable length of time before giving a "do it" signal. This pause provides a general cue that a "do it" signal is coming and sets up a variable reinforcement schedule for good attending.

"Do it" signals are taught just like any other signal. Present several tasks using the same signal, reinforce appropriate responses, and correct inappropriate ones.

In multiple-segment tasks, a "do it" signal in one segment can be taught without going through the whole task. In a series task, the chain of responses should not be treated separately. If there is an error, the whole task is presented again.

Procedures Applying to the Post-Task Component

1   Reinforce correct responses. This is done by confirming the correct response and then giving praise, and so on.
2   As learning progresses make reinforcement more intermittent.
3   Correct all mistakes. Teach task directions where necessary.
4   When a child is having a lot of difficulty, reinforce trying.

The decision process in correcting mistakes in basic instruction is as follows. When an error occurs, determine whether or not the child responded to the R-direction. If not, repeat the direction to call his attention to it, and then model the task segment in which the error occurred. If the child responded to the R-direction, determine whether he does not know the answer or is having difficulty making the response. Do this by examining the response the child did make. If the child does not know the answer, give him the answer and repeat the task. If the child is having difficulty making the complete response, lead him through the response several times. If this fails, try to simplify the response requirements by breaking them down into smaller units and building them up again.

To see if the correction procedure has worked, present the task segment again, giving no help. Then the whole task is presented again and the program is continued. In advanced instruction, errors most commonly involve discriminative confusion between related concepts. By presenting a series of instances of both concepts, the teacher can improve the discrimination between them.

It is sometimes necessary to teach explicitly the operations involved in task directions ("look," "name"). To do this, design a general format containing the directions, construct a set of related tasks by following the general format, and teach the tasks using prompts, reinforcers, and corrections.

UNIT 4. Basic Requirements for Teaching Concepts

A concept can be defined as the set of stimulus characteristics uniquely common to a set of stimulus instances in a given universe and not common to other concepts in that universe. A general case has been taught when, after teaching some members of a concept class, any member of the class is identified correctly; and nonmembers are identified as not belonging to the concept class.

Concept learning can be viewed as bringing operant behavior under stimulus control. Basic to this learning is the principle of differential reinforcement. In the presence of instances of a concept class, one kind of response is reinforced. The basic teaching problem becomes one of determining which concept instances and not-instances should be presented to most efficiently teach the critical discriminations involved in concept learning.

Four procedures for establishing stimulus control over operant behavior were examined for their implications for teaching a general case. This examination indicated that a concept cannot be taught with a single positive and negative instance. A set of instances is required to isolate essential concept characteristics. In this set, all positive instances should possess all relevant concept characteristics, and negative instances only some or none of them. Within positive and negative instances, irrelevant characteristics must be varied to avoid teaching misrules and to isolate essential characteristics. When concepts fall into sets of related concepts that can easily be confused with each other, it is important to teach the set through a cumulative addition of new members to the set. Each time a new member is added, the set is brought to criterion. This procedure will insure that all essential discriminations will be learned and the members of the concept set will not be mistaken for each other.

Concept learning was thus viewed as a multiple discrimination problem where:

1 *Within* positive and negative concept instances, it is necessary to discriminate relevant from irrelevant characteristics; and,
2 *Between* positive and negative concept instances, it is necessary to discriminate between the relevant characteristics of the concept being taught and other (usually related) concepts.

Engelmann has proposed that concepts be defined only within finite sets. Once this is done, it is possible to analyze the logical properties of sets of related concepts and determine which discriminations are most important to teach.

UNIT 5.   Basic Requirements for Teaching Operations

An operation is the common effect of a set of behaviors under stimulus control. Behavior has a temporal dimension and, therefore, usually can be broken down into smaller units. From the point of view of the teacher and programer, the critical question is "What units?" The answer is, "No smaller than the smallest functional unit required to build behavior sequences (chains)." In naming things, the functional unit is the name word. In reading-by-sounds, the functional unit is the sound. Operations are functional units of behavior. The analysis of operations in programing seeks the minimum number of functional units of behavior which can be used as building blocks in the maximum number of response sequences when appropriately cued. With behavioral development, there is often a change in the size of the functional units under stimulus control. A whole chain of behavior may be the functional unit. The critical feature of an operation is not the size of the unit, but the existence of a class of responses under stimulus control which have a common effect on the environment.

Component operations can be built into habit chains and rule chains. They can also be used in the most creative human activities. In a habit chain, each response produces a stimulus that serves as the cue for the next response. The chain eventually becomes a functional unit. In a rule chain, each step in the chain provides the stimuli needed to carry out the next steps, but these stimuli will differ from problem to problem. They are not fixed as in a habit chain, but vary with the example. In a rule chain, the "habit structure" being learned is the general rules and their sequence of use which can then be applied to problems never solved before.

The *formal operations* of science, mathematics, and logic are usually singular rules, which can be used as building blocks in problem-solving behavior. For example, to find the rate of speed, given distance traveled and time taken, *divide distance by time*.

Concepts and operations are similar in several ways. Concepts refer to what is common to a set of stimulus instances. Operations refer to the common effect of a set of response instances. Instances of concepts and operations both have relevant and irrelevant characteristics. With concepts the response is arbitrary (a convention), with operations the controlling cue is a convention. For every operation, there is a potential concept about that operation. What is an example of an operation for the *doer* is an example of a concept for the *observer*.

Prompting and differential reinforcement are the basic procedures for teaching the operational requirements of a task. Beyond that, a sequence of tasks (a program) is required to isolate the essential requirements of the operations from non-essential characteristics and to differentiate a given operation from related operations. Cumulative programing is used to teach a set of related operations. To teach chains of operations, component operations are taught first and then put together as multiple-segment tasks. If the operations in behavior sequences are to be used in a variety of orders (as in language), then it is important to vary the order when teaching the operations. Otherwise, habit-chains will be learned. Once basic operations have been mastered, it is probably more efficient to teach new operations as concepts about the operations. The fact that some consistent signal is required to show the presence of an operation means that testing must use cues related to what has been taught. To infer that an operation has been learned, the teacher should look at a set of responses given under the appropriate cue conditions.

Programing can be smart or dumb depending on the building blocks used to teach the objectives of the program. For example, teaching reading by sounds is more efficient than the sight-word method. Operational approaches to mathematics are more efficient than rote habit approaches.

Thinking processes are assumed to involve no new principles beyond those involved in understanding overt conceptual and operational behavior. The processes are simply no longer observable.

Experimental studies in teaching language skills illustrate how a general case, such as learning the rules of grammar, can be taught through presenting a series of tasks involving operations to-be-differentiated-from-each-other.

UNIT 6. Teaching Experienced Learners

Beginning instruction must usually teach by example, since the concepts and operations necessary for teaching by rules are lacking. When basics have been mastered, rule learning is possible. Some rule learning simply involves the logic of an equivalency rule. New names are given to old concepts or operations. A code is an advanced form of an equivalency rule. In most instruction by rules, a rule or principle is given and then some positive and negative examples are used to teach the details of the rule and to test for acquisition. Markle and Tiemann have empirically shown that using examples along with a rule facilitates learning the rule. Carnine and many others have shown that teaching with rules and examples is often superior to teaching only with examples and letting the students discover the rules.

A danger in teaching with rules is that the student may only learn the verbal chain that is the rule (a verbalism) and not know how to use the rule to identify new examples. This problem can be avoided by being sure component concepts are taught before being used in a rule, and using specific testing procedures for each critical aspect of the rule. There are different requirements for selecting examples in testing rules and teaching rules. In *testing*, positive examples should broadly sample irrelevant characteristics, and negative examples should be designed to isolate one critical feature at a time. In *teaching* rules to experienced learners, it is probably more important to focus on discriminating S+ from S− than on discriminating S+ from Si. This can best be accomplished by changing only one element when going from a positive to a negative example, and by selecting pairs of examples so that each pair isolates a critical characteristic of the rule or concept.

When the visual stimulus properties of a concept are not obvious, rules specifying function or use can be helpful in teaching. "It's a vehicle if it can take you places." "It's food if you can eat it."

Teachers need to learn how to identify examples consistent with rules. This requires an understanding of the logic of rules. A rule has the form, "If A, then B; and if B, then infer A." Forward examples of a rule give A and ask about B. Backward examples give B and ask about A. It is important to understand the logic of rules in evaluating examples.

UNIT 7. Problem-Solving Behavior

The components of problem-solving behaviors are operations that can be chained together in a variety of ways to solve different kinds of problems. The "recombinability" of operations into new sequences results from each operation being under the control of a separate concept class. Additionally, problem-solving behavior involves problem-analysis skills. The guided discovery method is useful in teaching problem-analysis skills.

To illustrate what is involved in problem analysis and problem solution skills, a variety of problems were examined. With a fact problem, the problem is to find the answer. In contrast, judgment problems most often involve the design of creative solutions where there are multiple criteria for a good product. In judgment problems, it is necessary to continuously consider the alternative possibilities and operate tentatively until a variety of possible solutions have been produced and evaluated. Curricula to systematically teach problem-solving skills are needed.

review exercises

UNIT 1

1   What is instruction?
2   Name the procedures essential to instruction.
3   Describe the basic characteristics of an open classroom.
4   Discuss the potential strengths and weaknesses of the open classroom.
5   Why do behaviorists question the assumptions that learning is purposive, self-motivated, and must be self-directed?
6   Why would behaviorists question the assumption that what can be taught depends on the child's level of development (implying conditions related to physical maturation)?
7   Discuss the potential strengths and weaknesses of the large-group lecture method.
8   Describe the basic features of computer-assisted instruction.
9   What are the main weaknesses of CAI in its current form?
10   Describe the individually prescribed instruction model.
11   Discuss the potential strengths and weaknesses of IPI.

12 Describe the Distar small-group instruction method.

13 How does this method overcome problems common to traditional small-group instruction?

14 What are some potential weaknesses of the Distar method as a general approach to instruction? (Go beyond the text in your thinking.)

15 Suggest some ways in which the different models of instruction might be combined at various stages of education to achieve different objectives.

UNIT 2

1 Define the term *task*.

2 How is programing different from teaching a task?

3 Define *task stimulus*.

4 Define *task response*.

5 Define *"do it" signal*.

6 Define *attention signal*.

7 Define *task directions*.

8 Define *prompts*.

9 Why is it that the teacher does not actually teach concepts and operations?

10 What is required to teach a task in addition to presenting task signals?

11 Compare prompts and directions. How are they similar and how do they differ?

12 Give a task and analyze it in terms of task stimulus, S-directions, R-directions, and task response.

13 Draw the general model of teaching, excluding the program components.

UNIT 3

1 Demonstrate a procedure for teaching children to respond to an attention signal.

2 Demonstrate a correction procedure for failure to respond to an attention signal.

3 Describe how the teacher goes about eliminating reinforcers between the attention responses and the routine. Why is this done?

4 Explain why the teacher varies the length of attention signals before starting the routine.

5 How do you go about finding the "do it" signals in a program?

6 Why do you pause before a "do it" signal?

7 Give the basic procedure for teaching a "do it" signal.

8 State the difference between a multiple-segment task and a series task.

9 Specify how to teach the operations involved in directions.

10 Give an example of S-prompts.

11 Give an example of R-prompts.

12 How does good programing build and use prompts?

13 What is fading?

14 Demonstrate an example of fading.

15 Give three rules for the use of prompts in teaching.

16 Give an example of ineffective prompting where the task signal comes after the prompt.

17 Give an example of a prompt that detracts attention from the task signal.

18 Explain the difference between responding to the R-direction and not responding to the R-direction, and give an example.

19 Give the correction steps to follow when the child does not respond to the R-direction.

20 State two types of mistakes that can occur if the child does respond to the R-direction.

21 Give the correction steps used when the child does not know the answer.

22 Give the steps used when the child is unable to make the complete response.

23 Draw a diagram of the procedures used for systematic corrections in teaching basic skills.

Directions for items 24 through 27. For each of the following tasks and errors, classify the error and demonstrate an appropriate correction procedure.

24 Teacher: Let's hear you count to six.
Child: A ball.

25 Teacher: *(Presents an egg.)* What is this?
Child: A ball.

26 Teacher: This is a vehicle. Say the whole thing.
Child: Vehicle.

27 Teacher: *(Points to a bush.)* This is a bush. What is it?
Child: Green.

28 State the features to be considered in determining the pacing requirements of a task.

29 Give four procedures which apply to the pre-task component of a model of teaching.

30 Give four procedures which apply to the task component of a model of teaching.

31 Give four procedures which apply to the post-task component of a model of teaching.

UNIT 4

1 Give a definition of concept and provide an illustration.

2 What is the test for a "general case" in concept teaching?

3 Explain why conceptual behavior can be considered a special case of the stimulus control of operant behavior.

4 What is the basic procedure for bringing behavior under the control of a preceding stimulus? Give an example.

5 Stimulus control procedure 1 uses one positive and one negative example that differ in several ways. What implications for teaching concepts did analysis of this procedure yield?

6 Procedure 2 uses one positive and one negative instance with control of irrelevant stimuli (they were made the same).

   a) When tested with varying irrelevant stimuli (using only squares and circles), what is the likely outcome with this procedure?

   b) When tested with additional closed-geometric figures as negative instances (keeping irrelevant characteristics constant), what is the likely outcome of this procedure?

7 Stimulus control procedure 3 uses a set of positive and negative instances with varying irrelevant characteristics. What kind of "generalized" learning does this procedure produce?

8 Procedure 4 focuses on teaching the discrimination among a set of related concepts.

   a) When the successive-pairs method of programing is used, what is the outcome?

   b) When cumulative programing to criterion is used, what is the outcome?

9 Explain why (be explicit) cumulative programing "works" and successive-pairs programing is likely to fail.

10 Define S+, S–, and Si. Give an example of each.

11 Explain the difference between S^D as used in volume 1 of this text and S+.

12 Draw a diagram showing concept learning as a multiple-discrimination problem. Explain the multiple discriminations involved.

13 Summarize four basic requirements for teaching a concept by the inductive method.

UNIT 5

1 Define the term operation.

2 What is a component operation?

3 Consider the problem of driving a stick-shift car. Identify as many component operations and their controlling stimuli as you can.

4 Identify some of the component operations involved in cursive writing. Is writing single words a habit chain or rule chain? Does writing sentences involve habit chains or rule chains?

5 How do habit chains and rule chains differ? Give an example of each.

6 What determines the size of the functional unit of behavior used in designing a program?

7 What is a formal operation? Give examples.

8   How do creative design problems differ from problems that can be solved with rule chains?

9   Indicate two ways in which concepts and operations are alike and two ways in which they are different.

10   When is an operation a concept?

11   Summarize the basic requirements for teaching an operation.

12   What is required before chains of operations are taught?

13   Give a set of tasks you might use to teach the operation "placing on" (as in "Place the ball on the table"). Specify relevant and irrelevant characteristics, as well as the not-operations to be differentiated from placing on.

14   Give a set of tasks you might use to teach the operation of making a set equal to a sample set. Specify relevant and irrelevant characteristics of responses showing the operation, as well as the not-operations.

15   What operations are involved in generalized imitation?

16   Give an example of teaching an operation as a concept.

17   Why must testing be geared to the teaching formats or vice versa?

18   What is thinking?

19   Give an example to show how a rule of grammar can be taught as a general case through repeated examples that follow the rule.

20   Compare the advantages and disadvantages of teaching spelling with letter names as the component unit versus letter sounds.

UNIT 6

1   Suppose your students have been taught to call all examples where sets are combined into larger sets *plussing*. Now, you want them to also call these examples *adding*. Demonstrate a way to teach this. Explain the logic of an equivalency rule.

2   Present a simple code to your discussion group and test for its learning with some critical examples. Did you teach a general case?

3   Illustrate the basic procedures involved in teaching by rules by presenting a rule, presenting examples, and testing for acquisition.

4   Define a verbalism. How can the teacher avoid teaching verbalisms?

5   In *testing* for rule learning how are positive and negative examples selected?

6   In *teaching* with rules how should positive and negative examples be selected?

7   Suppose you are to teach the concept of *conservation of weight* using a rule method. The rule is: "If you have neither added any matter nor taken any away, it must still weigh the same." Specify the preskills necessary to teach this rule. Specify your teaching examples (three instances and three not-instances). Specify your test examples, both positive and negative.

8   What are function rules? Give an example.

9   What are the three major skills taught in *Distar III, Reading to Learn*?

10   State the basic logic of rules or principles.

11 Give a rule. Then give two forward test examples of the rule and two backward test examples of the rule.

12 Identify the rules about reflections in Story 120.

UNIT 7

1 Why is *insight* an inadequate explanation of problem-solving behavior?

2 What did Birch contribute to the understanding of the stick-joining problem first studied by Kohler?

3 What are the components of problem-solving behavior?

4 What kinds of problems can be solved with rule chains?

5 What is a problem-solving strategy?

6 Give examples of problem analysis strategies and problem solution strategies.

Questions 7, 8, and 9 are examples of problems. For each one, specify whether it is a fact or a judgment problem, and tell what is given and what is not given.

7 The problem is: "What is a lemon?"

8 The problem is: "What does this mean: 'Great oaks from little acorns grow'?"

9 The problem is: "Use a 4-pint can and a 7-pint can to bring back exactly 3 pints of water."

10 If you were given a concept-identification problem and no instances of the concept, what kind of search strategy would you use to solve the problem?

11 If you were given a concept-identification problem with some instances of the concept, describe the kind of search operation you would use to identify the essential characteristics of the concept.

12 Suggest some procedures that could be used to overcome habits.

13 How do creative design problems differ from "cookbook" construction problems?

14 Suggest some procedures for teaching creative behaviors.

unit 9

Concept Analysis in a Finite Universe
(Toward a Theory of Programing)

introduction

As indicated in unit 2, teaching can be divided into the activities of teaching tasks and programing task sequences. It is in the latter that the key to teaching the general case is found. We now have the background needed to look more closely at the procedures called programing. Three units are devoted to the topic. Unit 9 examines two logical analyses that are central to programing—the analysis of *concept structure* and *pairs of concepts*. Unit 10 presents an analysis of the basic steps in constructing a program, including component analysis. Unit 11 looks at the empirical and logical principles important in sequencing tasks within a program. The goal of these units is not to make every teacher a programer, but to make teachers aware of some of the minimal requirements for good programing. This should help teachers to be smart about examining and selecting programs.

objectives

When you complete this unit you should be able to—
1 Define the following:
   a) Sc
   b) concept structure analysis
   c) concept pair analysis
   d) stimulus generalization
   e) concept domains
   f) concept hierarchy
2 Specify three factors that lead to stimulus generalization errors.
3 State why each type of concept analysis is important in programing.
4 Do concept analyses with limited sets of concepts.

lesson

To teach concepts it is necessary to build mastery of a *set* of discriminations, among a *set* of concepts, through the presentation of sets of positive and negative instances. A little arithmetic will quickly show that if all possible pairs of discriminations among all possible concepts had to be taught, the job would be impossible. The number of pairs in a set of n things is $n(n-1)/2$. Assuming *only one* discrimination per pair (and there are usually more), to teach the twenty-six capital letters would require 325 discriminations. A concept vocabulary of 20,000 words would require mastery of 200 million discriminations, again assuming only one discrimination per pair. Fortunately, we can simplify the teaching process by the logical analysis of the similarities and differences among concepts and use of knowledge of where errors occur in discrimination learning. The product of this analysis provides one basis for a theory of programing.

Stimulus Properties Common to Two or More Concepts

A *concept instance* is an example that can be used in teaching. An example or instance of *red* might be a red ball or a red shirt. An example of *over* might be a ball held over a book. An example of *love* might be a story about a boy helping an injured animal.

Examples used to teach concepts can be analyzed for three kinds of stimulus properties. To illustrate:

Positive Instances		Negative Instances
S+		S−
Sc		Sc
Si		Si

As indicated earlier, S+ and S− are the relevant concept characteristics of positive and negative instances, respectively. Si characteristics are irrelevant stimulus characteristics. The notion of Sc characteristics is new. This symbol refers to stimulus characteristics common to the instances of two or more concepts. Sc characteristics are the bases for forming higher-order concepts. They tell about the structure among concepts.

Whether a characteristic common to instances of several concepts is treated as Sc or S+ depends on the set of concepts being analyzed. For example, instances of the concepts *horse* and *person* have in common the characteristics of being warm blooded, having mammary glands, and so on. These characteristics would not discriminate horse from person (would not be S+) in a universe of *mammals*, but in a universe of *animals*, they could be S+ for discriminating mammals from reptiles (see figure 9.1).

A. Concept Universe (teaching set): Mammals
   Concept Instances: Horses and People

	Horse	Person
S+	hoofs four legs "horsey shape" large hair-covered body	feet two arms, two legs "people shape" medium size skin-covered body
Sc	warm blooded mammary glands	
Si	position	

B. Concept Universe: Animals
   Concept Instances: Horses, People, Snakes, and Frogs

	Mammal	Reptile
S+	warm blooded mammary glands	cold blooded lays eggs
Sc	living moves eats	
Si	position	

Figure 9.1 Analysis of instances of horse in two concept universes

For more illustration of this type of the analysis, return to figure 4.1 (page 67). In this example, equal sides is common to *squares* and *equilateral triangles*. If there were only these two concepts in the analysis, equal sides would be Sc—common to both concepts and not useful in discriminating between them. However, in the *total set* of concepts to be discriminated, equal sides is essential (S+) to both square and equilateral triangle and is needed to discriminate these concepts from other closed-geometrical figures.

The Bases for Discrimination Failures (Errors)

A person has learned a discrimination when he responds appropriately to two or more classes (sets) of stimuli. Suppose a child is taught to say "Red" to instances of the color red within a specified range of red colors, and he is taught to say "Not red" to instances of blue, white, and black. What is likely to happen if he is presented with instances of orange? Very likely he would call them red. When someone responds to a new stimulus in the same way he responds to a previously taught stimulus having some of the same characteristics, the event is called *stimulus generalization*.

Stimulus generalization does not occur arbitrarily. If pure colors are ordered according to the wavelength of light being emitted or reflected (red, orange, yellow, green, blue, violet), generalization is more likely with colors of similar wavelengths than with those of dissimilar wavelengths. The same is true for other physical dimensions to which the human organism is sensitive, such as light intensity and variations in frequency and intensity of vibrations (pitch and loudness). Because our sensory systems are built the way they are, some stimulus events are more likely to be responded to as if they were identical when, in fact, they differ measurably.

Stimulus generalization implies a failure to make a discrimination. If the teacher or programer can predict when stimulus generalization is likely to occur, difficulties can be anticipated and possibly prevented. The programer who has an empirical knowledge of the psychophysical laws of similarity (often derivable from personal experience) is usually in a good position to judge which stimulus characteristics are most likely to be confused.

There are three factors that control the likelihood of new concept instances being responded to as if they were members of a previously learned class —that is, there are three factors that control stimulus generalization:

1 *The number of identical stimulus characteristics* (Sc) shared by the instances of two concepts.
2 *The number and magnitude of the differences in concept characteristics between two concepts* (S+/S− differences).
3 The degree of *prior discrimination training* with respect to the concept differences.

In the example of red and orange given above, all three factors enter into the prediction that orange would be responded to in the same way as red. First, red and orange share the characteristic of being colors (reflected or emitted light waves of specified frequencies). Second, red and orange are more similar in wavelength than orange and blue, orange and white, or orange and black. Third, the training history did not provide training that orange was *not* red.

The student should note that it is commonplace in educational psychology today to say that stimulus generalization occurs as a function of *stimulus similarity*. The concept of stimulus similarity is very imprecise and fails to recognize that similarity involves all three factors listed above: identical shared characteristics, number and sizes of differences, and prior training in the discriminations involved. With the above analysis the teacher and programer have a number of approaches to reducing or preventing errors in designing teaching sequences.

Consider the letters **a** and **d**. They share the characteristics (Sc) of being letters and being formed in the same manner. They differ only in the length of the stem. If the difference in the stem length is small, we can predict a greater difficulty in discriminating *a* from *d* than if the difference were large. Also, we can predict that these two letters are more likely to be confused with each other (one generalized to the other) than either would be with *s*. A programer could reduce the possibility of stimulus generalization by exaggerating the difference in stem length or by making *a* this way: **a**; and *d* this way: **d.** This eliminates some of the common characteristics (Sc). He could also focus training directly on the difference to be learned.

With a knowledge of the factors controlling stimulus generalization, we can prepare programs in which such errors are reduced or eliminated. In order to do this, it is first necessary to identify a teaching universe (a set of concepts to be taught) and to determine the common characteristics of, and differences between, instances of concepts in that universe.

Analysis of Concept Structure

Concept analysis is used in the design of instructional sequences (programing) in two places: to analyze the structure of a set of objectives and to analyze pairs of related concepts. In analyzing concept structure, one looks for characteristics common (Sc) to two or more concepts. These are the characteristics that define higher-order concepts. Efficient programing must attend to this structure. In analyzing pairs of related concepts, one looks again for shared characteristics (Sc) and minimal S+/S– differences. One looks for concepts most likely to be confused with each other. The programer must give special attention to highly similar concept pairs. We will first examine some of the implications that come from the analysis of *concept structure*.

Concept Domains

When looking at the ways in which concept instances share common characteristics, it is helpful to begin with some major structurings. An analysis of all concepts would reveal matter, space, and time to be the most inclusive and independent. All other concepts can be grouped into the following domains based on the higher-order concepts of matter, space, and time.

1 Concepts about *objects:* living things and man-made things, such as cars, fish, plants, and so forth.
2 Concepts about *object properties:* mass, heat, state, structure, parts, shape, size, surface properties, and color, for example.
3 Concepts about *object relationships in space:* order, location, direction, relative position, relative size, number, family relationships, arbitrary relationships, and so on.
4 Concepts about *events in time and space:* conservation of mass, movement, change in energy, changes in group composition (such as addition), and changes in government, for example.
5 Concepts about *relationships among events in time and space* (cause and effect): "For every action there is an equal and opposite reaction"; "Responses followed by reinforcement are strengthened."

Analysis shows that as one goes from domain 1 to domain 5, as listed above, there is an increasing dependence of the higher-numbered concepts on the lower-numbered concepts. That is, teaching higher-domain concepts would be very confusing if lower-domain concepts were not taught first. For example, in teaching about color, if a child has not been taught what a car is, and you point to one and say "This is red," the child might think that red is just the name for cars. Similarly, if relative size is being taught, the children should already know the names and properties of the concepts being compared in size. Just as relationship-concept instances always involve object (or object-characteristic) concepts, event concepts always involve objects in space and time. Thus, to make the event concepts clear, the object concepts used in various instances of the event are best taught beforehand. Finally, causal concepts involve characteristics common to pairs of events in space and time. Some familiarity with concepts from all of the other domains is usually necessary in order to understand instances of causal concepts.

In general, the teacher should first teach concepts that can be demonstrated readily through the direct presentation of instances and not-instances. Then she can move on to more complex concepts that assume knowledge of simpler concepts, so that *only one new concept is taught at a time.*

Concept Hierarchies

Within domains, concepts can be ordered into many kinds of hierarchies. In a hierarchy, instances of lower-order concepts are joined together to form higher-order concepts on the basis of shared characteristics (Sc). The rule for forming a hierarchy is that a higher concept has more instances than a lower concept. The following is an example of a hierarchy from the domain of object concepts:

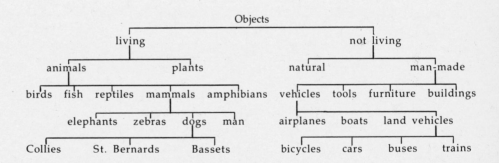

Figure 9.2 A concept hierarchy based on objects

Instances are grouped into larger and larger sets on the basis of common shared characteristics (Sc). Once you leave the domain of objects, there are usually fewer levels in a hierarchical structure. For example, Object Characteristics might be structured like this:

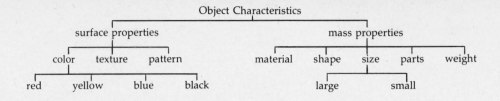

Figure 9.3 A concept hierarchy based on object characteristics

Relationship concepts have an interesting structure:

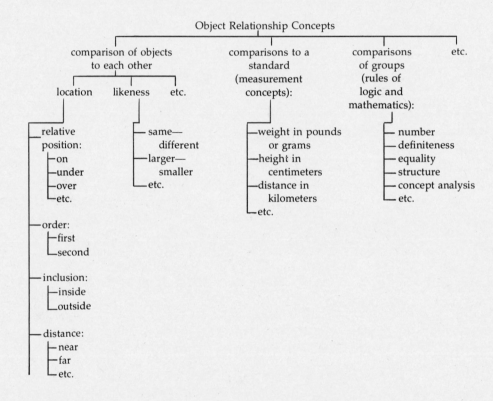

Figure 9.4 A concept hierarchy based on object relationship concepts

As figure 9.4 suggests, a complete analysis of Object Relationship Concepts would be quite an extensive venture into the world of logic.

An examination of Object Event Concepts (figure 9.5) takes us into the world of science. The basic structuring of events centers on the concepts of conservation and change. Conservation concepts focus on things that do not change from one time to another. Change concepts refer to things that are different from one time to another. Beyond this crude analysis we have not attempted to suggest what a structuring might be in this area.

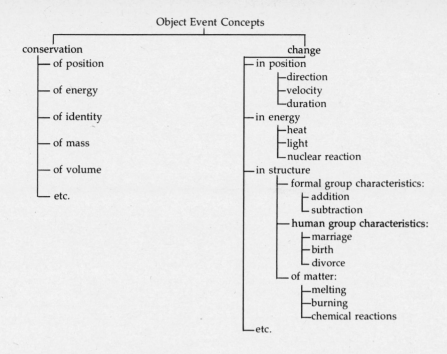

Figure 9.5 A concept hierarchy based on object event concepts

The analysis of the structuring of concepts is important for efficient pro-graming. For example, in teaching language concepts, one would first recognize the primacy of object concepts (nouns). After a student masters the required object concepts, he can move to object characteristics (adjectives), object relationships (adjectives and prepositions), and object actions (verbs). A particular format is designed for teaching object concepts and is different from that for object characteristics. For example, "This is a (an) ————— . What is this?" The common format is used to teach that the task involves *identifying* and *naming*. All tasks of the same format involve the same operations (directions). When teaching object characteristics, use of the format for objects might lead the child to think that *red* is another name for *truck*. Therefore, a new format is used: "This *(object)* is *(attribute)*. What *(attribute class)* is this?" In the case of the red truck, the format is filled in as follows: "This *truck* is *red*. What *color* is this *truck*?" This format teaches that the task involves identifying an object characteristic of the class given and naming it. With repeated examples, the child learns how to do problems of a given type more efficiently. The child learns how to learn when he is taught directions that apply to a large group of concepts.

Polars are a subgrouping of object characteristics that have an additional structure of their own. The logic of the structure of polars is this: "If it is not A, it is B." "If it is not wet, it is dry." "If it is not hard, it is soft." Polars are a two-member group, so if you know it is one, you also know it is not the other (and vice versa). The use of a common format can teach the higher-order logical structure. For example, "This rag is wet. What else do we know if we know it is wet? We know it is not dry."

In a similar way, to teach about object relationships and action concepts, the program should first ensure that the objects being related or the objects of action can be identified and then use distinctive formats, such as:

Relationships: "The *ball* is *over* the *book*. Where is the *ball*?"
Actions: (Point to the *man*.) "What is the *man* doing?"

In programing hierarchical concepts when the goal includes teaching the hierarchy itself, the teaching universe should include concepts from two levels. For example, to teach about varieties of mammals, first distinguish mammals from not-mammals, and then teach the subgroupings of mammals: "This mammal is an elephant." To teach varieties of dogs, first be sure the concept of dog is clear, and then teach subclasses such as Collie, St. Bernard, and Basset. This approach permits a direct teaching of the ways in which concepts are related to each other—that is, it teaches about concept hierarchies; it also teaches that an instance of one concept can also be an instance of another concept; and it focuses instruction on the groups of concepts and their instances that share many characteristics and must be carefully discriminated from each other.

The primary goal in the analysis of concept structure is to determine groups of interrelated concepts and independent groupings. Independent groupings can sometimes be taught concurrently as separate tracks. Interrelated groupings are analyzed for hierarchical structuring, with the higher-order structures being given priority in setting up teaching formats. After that, the focus is on analysis of pairs of concepts within the interrelated groups to determine which ones are most similar and therefore deserve special programing attention. Finally, a cumulative program to teach the set is designed.

Analysis of Pairs of Concepts Within a Specified Teaching Universe

Return to the concept set presented in figure 4.1 (page 67). Inspection of the connecting lines gives an analysis of the S+/S– differences for each concept. The ten pairs of concepts can be ordered in terms of number of differences as follows:

One difference: (two the same)	square — rectangle	
	square — equilateral triangle	
	rectangle — parallelogram	
Two differences: (one the same)	square — parallelogram	
	rectangle — equilateral triangle	
	parallelogram — equilateral triangle	

Three differences: (none the same)	circle — square	
	circle — rectangle	
	circle — parallelogram	
	circle — equilateral triangle	

Pairs of concepts differ in the number of ways in which they are the same (Sc) or different (S + versus S–). When concepts differ in many ways, only a sampling of ways in which they differ need be taught. It is only necessary for the student to learn to respond to one of the differences to be right. When there are few differences, each of the differences must be taught. In the set given above, programing would focus extensively on the three pairs showing only one difference, and moderately on those showing two differences, and briefly on those showing three differences. The programer might also consider the relative difficulty of each of the differences if evidence were available on this.

In a like fashion, the more common characteristics (Sc) between two concepts, the more likely a need for instruction to minimize errors. For example, it would take more teaching to discriminate *dog* from *horse*, than *dog* from *tree*.

Let us consider another example from a universe of letters. For simplicity in exposition, the analysis will be restricted to these five letters:

c a d l t

These letters can be broken into these components, which we will number in order of their line length.

4 C
3 |
2 —
1 |

This gives us a crude weighting of the contribution of the components to a discrimination, assuming shorter lines are less discriminable.

We can now identify each letter by component numbers which reflect discriminability weights:

C = 4

a = 4 + 3

d = 4 + 3 + 1

t = 3 + 1 + 2

l = 3 + 1

The pairs of letters can then be analyzed for weighted* sameness and difference as follows:

	Sameness weight (SW)	Difference weight (DW)	Discriminability = $\dfrac{DW}{SW + DW}$
a – d	7	1	.13
l – t	4	2	.33
c – a	4	3	.43
c – d	4	4	.50
d – l	4	4	.50
d – t	4	6	.60
a – l	3	5	.63
a – t	3	7	.70
c – l	0	8	1.00
c – t	0	10	1.00

*To obtain sameness weight, total the numbers which are the same. To obtain the difference weight, total the numbers which are different.

This analysis suggests that c and t are most discriminable and a and d are the least discriminable. More training would have to be given on the latter than the former. We have detailed this analysis to show some of the assumptive processes involved in the judgment of sameness and differences. The analysis might have started with a different set of component characteristics and a different weighting assumption might have been used. While somewhat arbitrary judgments do enter into the process of concept analysis, to be effective the process need not be absolutely perfect. The key is to isolate the more difficult discriminations where program modifications or more teaching can be used to be sure they are learned. As illustrated earlier with the example of a and d, sameness can be reduced, or differences exaggerated.

The analysis of pairs of concepts within finite sets of concepts is essential in making programing decisions to minimize errors due to stimulus generalization. This topic is pursued further in unit 11.

summary

Concept learning involves building up sets of discriminations. With knowledge of where errors occur in discrimination learning and skills in the logical analysis of concepts, it is possible to devise workable programs that focus on only *some* of the larger set of possible discriminations that could be taught.

The examples used to teach concepts are called positive and negative instances. Each can have three types of stimulus properties. Positive instances can have S+ and Si characteristics. Negative instances can have S– and Si characteristics. Both can also have Sc characteristics, which are those common to more than one concept within a set under analysis. Sc characteristics are the bases for forming higher-order concepts. Whether a specific characteristic is called S+ or Sc depends on the set within which the analysis takes place.

Stimulus generalization consists of treating new stimuli in the same way as some previously taught stimuli. This implies a failure to discriminate differences. Three factors control the likelihood of stimulus generalization:

1 The number of identical stimulus characteristics (Sc) shared by instances of two concepts.
2 The number and magnitude of the differences in concept characteristics between two concepts (S+/S– differences).
3 The degree of prior discrimination training with respect to the concept differences.

With knowledge of the factors controlling errors, the programer is able to design and sequence tasks to circumvent possible errors. The number of common characteristics can be reduced, the magnitude of differences can be increased, and explicit training can be provided where it is needed most.

Two logical analyses are important in programing. In the analysis of concept structure, the programer is looking for interrelated groups of concepts and independent groupings. Interrelated groupings are analyzed for hierarchical structuring, with the higher-order structures being given priority in designing teaching formats. Five concept domains (which are largely independent from each other) must be considered, from domain 1 (object concepts) to domain 5 (causal events). Each higher numbered domain uses concepts from the domains below it. To be teaching only one new concept at a time, it is important to present concepts from lower numbered domains before those from higher numbered domains.

Once related groups of concepts have been identified, a second kind of concept analysis focuses on pairs of concepts within a related set to be taught with a common format. In analyzing pairs of concepts one looks for shared characteristics (Sc) and minimal S +/S− differences. One looks for the concepts most likely to be confused with each other, that is, concepts most likely to show stimulus generalization from one to the other. Once identified, steps can be taken to minimize possible errors by modifying the initial teaching concepts and by selecting the critical discriminations for direct teaching.

self-test

1 errors;
  logical

2 common

3 stimulus
  generalization

4 shared;
  differences;
  discrimination

5 domains

6 many;
  few

1 Knowledge of where _____ occur in discriminating learning and the _____ analysis of the similarities and differences among concepts can be used to simplify the teaching process.

2 Sc refers to stimulus characteristics _____ to the instances of two or more concepts.

3 If a child is taught to say "Red" to red stimuli and "Not red" to blue and black stimuli, and the first time orange is presented he calls it red, the child would be said to be showing _____ _____ .

4 Three factors determine whether or not stimulus generalization will occur: (1) the number of identical stimulus characteristics _____ by the instances of two concepts; (2) the number and magnitude of the _____ in concept characteristics between two concepts; and (3) the degree of prior _____ training with respect to those concepts.

5 Concept _____ are based on the concepts of time, space, and matter.

6 More teaching needs to be devoted to concept differences when instances of two concepts have _____ common characteristics (Sc) than when they have _____ common characteristics.

NUMBER RIGHT _____

exercise 1 programed practice

1 discriminations

2 concepts

3 errors;
logical

4 example

5 common

6 higher-order

7 S+

8 stimulus
generalization

9 same
characteristics

10 Stimulus;
concepts

11 prior learning,
prior teaching

12 discrimination

13 stimulus
generalization

1 To teach concepts it is necessary to cumulatively build up the mastery of a set of _____ , among a set of concepts, through the presentation of sets of positive and negative instances.

2 If all possible pairs of discriminations among all possible _____ had to be taught, the job would be impossible.

3 Knowledge of where _____ occur in discrimination learning and the _____ analysis of the similarities and differences among concepts can be used to simplify the teaching process.

4 A concept instance is an _____ of a concept which can be used in teaching.

5 Sc refers to stimulus characteristics _____ to the instances of two or more concepts.

6 Sc characteristics are the bases for forming _____ - _____ concepts.

7 Whether a characteristic common to instances of several concepts is treated as Sc or _____ depends on the set of concepts being analyzed.

8 If a child is taught to say "Red" to red stimuli and "Not red" to blue and black stimuli, and the first time orange is presented he calls it red, the child would be said to be showing _____ _____ .

9 When someone responds to a new stimulus in the same way he responds to some other stimulus having some of the _____ _____ , the event is called stimulus generalization.

10 _____ generalization is the failure to discriminate between instances of different _____ .

11 In stimulus generalization, a new stimulus is responded to in the same way as a stimulus used in _____ _____ .

12 The opposite of stimulus generalization is _____ .

13 If a young girl calls all male adults "Daddy" after being taught to call her father "Daddy" she is showing _____ _____ .

14 For most physical dimensions of stimuli to which the human organism is sensitive, the greater the physical _____ of two stimuli, the more likely it is that stimulus generalization will occur.

15 Three factors determine whether or not stimulus generalization will occur: (1) the number of identical stimulus characteristics _____ by the instances of two concepts; (2) the number and magnitude of the _____ in concept characteristics between two concepts; and (3) the degree of prior _____ training with respect to those concepts.

16 Concept analysis is used to analyze the _____ of a set of objectives and it is used to analyze _____ of related concepts.

17 In analyzing concept structure, one looks for characteristics _____ to two or more concepts.

18 In analyzing pairs of related concepts, one looks again for shared characteristics (Sc) and minimal _____/_____ differences.

19 The most inclusive independent concepts are _____ , _____ , and _____ .

20 Concept _____ are based on the concepts of time, space, and matter.

21 Matter concepts are _____ concepts.

22 Concepts relating primarily to objects in space are _____ concepts.

23 Concepts relating primarily to objects in time and space are _____ concepts.

24 Concepts relating to relationships of events in time and space are _____ concepts.

25 As one goes from the domain of object concepts to the domain of causal concepts, there is increasing _____ of higher-order concepts on lower-order concepts.

26 If a child is being taught the object property "color," and he has not been taught the name of the _____ being used as an instance of the color,

14 similarity, likeness

15 shared; differences; discrimination

16 structure; pairs

17 common

18 S+/S−

19 matter; time; space

20 domains

21 object, thing

22 relationship

23 event

24 causal

25 dependence

26 object;

he is likely to confuse the name of the color with the name of the _____ .

27 A good teaching strategy is to build from lower-order concepts to higher-order concepts, so that each new teaching task requires that only _____ new concept be learned at a time.

28 The rule for forming a concept hierarchy is that a concept placed higher in the hierarchy has more _____ than a concept placed lower.

29 A complete analysis of Object Relationship Concepts would be quite an extensive venture into the world of _____ .

30 An examination of Object Event Concepts takes us into the world of _____ .

31 When the teaching goal is to teach a hierarchy, teach _____ levels at once.

32 Teaching two levels at the same time helps to teach the ways in which concepts are _____ and teaches that an instance can be an instance of more than one _____ .

33 Teaching at two levels is also a good rule because the teaching set then includes instances that _____ many characteristics—instances that must be discriminated from each other.

34 More teaching needs to be devoted to concept differences when instances of two concepts have _____ common characteristics (Sc) than when they have _____ common characteristics.

35 When there are few differences between concepts, _____ of the differences must be taught.

36 The more common characteristics (Sc) between two concepts, the more likely a need for instruction to minimize _____ .

37 The key in analyzing pairs of concepts is to isolate the more difficult _____ where program modifications or more teaching can be used to be sure they are learned.

---

object

27 one

28 instances

29 logic

30 science

31 two

32 related;
   concept

33 share

34 many;
   few

35 each

36 errors

37 discriminations

discussion questions

1 What are the three types of stimulus properties possessed by concept instances and not-instances?

2 Define Sc and give an example.

3 What determines whether a characteristic is S+ or Sc?

4 Define *stimulus generalization*.

5 Give an example of stimulus generalization.

6 How does stimulus generalization differ from the "generalization" involved in responding to "new" members of a concept class?

7 Specify three factors that influence the occurrence of stimulus generalization.

8 Give one example to illustrate each of the three factors influencing stimulus generalization.

9 What are some of the things a programer might do to reduce the probability of stimulus generalization occurring?

10 Define two types of concept analysis and give an example of each.

11 Relate matter, space, and time to the five concept domains.

12 What is a concept hierarchy?

13 Give an example of a hierarchy.

14 When concepts are ordered into hierarchies, why is it important to teach two levels at one time?

15 What are the goals for the programer in analyzing concept structure?

16 What are the goals for the programer in analyzing pairs of concepts in a related set?

17 Give examples of how the structure of concept domains influences programing (or teaching).

18 Give examples of how the structure of concept hierarchies influences programing (or teaching).

19 Suppose your concept universe involves only instances of ponies, horses, dogs, fish, and snakes. Analyze the possible S+ and Sc characteristics for these concepts. (Hint: Start by making a hierarchy.)

20 Do a pair-by-pair analysis of the number symbols

$$4, \quad 7, \quad 1, \quad \text{and} \quad 6$$

to determine the rank order of similarity (or discriminability index). Use the method of assigning weights to component parts suggested in the text.

21 Piaget has argued that the mental development proceeds from the immediate dealing with objects (sensorimotor stage), through a preoperational stage where there is much language development, through a stage of concrete operations, and on to a stage of formal operations where hypothetical and causal thinking occur. Central to this stage theory is that later stages build on earlier ones. The earlier stages are essential to the later ones. How might the five domains discussed in this unit be used as a basis for a stage theory of mental development?

unit 10

Basic Steps in Programing

objectives

When you have completed this unit you should be able to—

1 Describe the kinds of concept and component analyses important in programing.
2 Describe ten steps to follow in designing a program.

lesson

Programing is a design problem—a variety of judgment problems rather than a fact problem. As such, there may be good and bad programs, but no *right* ones. The problem becomes one of utilizing what we know about teaching the general case to design better programs and to develop procedures for evaluating the effectiveness of programs.

Good programing requires several different kinds of logical analysis.[1] In the last unit, we focused on: (1) the analysis of *concept structure* to isolate common characteristics (Sc) and (2) the analysis of *pairs of concepts* within sets of related concepts to determine S+ versus S−, Si, and Sc characteristics. These two forms of analysis, when coupled with the analysis of tasks into component operations and prerequisite skills, are at the heart of programing. In this unit we will outline the steps required in designing a program, showing where the various forms of logical analysis fit into the process. As an example, we use reading with comprehension to illustrate the process. The example does not represent a complete analysis of the problem of reading, but only illustrates some of the major considerations.

Preliminaries

The first job is to make a preliminary statement of the program objective(s). What is the program to teach? For example, it should teach reading with comprehension.

Next, analyze the preliminary objective for its possible relations to other objectives to come later, parallel, or earlier. This analysis permits an appropriate placement of a program in relation to other programs in order to build efficiently on earlier programs and feed into later ones. For example, the program should build on the language comprehension the students bring to school. It should feed into the work to follow. Since comprehension of lecture information requires many of the same skills and reading-to-learn skills are required for all courses with textbook assignments, reading comprehension should be an early goal in education.

This particular example, because it is so inclusive, does not demonstrate how important this step in analysis can be. An example from math is more to the point. Suppose the program deals with addition and subtraction. The programer needs to consider how multiplication and division will be taught later. The programer also needs to consider the larger structure of math concepts, including work with equations. To facilitate later work with equations, addition formats using the equality rule, such as $2 + 4 = \boxed{}$, would be more important than formats using column operations, such as

$$\begin{array}{r} 2 \\ + 4 \\ \hline \end{array}$$

With these preliminary considerations out of the way, we can begin the formal building of a program.

Step 1

Analyze the preliminary objective into sets of component terminal skills that involve common concepts and operations. What generalized sets of skills are involved in performing the objective? These might be called the "terminal cognitive objectives."

Example

Reading comprehension can be analyzed into decoding skills (word reading), knowledge of word meanings (concepts), and the operations involved in reading for information and reading to learn.

Step 2

Restate the objective as sets of related tasks, any one of which the student can perform. These might be called the *terminal behavioral objectives* of the program. They provide the basis for construction of tests of the terminal components of the program.

Example

1 Decoding. The student will correctly read any word from set x.
2 Word meanings. The student will state the essential concept characteristics, give a synonym, give an antonym, and/or identify instances and not-instances of concepts from the set x.

Step 3

Analyze each of the terminal objectives (where possible) into component skills that involve related sets of concepts and operations. This process is repeated until the programer identifies sets of components that involve a *common teaching strategy*.

The analysis of operations seeks the fewest components possible that can be used as building blocks for the largest number of complex response sequences. The analysis of concepts seeks higher-order structurings of related sets of concepts. In the case of both concepts and operations, the goal is to minimize the number of different teaching strategies (formats) used in the program. When many things are taught within a common set of directions, later members of the set are learned faster than earlier ones. Thus, larger sets promise a more rapid learning rate per member.

Example

1 Decoding. Decoding can be divided into separate operations for decoding *regular* words and *irregular* words.

   Regular-word reading can further be analyzed into *reading individual sounds* and *blending sounds into words.* Blending sounds requires different procedures for *stop sounds* ("t," "b") and *continuous sounds* ("aaaaa," "mmmmm").

   Irregular words form two functional classes, those falling into *irregular-word families* and *sight words.*
2 Word meanings. Since word meanings cover nearly all knowledge, restrictions must be placed on the set of concepts to be included in an initial reading comprehension program. (A lack of such specifications is a problem for many current reading achievement tests.) As suggested in the last unit, the structurings among concepts are many. A program in this area would begin with a basic language program such as that provided by Distar Language I and II. The scope and sequence chart of Language I (figure 10.1) provides some picture of the possible structuring in teaching word meanings.[1] After basic language instruction, vocabulary development progresses through subject-area programs.
3 Reading for information. One component skill in reading for information is *statement repetition*. If one cannot repeat the statements, it is unlikely that the statements can be operated on in other ways. Reading for information also involves skills in *following directions*. This means coordinating your behavior with that implied by the statements. A set of task formats is implied here, beginning with simple directions and building to tasks like using a cookbook to make a cake. *Answering questions* based on a set of

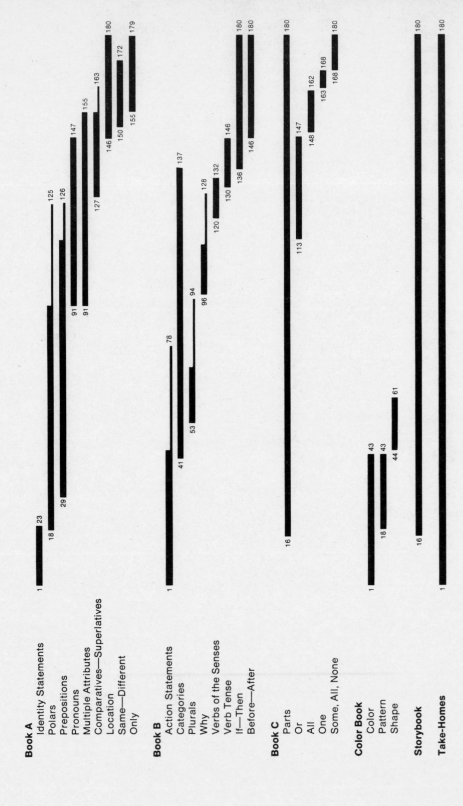

Figure 10.1 Distar Language I scope and sequence chart. The numbers at the beginning and end of each bar indicate the first and last presentations in which a concept is taught. The narrowing of a bar indicates that presentation of a concept is tapering off; the concept is not being taught every day.

statements is another set of skills. One could start by teaching types of questions (what questions, why questions, and so on) and then build to a random presentation of questions forms. Also, it might be important to separately train for operations involved in answering factual and inferential questions, or to treat them as preskills.

4 Reading to learn. A number of possible component skills can be found in this area. A few examples are:
   a. Identifying key rules and principles in a text.
   b. Studying a text to determine the essential features of a principle or rule (understanding).
   c. Using procedures for remembering rules, such as rehearsal and fading prompts.
   d. Analyzing new examples to see if they are instances of a rule.

Step 4

Specify the general-case task formats for each of the groupings identified in step 3. A task format is a general framework that can be filled in to provide examples of lots of related concepts and operations.

Examples

1 Decoding.
   a. Reading by sounds format: (Point to word.) "Read this word by sounds." "Mmmmmaaaaannnnn."
      "Say it fast." "Man."
   b. Reading irregular words—vowel conversion format: Present a short-vowel stem-word (for example, *tap*, *tin*, *ton*, *pet*) and have the students read the word. Then say, "Here's a rule." (Point to vowel.) "If I put an *e* on the end of a word, you say the name of this letter when you say the word. What's the name of this letter?" Go back and forth between long-vowel and short-vowel form. (*Note:* The prompts in a format, such as the rule about *e*, are faded over time.)
   c. A sight-word format: After a sight word is read by sounds say, "The sounds say '_____' but we say '_____.' What's the word?" For example, "The sounds say *'was'* but we say *'wuz.'* What's the word?" *"Wuz."*
2 Word meanings.
   a. Object-names format: (Point to object.) "This is a *ball*. What is this?"
   b. Object-characteristic format: (Point to characteristic.) "This *dog* is *brown*. What *color* is this *dog?*"
   c. Action-word format: (Point to boy running.) "This *boy* is *running*. What is this *boy* doing?"
   d. Several other language concept formats are illustrated in figure 10.2.[2]
3 A reading-for-information format. Read these sentences:
   a. If the teacher raises her hand, hold up a green card.
   b. If the teacher stands up, raise your hand.
   c. If the teacher says "stand up," hold up a blue card.
   d. If the teacher holds up a blue card, stand up.

47 CATEGORIES

Praise the children for correct responses. Correct mistakes immediately.

Task 1   Vehicles

Group Activity

a.   Point to the motorboat. This is a vehicle.
Is this vehicle a car? *No.*
Is this vehicle a bus? *No.*
Is this vehicle a boat? *Yes.*
This vehicle is a boat. Say the whole thing.
This vehicle is a boat.

This vehicle is a boat. This boat is a motorboat.

b.   Point to the rowboat. Is this vehicle a boat? *Yes.*
Is this vehicle a bus? *No.*
Is this vehicle a train? *No.*
This vehicle is a boat. What kind of vehicle is this?
Say the whole thing. *This vehicle is a boat.*

This vehicle is a boat. This boat is a rowboat.

Individual Activity

c.   Point to a picture and ask: Is this vehicle a car?
What kind of vehicle is this? **Require full responses.**

Task 2   Vehicles

Fooler Game

a. I'm going to name some vehicles and see if I can trick you.
What am I going to talk about? *Vehicles.*

When I name something that is **not** a vehicle, you say ''stop.''
Listen now. What am I going to name? *Vehicles.*
Here we go: airplane, truck, boat, **apple,** bicycle.
Stop. You said ''apple.''

What's wrong with apple? Can an apple take you places? *No.*
Is an apple a vehicle? *No.* Say the whole thing.
An apple is not a vehicle.

That's right. An apple is not a vehicle. I couldn't fool you.
● **To correct:** If the children don't catch the mistake, **act amused.**
I said ''apple.'' I fooled you. Is an apple a vehicle?
Can an apple take you places? No, that's silly.
An apple can't take you places, so it's not a vehicle.
You should have stopped me when I said ''apple.''

b.   Repeat the game. Use only a few examples if the children have trouble.
Let's see if I can fool you this time: truck, boat, snake, bicycle.
Stop. You said ''snake.''
What's wrong with snake? Can a snake take you places? *No.*
Is a snake a vehicle? *No.* Say the whole thing.
A snake is not a vehicle.

That's right. A snake is not a vehicle.

Figure 10.2   Example of a task format

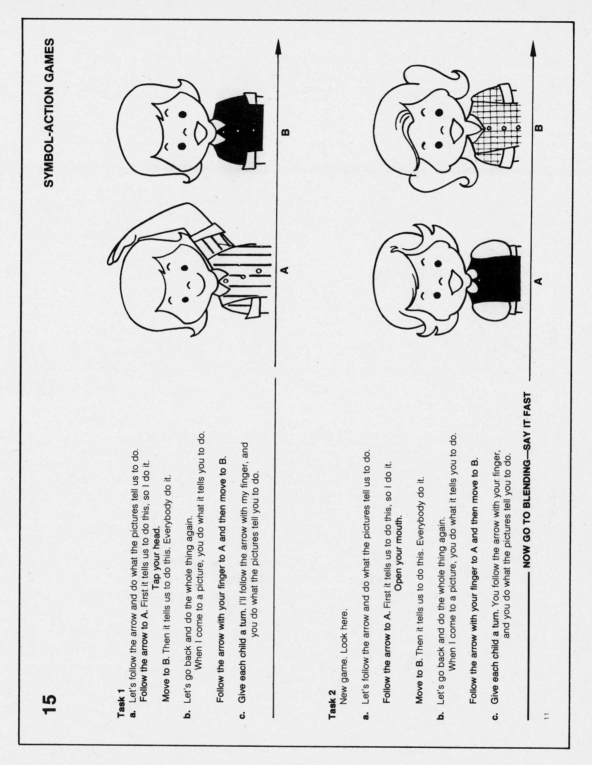

SYMBOL-ACTION GAMES

15

Task 1

a. Let's follow the arrow and do what the pictures tell us to do.
Follow the arrow to A. First it tells us to do this, so I do it.
   Tap your head.

Move to B. Then it tells us to do this. Everybody do it.

b. Let's go back and do the whole thing again.
   When I come to a picture, you do what it tells you to do.

Follow the arrow with your finger to **A** and then **move to B.**

c. Give each child a turn. I'll follow the arrow with my finger, and
   you do what the pictures tell you to do.

Task 2

New game. Look here.

a. Let's follow the arrow and do what the pictures tell us to do.

Follow the arrow to A. First it tells us to do this, so I do it.
   Open your mouth.

Move to B. Then it tells us to do this. Everybody do it.

b. Let's go back and do the whole thing again.
   When I come to a picture, you do what it tells you to do.

Follow the arrow with your finger to **A** and then **move to B.**

c. Give each child a turn. You follow the arrow with your finger,
   and you do what the pictures tell you to do.

───── **NOW GO TO BLENDING—SAY IT FAST** ─────

11

Figure 10.3 Example of a format to teach following a left-to-right visual sequence

The teacher then does one of the actions or another. This format can have many variations (see Distar II Reading, Read-the-Item).

4   Reading-to-learn formats.
See the example given in unit 6, page 101.

Step 5

Analyze the task formats for prerequisite skills. Determine prerequisite skills by analyzing the components. The analysis is used to specify program-entry skills and to develop programs to teach the preskills.

Examples

1   Reading individual sounds has as prerequisite skills discriminating letters, imitating sounds, and following the directions *look and say* when the teacher says, "Read this sound."
2   Reading-by-sounds has as a prerequisite skill the following of a left-to-right sequence of visual symbols in making a series of responses. Figure 10.3 illustrates one format for teaching this preskill.[3]

Step 6

Use the information derived so far to construct a program-sequence chart for terminal objectives, component skills, and prerequisite skills. The chart shows the dependencies and independencies among the objectives, components, and prerequisites. Component tasks are always taught before more complex chains involving those components. The goal in good programing is to try to teach only one new thing at a time.

Example

See figure 10.4.

Step 7

Within sets of terminal, component, and prerequisite tasks sharing a common task format, determine by analysis which pairs of concepts and/or operations lead to tasks that are more alike and which are more difficult because of their length.

Examples

1   Reading individual sounds. Visually, *m* and *n* have more in common than *m* and *a*. Auditorily, *p* and *b* have more in common than *p* and *a*. The responses in making an *e* (as in *e*gg) and an *i* (as in *i*s) have more in common than *e* and *k* (as in *k*it). The analysis has to go far enough to determine those pairs most likely to be confused with each other and those least likely.
2   Animal names. Visually, *German shepherds* and *wolves* have more in common than *German shepherds* and *elephants*.

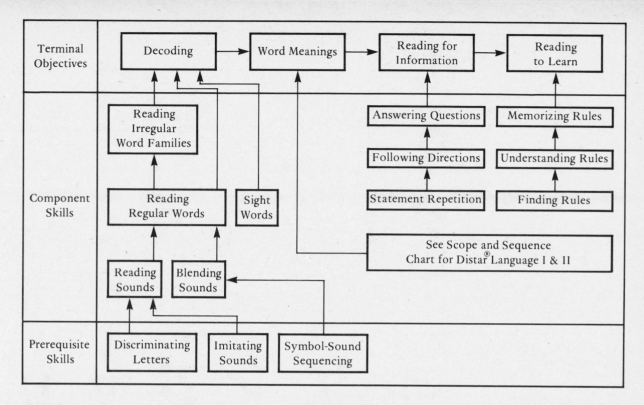

Figure 10.4 Program Sequence Chart for Reading Comprehension. Arrows show dependent relations among terminal objectives, component skills, and prerequisite skills.

3 Reading words. Visually, *not* and *note*, *his* and *this*, *rober* and *robber* have more in common (as pairs) than *not* and *his*, *note* and *this*, or *not* and *robber*.

4 Relationship concepts. The concept *over* has more in common with the concept *on* than *over* has with *beside*.

5 Reading sentences. Reading sentences is more difficult than reading words because the task is longer.

Step 8

Modify initial teaching concepts (or operations or rules) as needed to reduce shared characteristics or to simplify them.

Examples

1 Reading individual sounds. Figure 10.5 shows the symbols for sounds used in the Distar Reading Program.[4] The letters *a* and *d* are not confused because they are purposely drawn differently. The same is true for *b* and *d*. When different sounds can go with the same symbol, such as *e* in edit, *e* in be, or *e* in write, the symbols are modified to signal the differences. Long *e* has a bar over it, and silent *e* is made smaller. When two symbols make only one sound, they are physically tied together. To make learning to read letters less confusing, for the first year the program does not include

Figure 10.5 Sounds from revised Distar® Reading I

capital letters (except I), and does not teach letter names, since these are not important to reading. These objectives are added to the program only after the initial objectives are mastered.

2 Object concepts. In teaching the concept *vehicle*, an initial rule (simplified) might be, "It's a vehicle if it can take you places." The fact that horses can take you places is ignored for the moment. Later, the characteristic "man-made" can be added to the concept rule for vehicles to handle the difference between vehicles and horses.

Step 9

Use the basic principles for teaching concepts and operations to produce and sequence tasks. Tasks are produced by filling in the general formats with specific examples. These procedures are the topic of the next unit.

Step 10

Evaluate the program. There are four basic points in the evaluation of a program.

a. *Are teaching demonstrations of new concepts consistent with only one interpretation?* If a demonstration is consistent with more than one interpretation, some children will fix on the wrong interpretation. If all instances of *boy* have red hair, the child might learn to call only redheads boys.

b. *Are the skills sequenced so that all component skills are taught before a complex skill is introduced?* The simplest test is to see if any error students make can be corrected by using a variation of what has already been taught.

c. *Does the program teach what it sets out to teach efficiently?* A comparison against other programs aimed at the same skills is helpful here. Be sure that the steps taken in fading prompts are neither too large nor too small.

d. *Are the teaching skills required by the program trainable?* This can be tested by trying to train teachers in the use of the program. If there is consistent difficulty in presenting some tasks, either the tasks need to be specified more clearly or changed to make them easier to present.

summary

First, make a preliminary statement of the program objective(s), and analyze the preliminary objective(s) for possible relations to other objectives to come later, parallel, or earlier. This provides the basis for efficient interconnecting of programs.

The basic steps in programing are:

1   Analyze the preliminary objective into sets of component terminal skills that involve common concepts and operations.
2   Restate the objective as sets of related tasks, any one of which the student can perform.
3   Analyze each of the terminal objectives (where possible) into component skills that involve related sets of concepts and operations. This process is repeated until the programer identifies components that can be taught by a common teaching format.
4   Specify the general-case task formats for each of the groupings identified in step 3.
5   Analyze the task formats for prerequisite skills.
6   Use the information derived so far to construct a **program**-sequence chart for terminal objectives, component skills, and prerequisite skills.
7   Within sets of terminal, component, and prerequisite tasks sharing a common task format, determine which pairs of concepts and/or operations lead to tasks that are more alike and/or which are more difficult because of their length.
8   Modify initial teaching concepts (or operations or rules) as needed to reduce shared characteristics or to simplify them.
9   Use the basic principles for teaching concepts and operations to produce and sequence tasks. (See unit 11.)
10 Evaluate the program.

self-test

1   objective(s)

2   objectives

3   common

4   related

5   component

6   task formats

7   prerequisite

1   The first job in programing is to make a preliminary statement of the program _____ .

2   Next, analyze the preliminary objective for its possible relations to other _____ to come later, parallel, or earlier.

3   Analyze the preliminary objective into sets of component terminal skills that involve _____ concepts and operations.

4   Restate the objective as sets of _____ tasks, any one of which the student can perform.

5   Analyze each of the terminal objectives (where possible) into _____ skills that involve related sets of concepts and operations.

6   Specify the general-case _____ - _____ for each of the groupings identified in step 3.

7   Analyze the task formats for _____ skills.

8 Within sets of terminal, component, and prerequisite tasks sharing a common task format, determine which pairs of concepts and/or operations lead to tasks that are more _____ .

9 Use the basic principles for teaching concepts and operations to produce and _____ tasks.

10 In evaluating a program, one criterion is to determine if the teaching demonstrations of new concepts are consistent with only _____ interpretation.

8 alike

9 sequence

10 one

NUMBER RIGHT _____

exercise 1 programed practice

1 design

1 Programing is a _____ problem.

2 As such, there may be good and bad programs, but not _____ ones.

3 In the last unit, we focused on: (1) the analysis of concept _____ to isolate common characteristics (Sc) and (2) the analysis of _____ of concepts within sets of related concepts to determine S + vs. S–, Si, and Sc characteristics.

2 right

4 These two forms of analysis, when coupled with the analysis of tasks into _____ operations and prerequisite skills, are at the heart of programing.

3 structure; pairs

5 The first job is to make a preliminary statement of the program _____

4 component

6 Next, analyze the preliminary objective for its possible relations to other _____ to come later, parallel, or earlier.

5 objective(s)

7 Analyze the preliminary objective into sets of component terminal skills that involve _____ concepts and operations.

6 objectives

8 For example, reading comprehension can be analyzed into _____ skills, knowledge of word _____ , and the operations involved in reading for information and reading to learn.

7 common

8 decoding; meanings

9 Restate the objective as sets of _____ tasks, any one of which the student can perform.

9 related

10 component;
related

11 teaching

12 minimize

13 faster

14 irregular

15 sight

16 task formats

17 examples

18 prerequisite

19 component

20 entry

21 imitating;
directions

22 chart

23 dependencies

24 alike

25 more;
a (or whatever)

10 Analyze each of the terminal objectives (where possible) into _____ skills that involve _____ sets of concepts and operations.

11 This process is repeated until the programer identifies sets of components that involve a common _____ strategy.

12 In the case of both concepts and operations, the goal is to _____ the number of different teaching strategies (formats) used in the program.

13 When many things can be taught within a common set of directions, later members of the set are learned _____ than earlier ones.

14 Decoding can be divided into separate operations for decoding regular words and _____ words.

15 Irregular words form two functional classes, those falling into irregular-word families, and _____ words.

16 Specify the general-case _____ _____ for each of the group-ings identified in step 3.

17 A task format is a general framework that can be filled in to provide _____ of lots of related concepts and operations.

18 Analyze the task formats for _____ skills.

19 Prerequisite skills are determined by another _____ analysis.

20 The analysis is used to specify program _____ skills and/or to develop programs to teach the preskills.

21 For example, reading individual sounds has as prerequisite skills discriminating letters, _____ sounds, and following the _____ *look and say*.

22 Use the information derived so far to construct a program-sequence _____ for terminal objectives, component skills, and prerequisite skills.

23 The chart shows the _____ and independencies among the objectives, components, and prerequisites.

24 Within sets of terminal, component, and prerequisite tasks sharing a common task-format, determine by analysis which pairs of concepts and/or operations lead to tasks that are more _____ .

25 Visually, *m* and *n* have _____ in common than *m* and _____ .

26 Modify initial teaching concepts as needed to reduce _____ characteristics or to simplify them.

27 There are four basic points in the evaluation of a program:

a) Are teaching demonstrations of new concepts consistent with only _____ interpretation?

b) Are the skills sequenced so that all _____ skills are taught before a complex skill is introduced?

c) Does the program teach what it sets out to teach _____ ?

d) Are the teaching skills required by the program _____ ?

discussion questions

1 In what two areas are logical analyses of concepts used in programing?

2 What additional analysis of tasks is also important in programing?

3 Relate your answer to question 2 to the analysis of component operations as discussed in unit 5.

4 What steps should be considered before actually starting to design a program?

5 How do the terminal cognitive objectives differ from the terminal behavioral objectives of a program?

6 Analyze the following terminal objectives into component skills involving related sets of concepts and operations:
a) When asked, the student will count to any number up to 20 by ones.
b) The student will solve any problem of the form $3 + 4 = \boxed{}$ with sums under 11 using a set of problem-solving operations (not by simple discrimination learning).
c) The student will write a story of ten sentences or more about a field trip.

7 a) Give a general task format for counting to a number.
b) Take another subskill found in question 6b and write a general task format for it.

8 Specify the prerequisite skills for the general formats written in question 7.

9 Draw a program sequence chart for the 6b analysis, including preskills.

10 Do a concept pair analysis of *over—under*, *on—over*, and *inside—outside*.

11 Give some examples of how initial teaching concepts might be modified to decrease shared characteristics between concepts.

12 Give four criteria for evaluating a program.

13 Explain why this is an efficient format: "This is a ball. This ball is red. What color is it?"

unit 11

Sequencing Tasks in Programing

objectives

When you complete this unit you should be able to—

1 State four principles for sequencing concepts within a related set.
2 Give three requirements to consider in building a set of tasks to teach specific concepts.
3 Define and illustrate fixed values of a concept characteristic and a range of values.
4 Define and illustrate the programing principles called focus, interpolation, extrapolation, and comparison.
5 Give five requirements to consider in selecting and sequencing tasks to teach operations.
6 Within limited concept sets, devise program sequences to teach the concepts.

lesson

From the program-sequence chart (as discussed in the last unit), we know the major dependencies between the prerequisite, component, and terminal skills. These dependencies govern the sequencing of major program components. The next step involves the sequencing of concepts (operations, rules) and the tasks designed to teach them within related sets of component tasks.

We will focus first on teaching concepts, in which the response requirements of the tasks are not important to the programing. We will then examine task sequencing in which the response requirements (component operations and chains) are the critical product of the instruction.

Sequencing Concepts Within Related Sets

According to our analysis of basic requirements, the programing of a set of related concepts should be cumulative. Begin with one pair of concepts and add new members to the set one at a time, always bringing the set to criterion before going on.

The analysis of basics also indicated that, if two concepts share many common characteristics (Sc) and differ in few ways (S+/S− differences), more instruction must be directed toward the discrimination between those two concepts, or the initial teaching concepts should be modified to reduce sameness and increase differences.

Two additional concept-sequencing principles are derived from logical considerations:

1 Concepts easier to discriminate from each other should be taught before those more difficult to discriminate.
2 Pairs of concepts likely to be confused with each other should be separated by time and space in the program.

Sequencing Tasks to Teach Specific Concepts

As shown by the analysis of basic requirements, the set of tasks built to teach a specific concept within some universe must meet these requirements:

1 Both positive and negative instances must be used.
2 All positive instances should possess all relevant characteristics, and all negative instances should possess only some or none of them.
3 Irrelevant characteristics *within* positive and negative instances must be varied to avoid teaching misrules.

Values of Concept Characteristics

Before going further, we need to introduce a new concept, *value of a concept characteristic*. Every concept characteristic has a value or a range of values. When a concept characteristic can take on only one value, the value is *fixed*. When a concept characteristic can take on more than one value, it has a *range* of values. For example, four angles is a fixed characteristic of squareness. However, there are a range of angles possible for not-square figures. The color red has a range of hues all of which are considered red. At some point, it is necessary to define when red becomes orange, or when red becomes violet. In other words, if a value is not fixed, its range must be defined.

The values of S+ and S− together form a set of values that are all instances of a higher-order concept. If S+ is red and S− is all other colors, this set of values defines the range of instances for the concept "color." If S+ is 4 and S− is all other numbers under 100, this set of values defines the concept "all numbers under 100."

The values of *Si characteristics constitute one whole set by themselves.* Irrelevant characteristics can take on any value within the set of possible values. Si always has a range. In teaching color, object *shape* is irrelevant (Si). Any instances of shape can be used in presenting instances of color. Shape can take on any value within the set of possible shapes. Saying that Si values constitute a separate set is another way of saying that irrelevant characteristics are instances of concepts that are *independent* of the concept being taught.

To teach a concept, the teacher must show which dimensions or characteristics are irrelevant and demonstrate the range of each relevant characteristic.

Within the restraints of the basic requirements already covered, there are four major principles for selecting and sequencing tasks. These principles are called focus, interpolation, extrapolation, and comparison.

Focus

Focus attention on critical discriminations by changing one thing at a time. The following example is designed to illustrate the principle of focus and its subrules.

What is a Kazoo? A Kazoo is a concept in a universe of linear letter sequences. This is a Kazoo: EJOPE. This is not a Kazoo: AytBi. What is a Kazoo? See how fast you can learn it. Follow the numbered sequence.

Instances of Kazoo		*Not-Instances of Kazoo*
1. ABCpD	→	2. ABCED
3. ABCPD		
4. ABCqD		
5. ABCQD		
6. SMNpD		
7. fgHQc		
8. Jfpqt	→	9. Jfpq
		10. Jfpqtz

Are these Kazoos?	*Circle One*	
1: LMQRS	Yes	No
2: ZYxpM	Yes	No
3: ABCPD	Yes	No
4: XYOQ	Yes	No
5: abcqP	Yes	No
6: LMNPRST	Yes	No

(Answers: No, Yes, Yes, No, Yes, No)

There are four subrules pertaining to focus:

1 *When a concept has more than one essential characteristic, begin teaching with the characteristic that leads to the greatest reduction in the alternative possibilities available.*

For example, Kazoo has three essential characteristics. Unless the learner looks at the fourth position in the five-position series first, the range of possibilities about what Kazoo is would be very great. So the first move is to focus on the fourth position.

2 *To teach a fixed characteristic, the basic strategy is to switch from an instance to a not-instance, changing only the fixed characteristic.*

This move is repeated as needed, perhaps using a different set of irrelevant characteristics that are kept constant from instance to not-instance. In the Kazoo example, the importance of the fixed characteristic *fourth position* was demonstrated by keeping the first, second, third, and fifth letters the same in the not-instance (frame 2), but changing the fourth letter to an *e*.

3 *To teach a range within S+ or S−, present a series of instances (or not-instances) in which nothing changes but the range of the characteristic being taught.*

To show that Kazoo had a range for S+, a series of instances were presented where only the range was changed (frames 3, 4, and 5). For a person experienced in learning concepts, it would not be necessary to show the range of letter shapes possible in S− as long as the range of S+ is shown. For inexperienced learners, a sample of the possibilities for S− shapes would be given.

4 *To teach the range of irrelevant characteristics (Si), present a series of instances in which all Si keep changing and S+ characteristics stay constant.*

If the range of S+ has already been shown, then it can also be varied while varying Si. After teaching the range of Si for instances, it may be necessary to do the same for not-instances.

In the Kazoo example, frames 6, 7, and 8 show that the shape of the letters can change in positions 1, 2, 3, and 5.

In frames 8, 9, and 10 rule 2 is used again to show the fixed characteristic *five letters*. Frames 9 and 10 define the range for that S+ characteristic rather than show the whole range of S− possibilities for number of letters.

There are many possible ways of structuring a teaching sequence. The method chosen depends on the concept being taught. The rules given above do not indicate the order in which different types of characteristics are taught, but the *ways* in which they can best be taught. Here is another example of a teaching sequence.

What is a Giz? Follow the numbers to learn what a Giz is and then take the test. A Giz is a concept in a universe of two figures on a surface.

Instance of Giz	Not-Instance of Giz	Instance of Giz	Not-Instance of Giz
1		9	
2		10	
3		11	
4	5	12	
	6	13	14
	7		15
	8		

Test 1.	Is this a Giz? Yes No	
Test 2.	Is this a Giz? Yes No	
Test 3.	Is this a Giz? Yes No	
Test 4.	Is this a Giz? Yes No	

Answers; 1. No; 2. No; 3. Yes; 4. No.

A Giz consists of a figure of any shape within the upper left quadrant of a square figure of any size, location, or surface pattern.

Concept Analysis For Giz

		S+	S−
1.	*Relationship:*	Smaller inside larger	Smaller outside larger
2.	*Location:*	Smaller figure in upper left quadrant	Smaller figure in any other quadrant
3.	*Shape:*	Larger figure square	Larger figure not square

Si

Shape of smaller figure
Size of square
Surface pattern of both figures
Location of square in the frame

The Giz example again illustrates the focus rules. First, focus on the S+ characteristic that most reduces the alternatives—namely, the location of the smaller object inside the upper left-hand quadrant of the larger object.

Frames 1 through 4 demonstrate the range of this characteristic. The only change is the position of the smaller object. Frame 5 shows that the smaller object cannot be in the upper right quadrant. Frames 6 and 7 show what other quadrant locations are not-Giz. To be safe, frame 8 explicitly rules out the possibility that the little figure could be outside the square.

Frames 9 through 13 rule out Si concerning the shape of the smaller object, the size of the square, the location of the square in the frame, and the surface pattern of the figures. Irrelevant characteristics are varied while relevant ones are held constant.

Going from 13 to 14 explicitly demonstrates the fixed characteristic of squareness for the outer figure, and frame 15 extends the range of outer figure shapes that are not-Giz. Note that in these frames only the fixed characteristic of squareness is changed. Frame 15, like frame 8, is probably unnecessary for most learners, but is included to be safe.

In this teaching sequence, fixed characteristics are demonstrated by switching from instances to not-instances, ranges are demonstrated by moving within instances or not-instances, and irrelevant characteristics are demonstrated by moving first within instances and then switching to not-instances.

Interpolation

In teaching a characteristic that has a range of values, *sample the range* with at least three instances, but do not be exhaustive. In the Giz example, frames 1 to 4 sample the range of S+ for "smaller figure in upper left quadrant." Frames 5 to 7 sample the range for S– for "smaller figure in upper left quadrant." Frames 9 to 13 sample the range of Si characteristics. If sampling is used in a series of programs, the student will learn the logical rule: "The range is a sample. Interpolate." In the illustration below, if the concept instances are those with an x under them, most students with some experience in sampling would say that y is also an x.

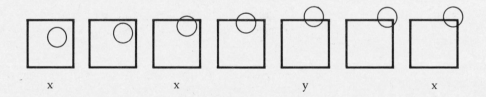

Extrapolation

In teaching a characteristic that has a range of values, sample the range of positive instances and then show the *boundary* starting the range of negative instances. The student will learn by extrapolation that "any negative instance more different than those demonstrated must also be a negative instance." In the illustration below, if the positive instances are x and the negative instance y, the z's will probably be called y.

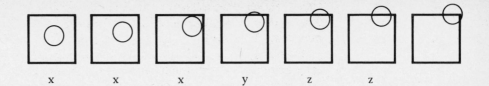

x	x	x	y	z	z	

In teaching Kazoo, only three not-instances were used. One not-instance was used to show that specific letters had to be in position four, and two not-instances were used to show that groups of four and six letters would not do. Could there be Kazoos with ten letters or fifteen? These were not ruled out. A Kazoo could have been defined as five *or* ten letters with a P, Q, p, or q in the fourth position. If this were the case, however, the teaching demonstration would have to show it. When the demonstration showed that four- and six-letter sequences would not do, the implication was this: "Look, if the closest thing to five won't work, it's got to be *only* five." In teaching Giz, it was probably unnecessary to give the last frame with the circle as the outside figure after presenting a rectangle because, "If the closest thing to a square won't work, it's got to be a square."

Comparison

Facilitate the comparison of positive and negative instances. Any procedure that reduces the number of stimuli to be attended to and remembered will facilitate concept teaching. Research comparing simultaneous and successive presentation of instances supports this conclusion.[1] Some of the basic steps for facilitating comparisons are:

1 Change one thing at a time when going from an instance to an instance or a not-instance. One effective way of doing this is to directly convert an instance into a not-instance: "Now the ball is *on* the chair. Now the ball is *not on* the chair." Note that this is the same procedure underlying the focus principle.
2 Present several instances and/or not-instances simultaneously so that there is opportunity to examine their likenesses and differences.
3 Where important to show the structure of instances and not-instances, present them in pairs or larger sets. The following example illustrates this point.

Teaching With Pairs of Instances.   See if you can figure out what an Eggbert is from these instances:

1 This is an Eggbert: TAM
2 This is *not* an Eggbert: SIN
3 This is an Eggbert: NAP
4 This is *not* an Eggbert: LID
5 This is an Eggbert: NET
6 This is *not* an Eggbert: APE
7 This is an Eggbert: TIPS

8   This is *not* an Eggbert: SAT
9   This is an Eggbert: BAD
10 This is *not* an Eggbert: NIS
11 This is an Eggbert: DAB
12 This is *not* an Eggbert: FLIP
13 This is an Eggbert: SPIT
14 This is *not* an Eggbert: TAS
15 This is an Eggbert: PAN
16 This is *not* an Eggbert: PILF
17 This is an Eggbert: TEN
18 This is *not* an Eggbert: PEA
19 This is an Eggbert: MAT
20 This is *not* an Eggbert: DIL

What is an Eggbert?

Now the same information is presented in sets of pairs. See if you can learn the concept now.

	Instances of Eggbert (Both are Eggberts)	Not-Instances of Eggbert (Neither is an Eggbert)
Set 1	MAT—TAM	APE—PEA
Set 2	NAP—PAN	SAT—TAS
Set 3	NET—TEN	SIN—NIS
Set 4	BAD—DAB	LID—DIL
Set 5	TIPS—SPIT	FLIP—PILF

Are these Eggberts?	*Circle One*
1. BUD	Yes No
2. SPAN	Yes No
3. FANS	Yes No
4. SUN	Yes No

(Answers: Yes, Yes, No, No)

The information available in the second presentation is the same as that given in the first. However, the second presentation shows pairs of Eggberts that are the reverse of each other, and pairs of not-Eggberts that either are not the reverse of each other, or are not both words. This comparison helps to isolate the essential features (S + and S–) for Eggberts and not-Eggberts. Eggberts are groups of letters that spell a word both forward and backward. Not-Eggberts will not spell a word in both forward and reverse order. The fact that you can make two words out of an Eggbert is not the key, since that can also be done with not-Eggberts. Neither is the number of letters critical.

Note the teaching strategy. In the first set, everything possible is kept the same in going from instances to not-instances, except the critical characteristic. Both examples involve pairs of three-letter words. Both examples use only three different letters to make two words. The only difference is that the letters are not reversed in the not-instance. Sets 2 through 4 show that reversal of letters alone is not sufficient—two *words* must be formed. Set 5 shows that Eggberts are not restricted to three-letter words.

A Note on a Common Confusion

A number of writers maintain that learning a concept involves generalization within the concept class and discrimination between classes of concepts. With the recognition that some concepts have a range of values and the introduction of the principle of interpolation, it would seem that there may be some truth to the generalization-discrimination notion. However, it is false on two counts. First, most writers in referring to "generalizations within a concept class" imply "generalization" across changing irrelevant characteristics. We have argued that such "generalization" is clearly a discrimination process between relevant and irrelevant characteristics within a concept instance. Second, if the writers are referring to "generalization" across a range of values for positive concept instances, we would have to argue that this too is a discrimination learning process. The limits of the range are discriminated and the intervening possibilities are filled in using the logic of interpolation, not stimulus generalization.

Sequencing Tasks in Teaching Operations

When the motor skill itself is not critical, teaching a concept about an operation often suffices. In such cases, we can follow the sequencing procedures for teaching concepts. For example, to learn the operation melting, the student does not actually need to melt iron or ice. Observing examples of melting or hearing descriptions of examples will suffice.

The analysis of the requirements for teaching operations indicated the importance of prompting, differential reinforcement, and gradual fading of prompts as key teaching procedures. As with concepts, it was also important to be sure that related operations are differentiated from each other by including one as the negative instance of the other, and that irrelevant response characteristics are differentiated from relevant characteristics by varying irrelevant characteristics in the examples chosen.

The most critical questions in sequencing specific tasks have to do with how much prompting to do, when to fade prompts, and the relative difficulty of specific examples of operations. Relative difficulty can often be determined by a logical examination of a set of possibilities, but decisions on prompts and fades must be based on tryout data.

Prompts and Fades

In making decisions on prompts and fades, the programer makes some preliminary guesses and field tests them. Then revisions are made and tested again. In the following example, taken from the *Corrective Reading Program*, the generalized task is to correctly read words with long or short vowel sounds using the final *e* as the cue. For example, tam/tame, rot/rote, hug/huge, pin/pine. At first the students are told this rule:

Here's a rule. (Point to *a* in first word.) *If I put an* e *on the end of a word, you say the name of this letter when you say the word. What's the name of this letter?* (Signal.) *Yes,* a.

In the first fade the students now give part of the rule:

(Point to *a* in first word.) *If I put an* e *on the end of each word, what are you going to say for this letter?* (Signal.) *Yes,* a.

In the next fade, the students are reminded of the rule, but it is not given out loud:

Everybody, get ready to tell me these words when I give you the signal. Remember what the e *on the end of the word does to that letter in the middle of the word.* (Point to each word. Pause.) *What word?* (Signal.)

Finally, examples are converted from short to long vowels without saying the rule. The students have learned to respond according to the rule without having to use it as a prompt. The prompt is completely faded. The empirical evaluation of this set of fades showed that it worked.

If the jumps used in fading prompts are too small, teaching time will be wasted and the tryouts will show very low error rates (say under 5%). If the jumps are too big (the more likely case), the tryout will show a breakdown in performance at the point where a fade is made.

In the next two situations, taken from the development of Distar Arithmetic I, the initial fades involved jumps that were too big. About half way through the program, the worksheet procedures, completed after a group teaching session, were changed from a structured teacher-directed activity to one in which the children worked completely on their own. Error rates became so high at this point that an intermediate step was added. The teacher reviewed the key points of the exercise and then let the children work the problems on their own while she observed and gave help as needed. After using this fade for a few weeks, the children could move to working on their own without a high error rate.

Another problem was confusion on worksheet exercises when both regular addition (3 + 4 = ☐) and algebra addition (3 + ☐ = 7) problems were randomly presented. The children had no trouble doing eight addition problems and eight algebra-addition problems when they were each grouped separately on the worksheet. But the error rate became very high with random presentation. This trouble was corrected by inserting two days on which the teacher carefully prompted looking at each problem (randomly presented) and deciding which kind of problem it was before going on. The children were given an added prompt in problem analysis and then this was faded.

Item Difficulty

The difficulty of specific tasks used in teaching operations is related to two main factors. First, the number of characteristics shared between a given task and related tasks, and second, the length of the task. For example, in teaching students to solve problems of this form by counting lines:

$$2 \; + \; 5 \; = \; \square$$
$$\text{II} \quad \text{IIIII}$$

the student encounters "five" on the way to "seven." The possibility is good that the student will stop at "five" since the number 5 is there to cue the previously learned task "Say 'five' and stop." Thus, a task of this sort would not be used in the earlier stages of teaching the use of counting to solve addition problems.

Longer tasks are more difficult than shorter tasks. Consider again the solving of addition problems by counting. In an advanced solution method, the lines under the first number are faded, and the student now counts from the first number until all the lines under the second number are counted. In this format:

$$2 \; + \; 9 \; = \; \square \quad \text{is more difficult than} \quad 9 \; + \; 2 \; = \; \square$$
$$\text{IIIIIIIII} \hspace{5.5cm} \text{II}$$

In number writing, two digits are harder than one. In number decoding, higher numbers are more difficult than lower numbers except zero. In general, easier tasks are taught before more difficult tasks, and as with concepts, operations likely to be confused with each other are separated in the teaching sequence.

A Suggestion

A good way to get a fuller picture of the sequencing of tasks in programing is to examine the complete programs for Distar Reading I, Arithmetic I, and Language I. Even more helpful in learning about programing strategies would be actually teaching one or more of the Distar programs for a period.

summary

In sequencing *concepts* within related sets, the programer needs to keep these principles in mind:

1 Begin with one pair of concepts and add new members to the set one at a time, always bringing the set to criterion before going on.
2 Where concepts have many shared characteristics and few or small differences, more teaching is required or the initial teaching concepts must be modified.

3 Concepts that are easier to discriminate from each other should be taught before those more difficult to discriminate.
4 Pairs of concepts likely to be confused should be separated from each other in the program.

In sequencing *tasks* to teach specific concepts, the programer should keep these principles in mind:

1 A set of positive and negative instances is required.
2 The set should be designed so that all positive instances possess all relevant characteristics and all negative instances possess only some or none of them.
3 Irrelevant characteristics within positive and negative instances must be varied to avoid teaching misrules.

Additional programing principles should consider the values a concept characteristic can take on. When a concept characteristic can take on more than one value, it is said to have *range*. When a concept characteristic has only one value, it is said to be *fixed*. The values of S+ and S− together form a set of values that are the instances of a higher-order concept. For example, if instances of red are S+, and instances of blue, green, and so forth are S−, together the S+ and S− instances are S+ for the higher-order concept "color." The values of Si characteristics are one whole set by themselves. Irrelevant characteristics (Si) are instances of concepts that are independent of the concept being taught.

The principle of *focus* states: focus attention on critical discriminations by changing one thing at a time. Four subrules help to specify the focus principle:

1 If there is more than one essential characteristic, begin with the characteristic that will lead to the greatest reduction in alternative possibilities.
2 To teach a fixed characteristic, switch from an instance to a not-instance, changing only the fixed characteristic.
3 To teach the range of S+ or S−, present a series of instances (or not-instances) in which nothing changes but the value of S+ or S−.
4 To teach the range of irrelevant characteristics, present a series of instances or not-instances in which only the values of the irrelevant characteristics change.

The principle of *interpolation* states: in teaching a characteristic that has a range of values, sample the range with at least three instances, but do not be exhaustive. The student is taught the logical rule: "The range shown is a sample. Interpolate."

The principle of *extrapolation* states: in teaching a characteristic that has a range of values, sample the range of positive instances and then show the boundary starting the range of negative instances. The student is taught the logical rule: "Any negative instance more different than those demonstrated must also be a negative instance."

The principle of *comparison* states: facilitate the ready comparison of positive and negative instances. This can be accomplished by:

1 Changing one thing at a time, as in the focus procedures.

2 Using simultaneous rather than successive presentation.

3 Presenting carefully chosen pairs of instances and not-instances.

When the target of the programing is the teaching of operations rather than concepts, the key teaching procedures involve prompting, differential reinforcement, and fading of prompts. It is important to build sets of tasks involving related operations to be differentiated from each other and to vary irrelevant response characteristics by the way in which examples are chosen.

The choice of prompts and fades starts with "good guesses" which must then be empirically tested out. If, when a fade is introduced, errors occur that are not easily eliminated, then smaller steps in removing the fade should be considered.

Another major consideration in sequencing tasks to teach operations is the difficulty of specific tasks. Tasks may be more difficult because the response is longer or because shared characteristics lead to confusions with other tasks.

self-test

1 An S+ characteristic has a _____ of values when it can take on more than one value.

2 The values of S+ and S− together form a _____ of values that are instances of a _____ concept.

3 Four subrules help to specify the focus principle:

a)   If there is more than one essential characteristic, begin with the characteristic that will lead to the greatest reduction in _____ possibilities.

b)   To teach a fixed characteristic, switch from an instance to a not-instance, changing only the _____ characteristic.

c)   To teach the range of S+ or S−, present a series of instances (or not-instances) in which nothing changes but the _____ of S+ or S−.

d)   To teach the range of irrelevant characteristics, present a _____ of instances or not-instances in which only the values of the irrelevant characteristics change.

4 The principle of interpolation states: In teaching a characteristic that has a range of values, _____ the range with at least three instances, but do not be exhaustive.

1 range

2 set;
   higher-order

3a) alternative

b) fixed

c) value

d) series

4 sample

5 The principle of extrapolation states: In teaching a characteristic that has a range of values, sample the range of positive instances and then show the _____ starting the range of negative instances.

6 If, when a fade is introduced, errors occur which are not easily eliminated, then _____ steps in removing the fade should be considered.

NUMBER RIGHT _____

exercise 1 programed practice

1 related

a) criterion

b) shared

c) before

d) separated

2 pairs

3 specific

4a) negative

b) all; some

1 In sequencing concepts within _____ sets, the programer needs to keep these principles in mind:

a) Begin with one pair of concepts and add new members to the set one at a time, always bringing the set to _____ before going on.

b) Where concepts have many _____ characteristics and few or small differences, more teaching is required or the initial teaching concepts must be modified.

c) Concepts which are easier to discriminate from each other should be taught _____ those more difficult to discriminate.

d) Pairs of concepts likely to be confused should be _____ from each other in the program.

2 A strategy for sequencing set members is designed on the basis of an analysis of concept _____ .

3 The next task is to sequence tasks to teach _____ concepts as they are introduced to the set.

4 In sequencing tasks to teach specific concepts, the programer should keep these principles in mind:

a) A set of positive and _____ instances is required.

b) The set should be designed so that all positive instances possess _____ relevant characteristics, and all negative instances possess only _____ or none of them.

c) Irrelevant characteristics within positive and negative instances must be _____ to avoid teaching misrules.

5 An S+ characteristic has a _____ of values when it can take on more than one value.

6 S+ or S− is fixed when it can take on only _____ value.

7 The values of S+ and S− together form a _____ of values that are instances of a _____ concept.

8 The principle of focus states: focus attention on critical discriminations by _____ one thing at a time.

9 Four subrules operationalize the focus principle:

a) If there is more than one essential characteristic, begin with that characteristic that will lead to the greatest reduction in _____ possibilities.

b) To teach a fixed characteristic, switch from an instance to a not-instance, changing only the _____ characteristic.

c) To teach the range of S+ or S−, present a series of instances (or not-instances) in which nothing changes but the _____ of S+ or S−.

d) To teach the range of irrelevant characteristics, present a _____ of instances or not-instances in which only the values of the irrelevant characteristics change.

10 The principle of interpolation states: in teaching a characteristic that has a range of values, _____ the range with at least three instances, but do not be exhaustive.

11 The principle of extrapolation states: in teaching a characteristic that has a range of values, sample the range of positive instances and then show the _____ starting the range of negative instances.

12 The student is taught the logical rule: "Any _____ instance more different than those demonstrated must also be a _____ instance."

13 The principle of comparison states: facilitate the ready comparison of positive and negative instances. This can be accomplished by:

a) _____ one thing at a time, as in the focus procedures.

b) Using _____ rather than successive presentation.

---

c) varied

5 range

6 one

7 set;
   higher-order

8 changing

9a) alternative

b) fixed

c) value

d) series

10 sample

11 boundary

12 negative;
   negative

13a) Changing

b) simultaneous

c) Presenting carefully chosen _____ of instances and not-instances.

14 When the motor skill itself is not critical, teaching a _____ about an operation often suffices.

15 The most critical questions in sequencing specific tasks have to do with how much _____ to do, when to _____ prompts, and the difficulty of specific examples of operations.

16 Difficulty level can often be determined by a _____ examination of the set of possibilities, but decisions on prompts and fades must be based on _____ data.

17 If, when a fade is introduced, errors occur that are not easily eliminated, then _____ steps in removing the fade should be considered.

18 Tasks may be more difficult because the response is _____ or because _____ characteristics lead to confusions with other tasks.

19 It is important to build sets of tasks involving _____ operations to be differentiated from each other and to _____ irrelevant response characteristics by the way in which examples are chosen.

c) pairs

14 concept

15 prompting; fade

16 logical; tryout

17 smaller

18 longer; shared

19 related; vary

discussion questions

1 State four principles or procedures that serve as guidelines in sequencing the introduction of concepts within a related set.

2 How do you determine whether concepts are easier to discriminate from each other? Give an example.

3 How do you handle pairs of concepts likely to be confused with each other in the program?

4 Give three requirements to consider in building a set of tasks to teach specific concepts.

5 Define the term *range of values* with respect to concept characteristics.

6 Define the term *fixed value* with respect to concept characteristics.

7 What does it mean to say that S+ and S− together form one whole set?

8 What does it mean to say that the values of any Si form one whole set?

9 State the focus principle.

10 State a rule for teaching a fixed characteristic.

11   State a rule for teaching a range within S+ or S–.

12   State a rule for teaching the range of irrelevant characteristics.

13   State the principle of interpolation and give an example.

14   State the principle of extrapolation and give an example.

15   What do you do to facilitate comparison of teaching examples?

16   Why do the authors reject the notion that concept learning involves "generalization" within the concept class?

17   Why is the procedure of converting instances into not-instances or new instances especially valuable to the teacher?

18   Give five requirements to be considered in selecting and sequencing tasks to teach operations.

19   How does the programer decide on what prompts to use and how to fade them in teaching operations?

20   Name two factors that determine task difficulty in teaching operations and give an example of each.

21   Take the sounds *m*, *n*, *a*, *b*, *p*, and *c*. Do a pairs analysis of the stimulus properties of the letters and suggest an order of introducing each new sound in a cumulative set based on this analysis.

22   Take the set of closed geometric figures (which includes squares, triangles, parallelograms, circles, rectangles, and ovals). Within this set (universe), design a sequence of tasks to teach the concept rectangle (vs. not-rectangles).

unit 12

Intelligence, Retardation, and Teaching

objectives

After completing this unit you should be able to—

1. Describe the kinds of items used on intelligence tests.
2. Discuss the relevance of intelligence test scores to teaching and learning.
3. List three bases for saying a child is retarded.
4. Name and describe three levels of retardation.
5. Identify some causes of retardation that can be treated or prevented.
6. Discuss the pros and cons of the heredity-environment issue in terms of its relevance for the teacher.
7. Describe several studies showing the importance of teaching to intelligence and academic progress.

lesson

What Is Intelligence?

We have suggested many times throughout this text that intelligent behavior is operant behavior and therefore is learned. Scholars have devoted much effort to the attempt to define the critical aspects of intelligent behavior. For example, Spearman focused on "the ability to educe relationships." Binet defined intelligence as "the tendency to take and maintain a definite direction; the capacity to make adaptations for the purpose of attaining a desired end; and the power of auto-criticism."[1] For many, these formal definitions have had little value and intelligence has become, "What the tests measure," especially the Stanford-Binet test. We begin this unit by examining the items on this test. Our objective is to show that the behaviors called intelligent are the same combinations of conceptual and operational skills we have been describing since unit 4. The analysis starts at the six-year level and works upward, dealing only with new tasks. Number jumps occur where repeated tasks have been omitted. The focus of the analysis is on the key concepts and operations involved. Common to most tasks are the operations involved in looking, listening, persisting, talking, and so forth.

An Analysis of the Stanford-Binet Intelligence Test

Year 6

1. *Vocabulary.* The subject is asked what is meant by a number of words. Acceptable answers give the essential concept characteristics. Vocabulary tests consist of concepts and the responses used to point out concept characteristics.

2. *Differences.* The task is to tell how two things differ. The subject has to point out an S+ for dogs that is S– for birds, or vice versa. Several specific concepts are tested along with the concept of difference and the operation of comparing two things.

3. *Mutilated Pictures.* The subject is shown a picture with some part missing and is asked to name the missing part. Parts are object characteristics that can be treated as separate objects ("the wheel is off the wagon"). The task involves concepts of parts and the operation of detecting missing parts.

4. *Number Concepts.* The subject gives the tester the number of blocks requested. The task involves number concepts and the operation of counting. The child must be able to discriminate nine blocks from eight or ten in order to give the examiner nine.

5. *Analogies.* Analogies involve concepts about relations between sets of concepts. The general form is "A is to B, as C is to D." The relation of C and D is the same as that of A and B. Given three parts of the statement, the task is to give the fourth. For example, "A table is made of wood; a window of . . . ."[2] The first statement reveals "We are talking about materials from which things are made." He is then asked, "What is a window made of?" Analogies are tests of various specific concepts and the operations involved in comparing relations of pairs of concepts.

6. *Maze Tracing.* This involves a complex set of concepts and operations. The task is to draw a line showing the shortest way for a boy to go to school, given that he has to stay on the sidewalk. The maze is a map, so the test requires knowledge of concepts about representations of things. It is a test for the concept "shorter," for the operation of comparing two paths, for the operation of drawing a line with a ¼" path, and for the operations controlled by the signals "*Start here* and *take* the *boy to school.*"

Year 7

1. *Picture Absurdities.* The subject is shown a picture in which something is wrong, such as it is raining and the man does not have his umbrella over his head. He is asked what is funny (foolish) about that. The task involves concepts about the right way to do things, the concept of foolish, and the operation of looking for what is wrong.

2. *Similarities.* The subject is asked, "In what way are wood and coal alike?"[3] Tasks such as this are tests of various concepts and the operation of comparing two concepts.

3. *Copying a Diamond.* The subject is asked to draw a diamond from a model. The primary task is the operation of drawing angles and lines from a model.

4. *Comprehension.* Questions are asked—some of fact, some of propriety. "What makes a sailboat move?" is a question of fact.[4] "What's the thing for you to do if another boy hits you without meaning to do it?" is a question of propriety.[5] The sailboat question involves concepts about sailboats, wind, and the causes of movements. To answer propriety questions, a child has to know concepts about proper behavior.

5. *Repeating Five Digits.* "Listen and say what I say. 3-1-6-4-7." This is a short-term memory task. While there may be some question about what is involved in memory span, it is known that listening and imitating are operations that can be taught, that practice with similar problems increases how much can be remembered, and that various operations for remembering things can be taught (grouping things, saying it to yourself, and so forth).

Year 8

No new types of tasks are presented at this level.

Year 9

1. *Paper Cutting.* The subject observes a paper being folded in half once or twice and a part being cut out of it. He has to make a drawing of how it would look if the paper were unfolded. The task deals with spatial concepts, halving operations, and drawing operations.

3. *Memory for Designs.* The task is to look carefully at two designs and then draw them from memory. Looking and drawing operations are clearly involved. As in the case of repeating digits, it is not clear what other operations are used to help retain what is seen.

4. *Rhymes.* "Tell me the name of a color that rhymes with *head*."[6] Rhyming is an operation that involves changing the initial sound, keeping the remaining sounds, and putting the new combination together. The task involves concepts (color, red, rhyming) and the rhyming operation.

5. *Making Change.* Story problems are given involving the subtraction operation with numbers under 25.

Year 10

2. *Block Counting.* The subject is asked to count stacks of blocks drawn as three-dimensional figures. The task requires counting operations and the concept of representing three dimensions in two. The child has to count what he can't see, using what he can see as the basis. Some training in stacking operations with blocks or bricks is probably necessary.

3. *Abstract Words.* More concepts are tested.

4. *Finding Reasons.* "Give two reasons why children should not be too noisy in school."[7] Reasons involve the causal relation of one event to another: "If they are too noisy, they can't do their lessons." The task is primarily a test

of completing a two-part task. Most failures occur because the child gives one reason and stops. Staying with a task is an operation.

5. *Word Naming*. To pass, the subject must say twenty-eight words in one minute. This is a fluency operation that is probably dependent on the strength of language responses and operations for cuing single-word responses such as "Look around the room and name what you see."

Year 11

2. *Verbal Absurdities IV*. A statement is made that contains a logical contradiction. Analysis of the meaning (essential characteristics) of the concepts involved in the statement will reveal the absurdity. The task involves concepts and operations for comparing characteristics of concepts.

4. *Memory for Sentences II*. A sentence containing about fifteen words must be repeated correctly from memory. As in the case of digits, the skills involved in repeating sentences are clearly related to training. Grammatical structure, word meanings, and a variety of operations to aid recall can be taught and are related to performance on memory tasks. Our only hesitation in forthrightly treating memory as a set of operations is the fact that the operations involved are not always observable. Logically, however, the behavior involved in memory tasks is no different than other behavior under stimulus control except for the imposition of a delay between the stimulus and response.

5. *Problem Situation II*. The subject is told something like, "A boy meets an animal in the woods and later his family burns his clothes." The problem is why. The problem is solvable if the subject has the right concepts about the behavior of skunks.

Year 12

6. *Minkus Completion*. This task requires writing in missing words to connect two phrases in a logical way. It involves concepts about relationships between events. "The streams are dry _____ there has been little rain."[8]

Year 13

1. *Planning a Search*. The subject has to show how he would search a field to find a lost purse. Planning a search is an operation that involves systematically eliminating alternatives.

Year 14

2. *Induction*. The task is to observe a paper being folded and cut on the last fold. The subject is asked how many holes the paper will have when it is unfolded. The demonstration is repeated several times, one new fold being added each time to show that each fold doubles the number of holes. When the sixth fold is made, the subject is asked to state how many holes there will be (thirty-two) and to give a rule about the relation of number of folds to number of holes. The subject has to know the concepts and operations involved in doubling.

3. *Reasoning*. The subject is given some facts about when a house was burglarized. The task is to determine when it happened. Alternatives are

eliminated by using the given information, leaving only one time period possible. Eliminating the alternatives in a closed set of events is a logical operation.

4. *Ingenuity*. This task is an arithmetic problem that involves using two cans to measure an amount of water that is not equal to that held by either can. The solution involves addition and subtraction operations.

5. *Orientation*. The subject is told that he is facing in a certain compass direction and then turns right or left several times. He is then asked, "What direction are you going now?" The task involves the concept of compass directions and their relation to one another and the operations of imagining that you are going in one direction and then turning left or right.

Average Adult

4. *Arithmetic Reasoning*. These are simply story problems involving the operations of addition, subtraction, multiplication, and division.

5. *Proverbs*. "What does this mean: 'Don't judge a book by its cover'?" Proverbs are analogies. To understand them, the person has to learn the rule that proverbs refer to things that are generally true about people or situations. The task operation is to translate the proverb into the general concept or statement ("Appearances may be deceiving").

Superior Adult I

2. *Enclosed Box Problem*. The task is to imagine a box that contains two smaller boxes that each contain two smaller boxes, and to state how many boxes there are all together. The subject has to be able to perform the operations of visualizing the situation and counting the boxes. The task combines spatial and number concepts.

Superior Adult II

6. *Repeating Key Ideas*. A paragraph is read in which many highly abstract concepts are presented in discussing the value of life. The task is to repeat the key ideas. If the subject knows the concepts involved, the task involves coding the ideas in some way and saying them back. It is a test of several higher-order concepts and many complex verbal operations.

A Conclusion

With the possible exception of memory tasks and word-fluency tasks (which involve less-observable operations), it is clear that the Stanford-Binet Intelligence Test measures whether or not the person being tested has learned various concepts and operations. If intelligent behavior is learned behavior, then teaching (by parents and teachers) should be vitally important in its development. We will return to this question after taking a look at the major factors related to retarding the acquisition of intelligent behavior.

Intellectual Retardation

Retardation is said to exist on the basis of three criteria:

1 *Retarded acquisition of physical skills.* Skills such as crawling, walking, and making sounds are acquired more slowly.
2 *Retarded acquisition of social skills.* Skills involved in playing and interacting with others are acquired more slowly.
3 *Retarded acquisition of intellectual skills.* Concepts and operations are learned more slowly.

Retarded children usually show slowed development in all three areas. The legal or medical decision as to whether a person is or is not labeled retarded is usually based on an evaluation of the pattern of the individual's adjustment to his environment. Can he make it there or must he be taken care of by the state?

Intelligence-test scores are often used to determine levels of retardation. The average person will receive a score of 100 on an intelligence test. Theoretically, 50 percent of the people tested receive scores between 90 and 110. The score a person receives on an intelligence test is called the intelligence quotient, or IQ. Persons whose scores are above 130 or so are considered to be very intelligent. Persons whose scores are below 75 are considered to be retarded. Three degrees of retardation can be defined as follows:

1 *Educable mentally retarded.* IQ between 50 and 75. This range is equivalent to an adult having a mental age of 7½ to 11 years. About 2.6 percent of all children born in a given year can be expected to fall in this range.
2 *Trainable mentally retarded.* IQ between 25 and 50. This range is equivalent to an adult having a mental age of 3 to 7½ years. About .3 percent of all children born in a given year can be expected to fall in this range.
3 *Profoundly mentally retarded.* IQ between 0 and 25. This range is equivalent to an adult having a mental age of 3 years or less. About .1 percent of all children born in a given year can be expected to fall in this range.

The distinctions between categories are often arbitrary. Generally, the *profoundly retarded* have severe brain damage and are usually given custodial care in state institutions. They can be trained to some extent, but, with present knowledge, it is unlikely that they can be trained to live independent lives.

Trainable children are said by most experts to require custodial care. As with the profoundly retarded, a high percentage of these children also have physical defects. They are not supposed to be able to learn to read or write, but some have been taught to do so through the effective use of learning principles. Usually, the aim is to teach self-care skills and simple work activities to be carried out under supervision. It is reasonable to expect that with improved training methods, many more children who in the past would have ended up in institutions for the trainable retarded will be educated to live largely self-supporting lives.

The *educable* group is the largest group and the one for which the most can be done in regard to developing behavior necessary for independent living.

Causes of Intellectual Retardation

Intellectual retardation can be caused by a variety of events. When causes are known, intellectual retardation can often be prevented or remediated.

Physiological Defects

Genetic defects, defective development during pregnancy, and a variety of destructive processes taking place during pregnancy or shortly after birth have been implicated as causes of retardation. For example, mongolism is caused by a defective structure of the chromosomes. Phenylketonuria (PKU) is due to a genetic defect in the child's metabolism that causes products that are harmful to the brain to enter into the blood stream. Phenylketonuria can now be easily detected in infants and retardation eliminated by diet control.

Many kinds of retardation have their basis in events related to pregnancy. If a child is born prematurely, his chances of being retarded for a variety of reasons are increased. A good diet and good medical care reduce the occurrence of premature births. Diseases such as German measles can produce a retarded child if the mother is infected during pregnancy. This is especially true during the first three months of pregnancy. If steps are taken to insure that women get German measles before having children, this cause of retardation will be eliminated. In the past, syphilis infection in the mother was an important cause of mental retardation. Compulsory blood tests and effective therapy have largely eliminated this condition. Rh blood incompatibility is another former cause of retardation that can now be detected and prevented. Recently, drugs such as LSD and thalidomide used by the mother during pregnancy have been implicated in birth defects. Many other events can happen to injure the brain. The birth process itself can involve mechanical injury or oxygen deficiency.

For a long time, a major form of mental retardation was cretinism, or dwarfism. The lack of iodine, which is important in building the thyroid hormone, leads to defective growth. With the addition of iodine to salt, a major cause of retardation was largely eliminated. Some retardation is related to defective growth of the skull. In microcephaly, the skull is abnormally small. In hydrocephaly, a deformation leads to the excessive accumulation of fluids inside the skull. The skull enlarges and the brain may be damaged if the pressure is not relieved. Surgical treatment of this condition has been fairly successful.

It is not necessary for our purposes to list the many other physiological bases for retarded development that have been identified, such as infections, tumors, and poisons. The main point is that many causes have been found and prevention and treatment programs established. More work in this direction is needed. It is most interesting, however, to recognize that for 75 percent of the retarded, no specific physiological causes can be identified. For some of these, new physiological causes may be found that can be treated or prevented at some time in the future. For the majority however, it is important to question just what is going on. The answer to that question will influence whether or not efforts are made to make such children "smarter."

Familial Retardation

With retarded children for whom there is no known basis for the retardation, it is often found that other members of their family are also labeled retarded and that their IQs are usually above 50.[9] Interpretation of findings of this sort and of more systematic studies of possible contributions of heredity to intelligence is extremely controversial. Some believe strongly that the retardation that runs in families is largely due to heredity and that the contribution of environment can at best be no more than 20 percent of the observed variation in intelligence. Others believe that the same evidence can be interpreted to support the idea that children with poorly educated parents, living in deprived surroundings, have less chance to learn the kinds of concepts and operations that intelligence tests measure. The inferential and complex statistical bases for understanding either side of this issue go beyond the scope of this text.

It is important to note, however, that the people who ask, "What is the relative contribution of heredity, and what is the relative contribution of environment?" are asking a question that has no meaning for the teacher. Current answers to this question are based on statistical comparisons of persons with "different" environments and/or "different" heredities. The statistical answers have no implications for answering these questions: "How much can I teach child X?" or, "Given the most ideal training environment that can currently be constructed, what would the results be?" or, "What could be accomplished by genetic control?"

In commenting on Arthur Jensen's paper on "The Culturally Disadvantaged and the Heredity-Environment Uncertainty,"[10] Edmund Gordon says: "There is enough evidence of hereditarily-determined physical characteristics to at least suggest that some psychological characteristics (intelligence, temperament, response tendencies, etc.) may be greatly influenced by genetics. But for the educator and social planner, establishing this fact is less important than determining the modifiability of these characteristics and the development of learning experiences appropriate to them. . . . Too often the retreat to a genetic theory in this area had led to defeatist attitudes."[11]

Suppose that 10 percent, or even 90 percent, of the "familial retarded" could be raised to average intelligence. Either outcome would have great social significance. The answer to this kind of question does not come from asking, "How much is due to heredity and how much to environment?" It must come from experimental teaching programs. Consider a contrary possibility. Dexter asks what would happen if more than half of the population were retarded and we could not make them smart by teaching?[12] If they had any political power or if people were morally committed to support each other, it would be necessary to devise different kinds of social systems, perhaps colonies where "dull" people would work in groups under the supervision of the "brighter ones." Many aspects of society would have to change to make it appropriate to the needs of its people. Machines would be simplified, contracts would be written in less complicated ways, teaching would be more explicit, and so forth. Regardless of the answer to the environment-heredity issue, we still need to know *who can be taught what and how*. This is learned by evaluating *teaching* with the best current technology.

It should be noted that our failures tell us very little about what can be done. They just eliminate possibilities. Only successes provide definitive information on what can be done. It is possible to cite many examples of significant changes brought about in children through better teaching. For example, Birnbrauer[13] has taught many trainables to read and do arithmetic problems and a striking example comes from the work of Heber.

Heber et al. selected forty mothers with IQs of less than 75 prior to the birth of a child.[14] At birth the families were assigned to experimental and control groups. The experimental-group mothers received adult education classes and training in vocational skills. The infant intervention program began at three months and was carried out at a child training center, all day, five days a week, until the children were six years old. The program focused on activities designed to enrich intellectual development, including motor skills, cognitive-language skills, and social skills. While the experimental and control groups did not differ on IQ tests at twelve months, they differed by nearly 30 points at 3 years and maintained this difference through 5½ years (IQs of 125 versus 95).

That the IQs of the control group children are much higher than their mothers' is to be expected because of regression effects (which occur when a group is selected deviant from the mean) and because father IQs were not controlled. But the 30-point IQ difference is remarkable and consistent with other evidence on what can be done with an enriched environment. Heber also reports differences on a variety of other measures of language and conceptual behavior and has produced some remarkable films illustrating the behavioral differences in the groups of children.

Hunt has reviewed much of the extensive literature on the effects of experience on intelligence.[15] It can be shown that many children are retarded not because they cannot be taught, but because they *have not* been taught by people or by their environment. A little extra training can rapidly change the behavioral development of infants living in a stimulation-deprived environment.[16] Most of the existing evidence shows that remarkable changes occur in intellectual development when children are moved from extremely barren environments to more stimulating ones.

In a recent study, Becker and Engelmann[17] selected the children in their Follow Through Program (disadvantaged) with IQs of 80 or less and examined their gains in reading and arithmetic using the Wide Range Achievement Test (WRAT) and the number of lessons taught in Distar Reading, Arithmetic, and Language over several years. For kindergarten-starting children, there were too few low-IQ children to make post-kindergarten/post-third comparisons. The analysis is primarily concerned with the teachability of low-IQ children when a technically advanced system of instruction is used. Figures 12.1 and 12.2 show the gain data for the children in the Follow Through classes. In the All groups, 78 percent of the children came from homes meeting federal definitions of economic poverty.

Figure 12.1 shows that disadvantaged children with IQs of 80 and under (an average IQ of 72 at the start of the program) gained more than a grade-level each year in reading on the Wide Range Achievement Test. Figure 12.2 shows that these same children also gained more than a grade-level each year in math in most cases. In math, the data show little difference between the Low-IQ groups and the All groups in average *gains*. The main difference is that the Low-IQ groups started lower and maintained that relative position. In reading, the All groups consistently gained more than the Low-IQ groups, although the Low-IQ groups were above grade level on the average at the end of third grade.

Examination of the number of Distar lessons taught to each group shows the main difference at the kindergarten level. In kindergarten, the Low-IQ group was taught eight lessons for every ten taught the All group. In first grade, the Low-IQ group was taught nine lessons for every ten taught the All group; in second and third grades the Low-IQ group was taught ten lessons for every ten taught the All group.

Pre- and post-tests show sizable IQ increases for the Low-IQ groups: 23 points for kindergarten children and 14 points for first-grade children. However, the magnitude of these gains is exaggerated by statistical regression effects. True gains would be on the order of 70 percent of the obtained gains. In the All groups, there is no such regression effect. For 1477 children pre-

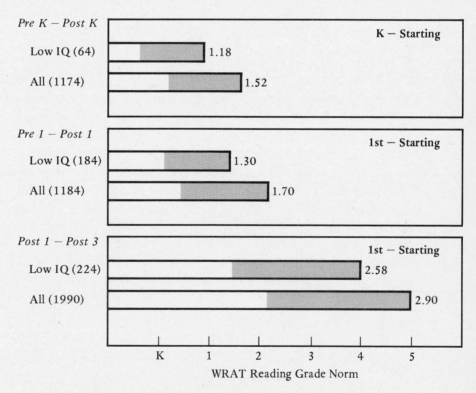

Low IQ = IQ of 80 or less in Follow Through Program

All = All children in Univ. of Oregon Follow Through Program
78% of whom are disadvantaged

Figure 12.1 Reading gains of low IQ and disadvantaged children (Shaded area indicates gain for the time period shown to the left of each chart.)

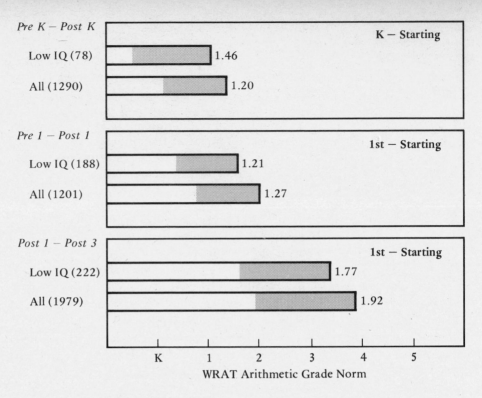

Figure 12.2 Arithmetic gains of low IQ and disadvantaged children (Shaded area indicates gain for the time period shown.)

and post-tested at the kindergarten level, there is a mean gain of 9.6 IQ points. For 1374 children pre- and post-tested at the first-grade level there is a gain of 5.1 points; and for 2024 children studied from post-first grade to post-third-grade, the gain is 3.6 points.

These findings should suggest some new perspectives on teaching and intelligence. How much children can be taught is not a simple function of IQ and grade-norm expectations. The amount of teaching and its nature are also very critical. This is not to say that most retarded children can be made normal in IQ, but many can, and we will only know how many by doing the job.

The Disadvantaged

Retardation is defined by the comparative performance of a child on an IQ test and by an evaluation of social and physical development. Cultural deprivation, on the other hand, is defined by the income level of the family and the characteristics of the home and neighborhood in which one lives. The above discussion of the familial retarded contains much that is relevant for the teacher of the disadvantaged, but there is more to be said. First, there are not many generalizations one can make about poor people. *On the average*, they test lower on IQ tests and achievement tests, but only *on the average*. Second, a large number of disadvantaged children are not prepared for school primarily because the language spoken in school is not the same as the language spoken at home. Third, the most common difference between children from disadvantaged and advantaged homes when they first go to school is their command of language *concepts*. We don't mean primarily dialectical differences. Some Black children have difficulty saying certain words in the standard way. But so long as they can translate, that's no great problem. The problem consists of a lack of basic language concepts. The child may not know the meaning of the words *or*, *big*, *long*, *hard*, *tall*, *animal*, *vehicle*, and so forth. It's not merely that he cannot say them; he doesn't know their meaning.

In an early study Engelmann showed the contribution that could be made to the intellectual development of disadvantaged four- and five-year-olds.[18] He raised the IQs of twelve disadvantaged children an average of 24 points with two years of direct instruction in reading, arithmetic, and language. Control children placed in a child-development-oriented preschool for two hours a day gained an average of 5 points in two years (see figure 12.3).

There are currently several major programs at the national level aimed at upgrading the teaching of disadvantaged children to reduce or eliminate the high rate of school failure among such children. Head Start and Follow Through are the most prominent of these programs. Head Start was initiated in 1965 and reached 561,000 poor children that year. Since then, close to 5 million children have been given preschool training, better medical and dental care, more nutritious diets, and various social and psychological services. Hundreds of thousands of parents and neighborhood people have worked as volunteers in the program. Several million children have entered first grade with more of the attitudes and behavior needed to succeed.

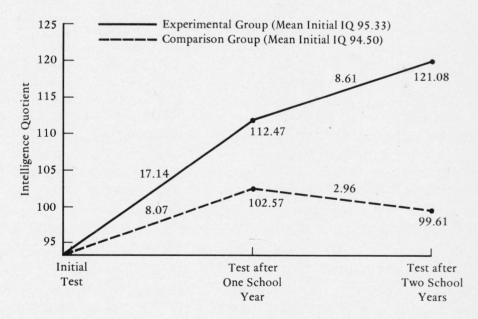

Figure 12.3 Stanford Binet IQ performance of disadvantaged subjects after one and two years of training

Evaluation of the academic gains of children in Head Start programs shows that children who were given direct instruction usually made the largest gains[19] Because follow-up studies showed that the initial gains of Head Start children were often lost within a year or two in regular school, the Follow Through program was initiated in 1967 as an experimental program to explore possible ways of continuing the gains until the children of the poor were assured of success. Like Head Start, the program provides comprehensive services in all areas, as well as an upgraded academic program. Many models for teaching disadvantaged children are currently being implemented and evaluated by the Office of Education through various sponsoring universities and research institutions. In 1973–74 Follow Through reached 84,000 children from kindergarten through third grade in 155 communities. This program has a promise of being one of the most significant educational experiments ever undertaken. Out of this work may come practical answers concerning how far schools can go in bettering the chances of the children of the poor for school success.

Preliminary results from the National Evaluation of Follow Through show strong positive results after kindergarten for two behavioral models (University of Oregon and University of Kansas) and one cognitively-oriented model (High/Scope Foundation).[20] Because of problems in designs and control groups in the earlier evaluation efforts, the National Evaluation does not offer

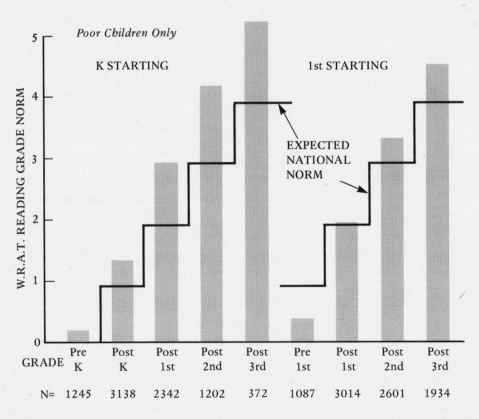

Figure 12.4 Reading progress for poor children in Follow Through, Engelmann-Becker Model, (University of Oregon)

data on the children who started the program five years ago. The two behavioral models have collected data on all children on their sites each year as a part of an information-feedback and self-evaluation program. IQ data from the University of Oregon program were presented earlier. Some achievement findings will be examined next.

University of Oregon, Engelmann-Becker Model. The small-group direct-instruction procedures described in unit 1 are the keystone of the University of Oregon E-B Model in Follow Through. When systematic behavioral principles are combined with effective programing strategies and effective classroom organization, the progress of economically disadvantaged children can be greatly facilitated. Data involving five successive entering groups from twenty communities are summarized in figures 12.4 and 12.5. The data presented are based on "poor children" only in our program who were continuously in the program at least 130 days per year. Poor children starting the program in kindergarten leave third grade with average reading decoding skills on the Wide Range at the 5.2 grade level. Those starting in first grade leave the third grade with an average reading level of 4.5 grades. The progress in arithmetic is not quite as strong (figure 12.5), but is far above current expectations for disadvantaged children.[21]

A number of analyses are available with within-community control groups. In several communities we started the program in kindergarten, first

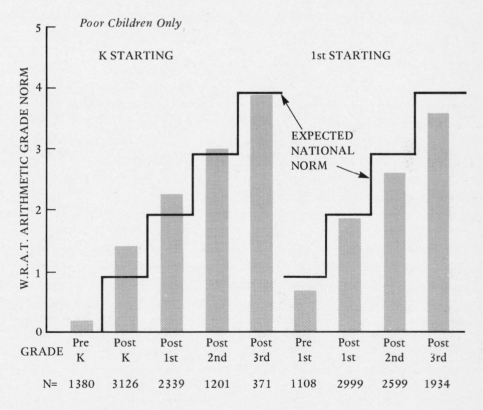

Figure 12.5 Arithmetic progress for poor children in Follow Through, Engelmann-Becker Model (University of Oregon)

grade, and second grade at the same time. This has made it possible to compare the effects of having two, three, or four years of the program. A typical result is presented in table 12.1 with data from an Indian community. The children starting the special program in second and first grade in 1970 have had only two and three years of the program, respectively. Those starting in kindergarten (1970, 1971, and 1972) will have four years of the program when they finish third grade. Examination of the tables shows progressive improvement in outcome when the special program was started earlier, and for successive entering groups (with more experienced teachers and aides). The differences between groups having four years of program and those having fewer (C vs. E groups) are highly significant.[22]

TABLE 12.1   SITE C—BIA SCHOOL
             ALL CHILDREN IN GAINS ANALYSIS

WRAT READING GRADE EQUIVALENTS

	Start of Program	Pre-K	Post-K [Pre-1]	Post-1 [Pre-2]	Post-2	Post-3
C	2nd-70			[1.80 (56)]	2.89 (81)	3.88 (81)
	1st-70		[.56 (45)]	1.64 (104)	3.18 (103)	5.21 (101)
E	K-70	.07 (35)	1.19 (84)	2.59 (93)	4.19 (85)	
	K-71	−.03 (35)	1.28 (99)	3.20 (92)		
	K-72	.05 (87)	1.68 (86)			

( ) indicates numbers children
C = Comparison
E = Experimental

WRAT ARITHMETIC GRADE EQUIVALENTS

	Start of Program	Pre-K	Post-K [Pre-1]	Post-1 [Pre-2]	Post-2	Post-3
C	2nd-70			[1.99 (57)]	2.60 (81)	3.32 (80)
	1st-70		[.91 (48)]	1.69 (105)	2.55 (103)	3.71 (101)
E	K-70	−.05 (46)	1.23 (84)	2.15 (92)	3.00 (85)	
	K-71	−.12 (34)	1.47 (99)	2.52 (92)		
	K-72	−.01 (85)	1.70 (86)			

Many will question the use of the Wide Range for giving a total picture of reading skills. The question is certainly appropriate. The Wide Range is a good measure of decoding skills (word reading) but does not measure comprehension. To overcome this problem, the Metropolitan Achievement Test has been used in the past year by many sponsors and in the National Evaluation. In spring 1973, tests of kindergarten-starting children show the following results, for "poor children" only.[23]

Table 12.2 METROPOLITAN ACHIEVEMENT TEST GRADE NORM SCORES,
SPRING 1973
E-B FOLLOW THROUGH MODEL
POOR CHILDREN ONLY— K STARTING

Test Form	Primary 1	Primary 2	Elementary
Grade Level	1	2	3
	Mean N	Mean N	Mean N
Word Knowledge	2.41 (591)	2.97 (553)	3.49 (252)
Word Analysis	2.25 (590)	3.11 (571)	—
Reading	2.22 (592)	2.88 (552)	3.25 (250)
Total Reading	2.28 (587)	2.92 (544)	3.33 (250)
Language			4.21 (224)
Spelling		3.23 (540)	3.78 (248)
Math Computation		2.98 (538)	4.13 (236)
Math Concepts	1.99 (591)	2.89 (570)	3.86 (236)
Math Problems		3.06 (542)	3.68 (237)
Total Math	1.99 (591)	2.83 (560)	3.86 (234)

Interpretation of these results is not easy. The lack of appropriate control groups poses one problem and the test itself another. Analysis of the Metropolitan Reading subtest shows that the vocabulary in the Elementary form (used in the third grade) extends far beyond the experiences of disadvantaged children even in an intensive program. If this test is the yard stick, the Oregon program is still a half year behind norms at the end of third grade. How the program could produce results far ahead of norms at earlier grades and behind in third grade can only be explained by the change in the character of the test. It is our judgment that it would take another two years of language-concept instruction to make the average disadvantaged child equivalent to the average advantaged child in language comprehension skills by the end of third grade.

University of Kansas, Behavior Analysis Model.   Under the direction of Don Bushell, the Behavior Analysis model uses programed instruction, carefully monitored goals for each child, and token reinforcement systems in its Follow Through programs. Figure 12.6 shows some results from the spring of 1973 in reading on the Wide Range from this program.[24] Comparative data are presented from children who have not had Follow Through. These non-Follow Through children were identified as comparable by the administrators of the school districts. Like Follow Through children, they attended schools receiving Title I funds, their neighborhoods were similar, and so were their family situations.

At each grade level, the mean performance of children with continuous Follow Through experience was at or above the national grade norm. Comparable children without Follow Through experience fell progressively

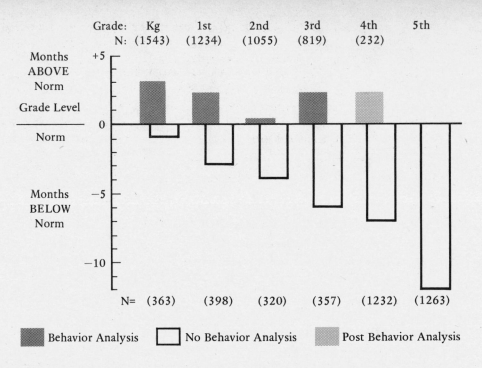

Figure 12.6 Results of WRAT Reading Post-test, 1973, Behavior Analysis Model (University of Kansas)

behind at each successive grade level. The mean score of the non-Follow Through fifth-graders was 1.2 years below the test's grade-level norm.

Two conclusions from this figure seem appropriate. First, the widely accepted notion that poor children fall progressively behind as they continue in school is confirmed by these data. Second, Follow Through has successfully broken this pattern. Additional support for this second conclusion is found in the Abt report on children entering the program in 1971.[25] This report found that the correlation of socio-economic status with achievement decreased from the beginning to the end of kindergarten for Follow Through children. This change indicates that learning progress became less dependent on socio-economic status for Follow Through children.

A Common Fallacy about IQ Scores

For years psychologists have been producing data to show that high-IQ children learn faster and low-IQ children learn slower. The assumption made is that high IQ is the cause of quick learning. But what is high IQ? It is a behavior sample of concepts and operations a person has learned. One set of academic-related behaviors (IQ-test performance) is found to predict another set of academic behaviors (school performance). That should be no surprise. To a certain extent, we may have two measures of the same thing. But it is probably true also that the more general concepts and operations measured on IQ tests are the very tools children need to benefit from instruction in large groups or through books. If these tools are lacking, learning does not occur.

It is likely that the correlation between IQ and gains from instruction will lessen when: (1) teaching is systematically designed to reach every child; (2) the instructional program starts from where the child is; (3) the programs build step-by-step on solid ground; and (4) effective motivational principles are used. Bloom has presented data supporting a very similar conclusion.[26] Elsewhere we have presented an analysis and data that also support this conclusion.[27]

Who can be taught what, and how fast, must be determined by trying to teach with the best procedures available. The teacher needs to maintain an open attitude toward the possibilities; although a child has a low IQ score, he can still be taught.

summary

The behavior tested by intelligence tests proves on examination to consist largely of concepts and operations that can be taught. This means that intelligent behavior can be taught. It is therefore reasonable to assume that teachers can make children "smarter."

Intellectual retardation varies in severity. More severely retarded children typically have defective nervous systems for one reason or another. A variety of physiological causes for retardation have been identified. In many cases, retardation can be prevented by early action or better medical care. The majority of children labeled retarded have IQs above 50 and have no identifiable physiological or physical defects. Often they come from families where other persons are labeled retarded. These "familial" retardates are a current source of controversy. Is the basic cause heredity or environment? How much does each contribute? Phrasing the problem in this way is of little use to the teacher. The answer to the question will not tell the teacher how to teach a given child. A more appropriate question is, "How far can teachers go in improving the mental capabilities of children labeled retarded, using a given teaching procedure?" The answer must come from the analysis of experimental teaching programs. Current evidence does not show that all or most retarded children can be made normal in intelligence. Some studies suggest, however, that systematic teaching following the model outlined in this text offers some promise.

Heber found that enriched instruction in the first six years with children whose mothers were retarded produced a 30-point IQ advantage. Engelmann and Becker found that children with IQs under 80 can gain more than a year in reading and math yearly when effective instruction is provided. Other findings from Follow Through, which provides for comprehensive and intensive school programs at beginning levels, indicate that disadvantaged children can be effectively taught using modern behavioral technology. It is no longer reasonable to assume that children do not learn because they are "dumb." It is necessary to examine teaching methods more carefully in order to determine why children fail. With systematic instruction, starting where the child is, building step-by-step on solid ground, and using good motivational procedures, the relation of IQ to gains from instruction is found to decrease. Who can be taught what is best determined by actually trying to teach with the best methods available.

self-test

1 concepts;
  operations
_____

2 educable
_____

3 brain
_____

4 educable
_____

5 IQ, intelligence
_____

6 IQ test
_____

7 24 (any number
  between 20 and
  25 is acceptable)
_____

8 concepts
_____

9 30

1 An examination of the Stanford-Binet test reveals that the tasks involved are combinations of _____ and _____ .

2 The _____ intellectually retarded have IQs between 50 and 75.

3 The profoundly retarded have severe _____ damage and cannot presently be trained to live independently.

4 For most retarded children in the _____ range, there is no known physical defect.

5 How much the _____ of the familial retarded child can be raised can only be determined by trying to do so through teaching.

6 Although a child scores low on an _____ _____ , he can still be taught.

7 Evidence gathered by Engelmann on the change of IQs of disadvantaged children shows that they gained an average of _____ points in two years.

8 The most common difference between children from disadvantaged homes and children from advantaged homes at the time they start school is their command of language _____ .

9 Heber found that when children of retarded mothers were given training, they scored _____ IQ points higher than those who were not.

NUMBER RIGHT _____

exercise 1 programed practice

1 concepts;
   operations

2 parts;
   detecting, finding

3 relationships

4 operations

5 essential, relevant

6 intelligence;
   taught

7 intelligent

8 smarter

9 intellectual,
   mental

10 100;
    intelligence

11 educable

12 profoundly

13 25; 50

14 brain

15 self-care

16 pregnancy

1 An examination of the Stanford-Binet test reveals that the tasks involved are combinations of _____ and _____ .

2 For example, Mutilated Pictures involve concepts of _____ and the operation of _____ missing parts.

3 Minkus Completion involves concepts about _____ between events.

4 Induction is a test of the concepts and _____ involved in doubling.

5 Vocabulary is a test of knowledge of the _____ characteristics of concepts.

6 Teaching is very relevant to _____ . Children get "smarter" when they are _____ .

7 This means that learning experiences are required for _____ behavior.

8 It also implies that teachers can make students "_____ ."

9 Retardation is said to exist when children are slow in acquiring physical skills, social skills, and _____ skills.

10 On an intelligence test, the average person receives a score of _____ . A person's score is called an _____ quotient, or IQ.

11 The _____ intellectually retarded have IQs between 50 and 75.

12 The _____ intellectually retarded have IQs below 25.

13 The trainable intellectually retarded have IQs between _____ and _____ .

14 The profoundly retarded have severe _____ damage and cannot presently be trained to live independently.

15 Many trainable children also have brain damage, but these children can be trained in many _____ - _____ skills. Some may be trained to do much more.

16 There are many physiological causes of mental retardation. Some defects are transmitted genetically, some occur during _____ , some at birth, and some after birth.

17 For most retarded children in the _____ range, there is no known physical defect.

18 Some believe the familial retarded are retarded because of _____ defects. Others believe the retardation is due to poor environment.

19 Whether the cause is hereditary or environmental is not important to the _____ .

20 The teacher needs to know how and what to teach a given _____ . The teacher can only find this out by trying to _____ the child.

21 It is possible to find out who can be taught what by using the best current _____ .

22 Current _____ shows that it is possible to do much _____ than is being done or has been assumed could be done.

23 It has been assumed for years that children who score high on intelligence tests learn _____ in school. This conclusion is based on findings that indicate that intelligence-test scores can be used to predict _____ in school.

24 One set of academic-related behaviors (IQ test performance) is found to _____ another set of academic behaviors (school performance). We may have only two measures of the _____ thing.

25 But it is probably true also that the more general _____ and _____ measured on IQ tests are the very tools children need to benefit from instruction in large groups or through books.

26 When the children do not know some of the concepts and operations assumed by the teacher's program, they are likely to _____ .

27 Such failure has often been blamed on the child's lack of ability, rather than on inadequate _____ .

28 It is likely that the correlation between IQ and gains from instruction will lessen when:

a) teaching is systematically designed to reach _____ child;

b) the instructional program starts from where the child _____ ;

c) the programs _____ step-by-step on solid ground;

d) effective _____ principles are used.

29 To learn what can be taught, the teacher must _____ using the best _____ available.

30 Evidence gathered by Engelmann on the change of IQs of disadvantaged children shows that they gained an average of _____ points in two years.

31 Retardation is determined in large measure by IQ test scores. Cultural deprivation is determined by the _____ level of the family, the home, and the neighborhood in which one lives.

32 While many disadvantaged children score in the retarded range on intelligence tests, many do _____ . As a group, the disadvantaged only score lower on the _____ .

33 Few generalizations are true for all _____ persons.

34 Many disadvantaged children are not prepared for school because the _____ used at home is different from the one used at school.

35 The most common difference between children from disadvantaged homes and children from advantaged homes at the time they start school is their command of language _____ .

36 Heber found that when children of retarded mothers were given training, they scored _____ IQ points higher than those who were not.

37 Head Start and _____ _____ are the two most prominent national programs attempting to reduce the _____ of poor children.

38 Current Follow Through results show that disadvantaged children learn if they are _____ .

29 try; procedures, technology

30 24 (any number between 20 and 25 is acceptable)

31 income, economic

32 not; average

33 disadvantaged

34 language

35 concepts

36 30

37 Follow Through; failure

38 taught

discussion questions

1 Defend the statement that tests of intelligence are primarily measures of the concepts and operations that a child has been taught (or has learned on his own).

2 List three bases for saying that a child is retarded.

3 Name three levels of retardation and give the important characteristics of each.

4 Name two causes of retardation that can be treated or prevented.

5   Why do some people believe that some types of retardation may be due to heredity? Why do other people question this?

6   Why is Jensen's concern with the extent to which heredity or environment influences intelligence of little importance to the teacher?

7   How do you find out who can be taught what?

8   What kinds of changes in IQ did Engelmann observe in disadvantaged children after two years of direct teaching?

9   Describe Heber's study of children with retarded mothers. What was the outcome?

10 What kinds of gains in achievement did Engelmann and Becker find in their study of low-IQ children in Follow Through?

11 What kinds of gains did Engelmann and Becker find for poor children in their Follow Through Program on the Wide Range Achievement Test?

12 Describe the E-B Follow Through scores on the Metropolitan Achievement Test in Reading.

13 What are the two conclusions that can be drawn from the data presented on the University of Kansas Follow Through Model?

14 How is IQ related to learning in the traditional classroom? How might this relationship be changed?

unit 13

A Comparison of Piaget's Cognitive-Development Theory with Behavior Theory

objectives

When you complete this unit you should be able to—

1 Describe the assumptions, methods, and major constructions of Piaget's cognitive-development position.

2 Compare and contrast this theory with behavior theory.

3 Identify the places where there is a convergence in viewpoints between cognitive and behavioral theories.

4 Indicate the major weakness in Piaget's cognitive-developmental theory as a basis for a theory of instruction.

5 Analyze and critique several major assumptions of cognitive theory.

lesson

Most educators, regardless of their diverging views of method and theory, are likely to agree that a major goal of education is to teach students to behave more intelligently in the face of life's problems. This goal implies that teaching should be focused on the most generalized adaptive skills, that is, concepts and operations, and their use in solving problems.

As the behavioral analysis of more complex human behavior evolves, it converges with studies of higher mental processes from a cognitive-developmental point of view. A common focus on concepts and operations is emerging. The work of Jean Piaget is preeminent in the cognitive-development area and is currently a popular basis for justification of many educational practices in the United States. Because of the popularity of the theories of Piaget and because of a common focus on concepts and operations by both the Piagetians and modern behaviorists, a closer comparative examination of these positions is useful. Our goal is to clarify similarities and differences between the two positions and their instructional implications.

Basic Assumptions

The Cognitive-Development Approach

The term *cognition* refers to the act of *knowing*, which is an unobservable internal event. The basic concern of cognitive theory is to understand the processes called thinking, and the focus is on internal structures called schemas and mental operations.

Cognitive theorists object to an S-R model of behavior that pictures man as a set of reflexes. Cognitive theorists assume that thinking occurs between a stimulus and a response and that thinking is a determinant of action. They also assume that what a man knows cannot be reduced to previously learned S-R connections since cognitive structures (the basis of thinking) always modify stimulus inputs. In this sense, later structures always depend to some extent on earlier structures. Most cognitive theorists take the position that it would not be possible to account for man's ability to deal with *new* situations and show *novel* behavior unless the cognitive structures do modify stimulus inputs and add the "creative" component to behavior.

Central to Piaget's view of the child is the assumption that the child actively *constructs* his own ways of thinking through his interactions with the environment. The child constructs an internal model of what the world is like according to his experience and actively tests this model with day-by-day experiments.

The Behavioral Approach

Behavior is action—and for the behavioral scientist this means *observable* action. The behaviorist is committed to a method of science which insists that the main independent and dependent variables dealt with be observable and subject to a test for reliability of observation. Currently, thoughts, feelings, and other internal events do not meet this test. It is possible to hypothesize about their origins and nature by *extending* principles developed through the study of observables, but thoughts and feelings should not be the starting place for the study of man.

The behaviorist believes that *all* behavior is *determined*. The individual's unique genetic history and prior learning experiences determine what is brought to a new learning situation and what interacts with the stimulus variables operating in that new situation.

Modern behaviorists object to the cognitive theorist's characterization of behavior theory in terms of an S-R reflex model. The S-R-S model of operant behavior, as developed in this text, can be clearly demonstrated to be adequate to deal with man's "ability" to respond to new situations and show novel behavior.

Modern behavior theory and cognitive theory have in common the concept that each new stimulus may be responded to uniquely. However, rather than attributing individual uniqueness to a "thinking process," the behaviorist would attribute it to a unique genetic and learning history. As will be seen, these "historical" effects can potentially be studied in an objective manner (where a general principle is involved) by generating known genetic or learning histories which then can interact with current stimulus events or training sequences. In this way, we can avoid the mystique of attributing uniqueness to an unobservable thinking process. For example, in unit 7 we discussed how Birch demonstrated the importance of prior experience in solving the "banana problem" that Kohler presented Sultan. Unless chimpanzees had prior learning in the use of sticks as extensions of their arms to rake, pull, and so on, they did not solve the problem. Thus, the historical-learning basis for "insightful thinking" was given an observable basis.

Behaviorists generally believe that instructional methods can do much to reduce individual variations in the outcome of instruction. They believe that the importance of individual "history" in determining what is learned can be reduced as instruction becomes more effective.

Methods of Investigation

Cognitive-Developmental Approach

Many of Piaget's formulations about the development of intelligence came from observations of his own children in their early years. Piaget made systematic daily observations of responses to various stimulus conditions, and he "experimentally" varied the conditions to see what-led-to-what (as a behaviorist would do). The following quote is an example of the precision in his descriptions of stimulus and response events:

From Observation 120: At six months one day, Laurent tries to grasp a piece of paper that I offer him. I finally place it on the hood of his bassinet. Laurent begins by stretching out his hands. As soon as the object is placed, he reacts as he always does in the presence of distant objects: he shakes himself, waves his arms, etc. I regulate the situation by removing the paper from the hood for a few seconds in order to move it progressively closer and further away. It is when the paper seems inaccessible to the hand that Laurent shakes himself. After having thus behaved for a moment, he seems to look for the string hanging from the hood with which he had learned to shake various objects. He pulls it harder and harder while staring at the paper. At the moment when the paper is ready to fall from the hood, Laurent lets go of the string and reaches for the paper of which he immediately takes possession. Several subsequent attempts yielded the same result. It goes without saying that it cannot be demonstrated that Laurent pulled the string in order to grasp the paper, but the whole behavior pattern gave me the impression of being performed with this end in view, and of being perfectly coordinated.

Observation 121: At age eight months 20 days, Jacqueline tries to grasp the cigarette case which I present to her. I then slide it between the cross strings which attach her dolls to the hood. She tries to reach it directly. Not succeeding, she immediately looks at the strings which are not in her hands and of which she sees only the part in which the cigarette case is entangled. She looks in front of her, grasps the strings, pulls and shakes them. The cigarette case falls and she grasps it . . . Second experiment: same reactions but without trying to grasp the object directly.[1]

These observations were used to support the hypothesis that the children, at this stage, were discriminating between *means* and *ends*.

The main method of investigation used by Piaget and his associates is to pose a series of questions or problems covering a conceptual area such as spatial relations, conservation of mass, or the causes of common events, and use probe questions that vary according to the response given. The inquiry is adapted to the child's view of things in a flexible, natural way. The following are examples:

> Here are two children, Raoul and Gerald (4; 6 and 7; 2): "Raoul, have you any brothers?—*Gerald.*—And has Gerald a brother?—*No, only me has a brother.*—Oh, come! Hasn't Gerald got a brother?—*Raoul? . . . No, he hasn't got one.*" Gerald, after giving the same answers in respect to Raoul, hits upon the right solution.
>
> Jacq (7; 6): "Have you any brothers?—*Two* [Paul and Albert].—Has Paul any brothers?—*No.*—You are his brother?—*Yes.*—Then Paul has some brothers?—*No,*" etc. He is then told the solution and seems to understand it. "And has your sister any brothers?—*Two, one brother Paul and one brother Albert* [he leaves himself out again]. An hour later: "Has Albert any brothers?—*One* [Paul].—And Paul?—*One* [Albert].—And your sister?—*Two.*"
>
> Labert (8; 6): "Have you any brothers?—*Arthur.*—Has he got a brother?—*No.* —How many brothers are there in the family?—*Two.*—Have you got any?—*One.*— Has he got any?—*None at all.*—You are his brother?—*Yes.*—Then he has got a brother?—*No.*"
>
> Di (9; 6) one of our 1st type subjects examined three months after the Binet-Simon test: "Have you any brothers?—*One.*— Has he got a brother?—*No.*—You are his brother, aren't you?—*Yes.*—Then he has a brother?—*No.*"[2]

The answers from groups of children at various ages are then analyzed to see how properties of "mental structures" change with age. In this case, many of the examples on the relationship *brother* are consistent with a more general egocentrism (personal frame of reference) in the young child's thinking.

The Behavioral Approach

Behavior methods are experimental in the sense that independent variables (stimulus events, setting conditions) are varied to see what the effects of variations are on dependent behaviors. Two or more groups may be compared using changing conditions. The basic strategy is to attempt to control for the influence of all independent variables except the one being experimentally varied. In this way, a causal relationship can be demonstrated. Piaget refers to this as the "all other things being equal" strategy, which is recognized as a canon in scientific investigation. For example, Carnine compared the effect on concept acquisition of two methods of sequencing teaching examples.[3] In the one case, pairs of positive and negative concept instances followed a sequence wherein only one essential characteristic was changed at a time. A comparison sequence used a random sequencing of the same examples. Students receiving the first sequencing procedure reached criterion significantly faster (17.6 trials versus 30.3 trials) and scored significantly higher on a post-test (77 percent versus 64 percent).

In behavioral research, a key to the control of an individual's unique genetic and learning history is the use of individual-subject designs where a *baseline performance* is first obtained before a *change procedure* is introduced. Demonstration of control by the independent variable is then made explicit by using a reversal of conditions (return to the baseline condition) or by use of multiple baselines (first change one behavior, and then another to show a consistent effect of the causal variable). When groups of subjects are used, appropriate pretesting and posttesting can sometimes be used to control for individual histories.

The Development of Cognitive Structures

The Cognitive-Development Approach

A cognitive structure is a mental structure or framework that can be used to process a variety of contents. In beginning math, a cognitive structure might involve the concepts and operations for combining and separating sets of objects in one's head; for example, it is understood that if 2 plus 3 equals 5, then 5 minus 3 must equal 2. The implicit rules of grammar, the principles of physics, and basic logic are examples of mature forms of cognitive structures. Cognitive structures are the rules we use in thinking.

In the developmental analysis of cognition, Piaget tries to *describe* what a person *can do*, given a certain kind of structuring (which is inferred from observation of behavior in a variety of situations). The varieties of structuring are seen to progress through developmental stages. Development is a continuous process, but stages can be described according to the nature (form) of the thinking structures predominant in a stage. The major stages are called the sensorimotor, the preoperational, the stage of concrete operations, and the stage of formal operations. Because of the qualitative differences in cognitive structures at different stages, competencies differ also. We will summarize each of these stages to give the student a fuller picture of Piaget's view.

The sensorimotor stage (birth to 1½ to 2 years). Central to the structure of cognition at this sensorimotor stage is its dependence on external stimulation and overt actions. *To "think" is to act. Cognition and behavior are one.* This earliest period can be broken down into a series of accomplishments that build on one another. The newborn begins dealing with his environment with built-in sensorimotor schemas. When his lips are stimulated he sucks; a touch on the palm leads to closing of the hand; a bright light draws the eyes toward it. As these reflexive schemas become well-practiced, coordinations between them occur. Hearing a sound leads to looking. The eye tries to follow the hand. Then occasionally, an interesting new effect is produced, like the shaking of a rattle, and attention focuses on reproducing the event. The reproduction of these events is said to represent the beginning of intention.

It is often observed that a familiar object is given recognition with a smile or with some part of the motor response used with that object in the past. For example, a six-month old infant might indicate recognition by shaking his hand if a rattle were held in front of him (if he had previously developed a rattle-shaking schema). At seven months, one might observe only a closing of the fist as a sign of recognition.

Slowly reality is constructed. Objects take on permanence as can be shown when the child searches for a ball hidden under a blanket. The beginnings of imitation occur. (It is of interest to note that Piaget's examples with Lucienne show a training process. Piaget imitated Lucienne's putting out her tongue, and this led Lucienne to do it again. This same kind of training was used with noises later.) Toward eight or nine months, there is evidence for the differentiation of means and ends. Different schemas are tried as the means to an end. The examples quoted earlier to illustrate Piaget's methods of observation illustrate how Laurent and Jacqueline tried a series of responses to get something held in front of them so it could be grasped and inspected.

Shortly after differentiation of means and ends, barrier problems are solved by using schemas for hitting, pushing, pulling, and so on, to remove a barrier to a goal. During this period, behavior is continually varied to produce novel effects on the environment. There is a beginning of active experimentation to find out what-leads-to-what (like playing with a light switch). This earliest stage ends with the development of mental invention. Schemas for problem solution are first "thought out" and then executed. For example, after looking for possible objects, a stick might be grasped and immediately used to reach a cookie that is otherwise not reachable. (Note that this is a variation on Sultan's problem as discussed earlier.)

By the end of the sensorimotor stage the child *can do* many things like finding hidden objects, making detours in space, and imitating speech sounds, but his intelligence is limited to here-and-now actions for the most part. Thought and behavior are still one.

The preoperational stage (2 to 7 years).   This is a period of massive growth in language skills and understanding the referents of words. Central to the structure of cognition in this period is the differentiation of signifiers and the things they stand for (referents). Piaget distinguishes two kinds of signifiers, signs and symbols. Signs, such as words, have an arbitrary relationship established by convention with their referents. Symbols bear some similarity to the referent. For example, the young boy, playing at being a hunter like daddy, might use a stick to represent his gun. The stick bears some similarities to a gun in that it can be held in the hand, is long, and can be pointed. Symbols can also be mental representations. An example comes from an observation of Lucienne when she was sixteen months of age. Piaget had several times before played with her by hiding a chain in a match box into which Lucienne had learned to put the chain. Lucienne at the time of critical observation could get the chain out by turning the box over if it was open or by using a finger to get the chain out. She had never *opened and closed* the box. At this point she was given the box with a very small opening. She could not get her finger in, and tipping did no good. She then studied the situation and several times in succession opened and shut her mouth, first slightly, and then wider. She appeared to be using a motor symbol for the mental representation. She then used her finger to enlarge the opening and get the chain.

In moving from the sensorimotor stage to operational thought, several things must occur during the preoperational period. There must be a speeding in thought or actions, so more critical information can be dealt with at once. There must be an expansion of the contents and scope of what can be thought about. And, there must be concern not only with the results of action, but also with understanding the processes by which a result is achieved. This later effect is said to be accomplished through the gradual growth of logico-mathematical operations for thinking about what is going on or might go on. Toward the end of the preoperational stage, the basis for logico-mathematical thinking has been laid in the use of language, but the child is still far from reaching operational thought. This latter point is often illustrated by experiments concerned with the conservation of liquid amount, conservation of quantity, or conservation of weight. In these experiments, a fixed amount of matter is transformed in shape. A liquid might be poured into a taller narrower glass or a fixed weight of clay might be reshaped. Usually, the preoperational child will say that the taller narrower glass contains more water than was in the shorter wider glass, when nothing was added or taken away; or that the longer piece of clay is heavier. The change in height or length has deceived him. He missed the reciprocal change going on in the other dimension. The preoperational child also lacks a test for conservation (for example, "They are the same before and after the change in shape because nothing was added or taken away").

Stage of concrete operations (7 to 12 years). For Piaget, an operation is a *mental action* that usually occurs in a structure with its counteraction—adding goes with its reverse operation subtracting, combining with separating, identity with negation. An operation is said to be *concrete* if it can be used only with concrete referents rather than *hypothetical* referents. In the concrete operational stage, thinking shows many characteristics of mature logic, but it is restricted to dealing with the "real." For example, an eight-year old might have no trouble ordering a set of sticks according to height, but might fail to solve the problem, "Bill is shorter than Mike; Bill is taller than John; who is the tallest of the three?"

Stage of formal operations (12 to 15 years and up). Formal operations involve thinking in terms of the formal propositions of symbolic logic and mathematics or in terms of principles of physics. One can deal with the hypothetical. One can deal with operations on operations. For example, the concept of density involves a ratio of weight to volume. A hypothetical object could be made more dense by adding to its weight while keeping volume constant or by subtracting from its volume while keeping its weight constant. But now consider the concept of specific gravity, which involves a ratio of two densities: the density of some matter to the density of water. In this case we have an operation on operations. At this stage, it is possible to generate many possible hypotheses (hypothetical statements) by combining various operations and setting out to test them.

Throughout the development of mind from the sensorimotor stage to the stage of formal operations, there is a parallel change in the orientation of the child to the world. Initially, the viewpoint is *egocentric* (self-centered); and gradually it becomes *objective*, as the child sees himself as an object in the world and learns to view reality from the point of view of others.

The Behavioral Approach

The behaviorist can find much of value in Piaget's descriptive studies of cognitive development. The framework provided is very useful in conceptualizing the longer-term process of change from infancy to adulthood. However, the behaviorist is more concerned with procedures for *developing cognitive structures than with describing how cognitive structures develop*. Procedures are sought that are effective in teaching concepts, operations, rules, and principles. Intelligent behavior is first and foremost operant behavior, in contrast to respondent behavior, which is reflexive in nature. Operant behavior operates on the environment and changes it in ways that increase the probability of reinforcing events and decrease the probability of punishing events. Operant behavior involves *operations* which come to be controlled by concept instances. An operation is a transformation or a change produced by an action, an effect on the environment. Whether an operation is actually carried out by responding to physical stimulus events (joining a group of 3 to a group of 2 to make a group of 5), whether it involves concrete mental operations (doing the problem in your head using symbols or signs to represent the changes), or whether it involves a hypothetical operation (adding a group of quantity x to a group of quantity y) should make no difference in delineating the fundamental procedures needed to teach operations (operant behaviors). In other words, the basic procedures that behaviorists have been studying for years for establishing classes of operant behaviors under the control of stimulus classes should be helpful in showing the teacher how to teach concepts and operations.

The behaviorist would not be concerned with stages except in the sense of preskills and component skills required to teach more complex objectives. Also, as we have noted earlier, there is a logical dependence of some concept domains on others, which implies an ordering in teaching. But the ordering arises not from the nature of man, but the nature of concepts.

Thus, the behaviorist would begin with an analysis of what it takes to teach certain concepts and operations, apply the procedures, and test to see that an appropriate general case has been taught.

A Convergence of Views

Piaget's descriptions are surprisingly consistent with the end product that a behaviorist would expect; and the structure of concepts and operations as described by Piaget is consistent with what we have presented in this text. The following discussion of Piaget's concept of a schema is taken from Flavell.[4]

> Another characteristic of schemas is hinted at by the phrase "class of similar action sequences" in our initial definition. A schema is a kind of concept, category, or underlying strategy which subsumes a whole collection of distinct but similar action sequences. For example, it is clear that no two grasping sequences are ever going to be alike; a grasping schema—a "concept" of grasping—is nonetheless said to be operative when any such sequence is seen to emerge. Schemas therefore refer to *classes* of total acts, acts which are distinct from one another and yet share common features. Although the terms *schema* and *concept* are not completely interchangeable, Piaget has recognized a certain similarity between them: "The schema, as it appeared to us, constitutes a sort of sensorimotor concept, or more broadly, the motor equivalent of a system of relations and classes."[5]

In this discussion, the formal similarity in structure between operations (schemas) and concepts is pointed out. Both involve what is common to a set of events. When the set of events involves motor events, we have a schema. When the set of events involves stimulus events, we have a concept. This view is entirely parallel to the view of concepts and operations presented in this text. Parallel distinctions are made between stimulus instances and the concepts about them, and specific responses and the operations they may follow.

Piaget does not see cognitive development as a process of responses being connected to stimuli. It is likely, however, that he would agree to a view of intellectual development that results in interrelated concepts and operations which can be flexibly recombined into new problem-solving strategies.

Piaget makes a distinction between overt actions (responses) and mental operations (thinking) that shows the relation of one to the other. An overt action *need not* be coordinated with other actions (but it could be); whereas operations, as mental actions, are linked together in reversible and transitive ways. "In other words, while operations presuppose the existence of an overall system, simple actions anticipate it. Nevertheless, they lead to such a system, and all that is required to pass from actions to operations is the progressive coordination of these actions."[6] The behaviorist would generally agree with this statement (even though it is vague), and then begin to describe *procedures* to produce the "progressive coordination."

We have noted the importance of teaching *sets of related concepts or operations,* so that concepts or operations sharing common properties are discriminated from each other. This view is consistent with Piaget's notion of an "overall system" of interrelated concepts and operations. In the following passage discussing the concept of *relative perspective in space*, Piaget shows another parallel with the view of concept presented here.

> Thus at this stage, relativity [e.g., relative perspective in space] is only partially attained; it remains global in character and is not analyzed in detail. It covers only relations between the entire group of objects and the subject and does not deal with relations between each of the single objects and the subject. Since the relationships are not 'grouped' we have here only a 'preconcept,' for a perceptual or mental relationship can only be regarded as a concept from the point when it can be co-ordinated with others in an overall grouping or group which combines the invariance of certain relations (in this case, the correspondence between viewpoints) with the variability of others (the relations of left-right, before-behind, and also distance and apparent shape).[7]

In the above quotation, the "invariance of certain relations" refers to essential characteristics of the concept, *relative perspective in space* ("correspondence between viewpoints"), and the "variability of others" refers to the irrelevant concept characteristics ("the relations of left-right, before-behind, and also distance and apparent shape"). This analysis of the concept of concept by Piaget is quite parallel to our own. The difference in position is mainly in the *use* of the analysis. Piaget uses the analysis of the nature of concepts and operations to *describe stages* in approaching the most flexible and mobile forms of thinking. The behaviorist uses this analysis to *design and test procedures* for inducing mature forms of thinking.

Educational Implications of the Cognitive-Development Position

The implications of the behavioral viewpoint for education are developed more fully in the final unit of this volume. At this point, we will examine the limitations and contributions of Piaget's work for educators.

Rohwer, Ammon, and Cramer have identified five limitations of cognitive theory for educational practice.[8] Our discussion is indebted to their analysis.

1   Cognitive theory takes behavior for granted. There is little said on how one gets from cognition to performance. There is no information given on teaching motor skills (overt operations), such as speech, handwriting, or athletic skills.
2   Noncognitive aspects of motivation tend to be ignored. If the child is not "intrinsically" motivated by the task, cognitive theory is of little help in telling the teacher what to do.
3   The teacher is not given any specifics of behavior to use as guidelines in deciding what to do or expect. The teacher has to clinically explore each child's performance, make an inference about structure, *and then decide what to teach next*. This could be a formidable problem with twenty-five students.
4   The focus on structure of the mind has led to neglect of analysis of conceptual contents to be taught in ways that could facilitate teaching. While many content areas have been studied, analysis has not focused on teaching implications.
5   Lastly, and most critically, Rohwer points out that cognitive theory has failed to study the environmental variables that bring about changes in cognitive structure. As a consequence there is a lack of teaching prescriptions that would help foster cognitive development. The theory, in focusing on the nature of mental structures, has failed to show the processes that lead to the development of mental structures. One might also note that the cross-sectional methods of research used in many studies are incapable of producing statements of what-leads-to-what (identifying causes). At best, they can describe what currently is the case *on the average*.

Positive contributions to education from Piaget's work can be summarized in five points. First, the evidence on the ways in which new structures are built in an orderly fashion out of old ones implies a need for a careful analysis of what each child brings to the learning situation. Second, Piaget clearly recognizes that learning is doing, especially for the young child. Active responding is important to learning operations, and thinking is to a large extent built out of initially overt operations. Third, there are strong suggestions, *at least by example*, that the development of cognitive structures can be fostered by the teacher's questions and probes that introduce contradictions. This is parallel to the notion of introducing negative instances in the work of Markel and Engelmann. Fourth, there are implications for the goals and design of curricula. The focus is on instruction to develop productive thinking that has the characteristics of what Piaget calls the operational stage.

Finally, Piaget has made major contributions to the analysis of many areas of knowledge, noting its structurings. He has explored concepts of physical causality, the properties of objects, space, time, mathematical logic, classification of objects, relations among objects, and propositional logic. He has also pursued the study of concepts in moral reasoning, in children's views on human behavior, and in language development. The logical analyses and descriptive material in his work can teach us to think more clearly about the world around us and to see more clearly what we need to teach others. Pertinent references to these major works are listed in the notes for this unit.[9]

summary

The cognitive theorist wants to understand thinking and how it develops. Through the study of children at various ages, an attempt is made to describe the major features of cognitive structures as they change with age. In the work of Piaget, this approach has led to the description of a series of developmental stages that grow one into the other. In the sensorimotor stage, thinking is doing. All thinking begins as overt behavior, which slowly comes to be represented by signs and symbols for actions. In the preoperational stage there is a differentiation between signifiers and the things signified. Thought and action are separated as language develops, but the child still lacks an understanding of causal processes. In the stage of concrete operations, an understanding of what-leads-to-what is achieved but is restricted to dealing with the real. Only in the stage of formal operations can the child deal with the hypothetical and perform operations upon operations.

The stages of mental development described by Piaget represent steps taken by the child in approaching the most flexible and mobile forms of mature thinking. Concepts and operations are the key components of mature forms of thinking. Piaget has noted a formal similarity in the structure of concepts and operations (schemas). Both involve what is common to a set of events (invariants), and examples of both have irrelevant characteristics (variants).

The behaviorist is concerned with the study of action. He is furthermore concerned with identifying those environmental variables (classes of stimuli) that lead to changes in behavior (social development). To find out what-leads-to-what, an experimental method is used in which independent variables are varied one at a time so that their effects can be studied. In approaching the problem of thinking, the behaviorist extrapolates from what is known about observable behavior and assumes the same processes are involved in behavior that cannot be observed. Explicit procedures have been identified for teaching concepts, operations, rules, principles, and problem-solving skills. The behavioral structures that can be built through using these procedures meet all of the requirements of flexibility and mobility characteristic of mature thought as described by Piaget.

A major difference between the cognitive-development and behavioral approaches is that the former is concerned with *describing* how cognitive structures develop while the latter is concerned with *developing* cognitive structures. However, there is a remarkable convergence in the actual concept of concepts and operations in both positions.

The weakness in the cognitive-development approach *as a basis for a theory of instruction* is its lack of concern with the processes and variables that can be used to induce learning. Thus, the teacher is not given the specifics needed to build cognitive structures. It should be noted, however, that instruction was (and is) of little concern to Piaget. The attempts to make Piaget's work the basis for a theory of instruction have been the responsibility of American educators. However, even without causal principles, Piaget's descriptive work does have implications for educational goals and methods. When coupled with knowledge of learning processes, Piaget's work has made important contributions to educational practice.

self-test

1 determinant

2 uniquely

3 mental structures

4 baseline

5 can do

6 overt actions

7 component

8 relevant;
  irrelevant

9 describe

1   Cognitive theorists assume that thinking occurs between a stimulus situation and a response and that thinking is a _____ of action.

2   Modern behavior theory and cognitive theory have in common the concept that each new stimulus may be responded to _____ .

3   In Piaget's work, the answers from groups of children at various ages are analyzed to see what they show about how properties of _____ _____ change with age.

4   In behavioral research, a key to the control of an individual's unique genetic and learning history is the use of individual-subject designs where a _____ performance is first obtained before a change performance is introduced.

5   In the developmental analysis of cognition, Piaget tries to describe what a person _____ _____ given a certain kind of structuring.

6   Central to the structure of cognition at this sensorimotor stage is its dependence on external stimulation and _____ _____ .

7   The behaviorist would not be concerned with stages except in the sense of preskills and _____ skills required to teach more complex objectives.

8   Another commonality in viewpoint is the recognition of the invariant and variant components in concept instances. This distinction parallels the distinction between _____ and _____ characteristics.

9   Piaget uses the analysis of the nature of concepts and operations to _____ stages in approaching the most flexible and mobile forms of thinking.

NUMBER RIGHT _____

exercise 1 programed practice

1 knowing

2 internal,
   unobservable

3 determinant

4 constructs

5 observable

6 internal

7 determined

8 uniquely;
   learning

9 questions

10 mental structures

11 varied;
   causal

12 baseline

1   The term cognition refers to the act of _____ .

2   The act of knowing is an _____ event.

3   Cognitive theorists assume that thinking occurs between a stimulus situation
    and a response and that thinking is a _____ of action.

4   Central to Piaget's view of the child is the assumption that the child actively
    _____ his own ways of thinking through his interactions with the
    environment.

5   The behaviorist is committed to a method of science which insists that the
    main independent and dependent variables dealt with be _____ .

6   Currently, thoughts, feelings, and other _____ events do not meet
    this test.

7   The behaviorist believes that all behavior is _____ .

8   Modern behavior theory and cognitive theory have in common the concept
    that each new stimulus may be responded to _____ . However,
    rather than attributing individual uniqueness to a "thinking process," the
    behaviorist would attribute it to a unique genetic and _____ history.

9   The main method of investigation used by Piaget and his associates is to pose
    a series of _____ or problems covering a conceptual area, and then
    use probe questions which vary according to the response given.

10 The answers from groups of children at various ages are then analyzed to see
    what they show how properties of _____ _____ change with
    age.

11 The basic behavioral research strategy is to attempt to control for the influence
    of all independent variables except the one being experimentally
    _____ . In this way, a _____ relationship can be demon-
    strated.

12 In behavioral research, a key to the control of an individual's unique genetic
    and learning history is the use of individual-subject designs where a
    _____ performance is first obtained before a change procedure is
    introduced.

13 A cognitive structure is a mental structure or framework that can be used to process a variety of _____ .

14 Cognitive structures are the _____ we use in thinking.

15 The major stages are called the _____ , the _____ , the stage of _____ operations, and the stage of _____ operations.

16 The newborn begins dealing with his environment with _____ sensorimotor schemas. When his lips are _____ he sucks.

17 This earliest stage ends with the development of mental _____ . Schemas for problem solution are first "thought out" and then executed.

18 By the end of the sensorimotor stage the child can do many things, but his intelligence is limited to here-and-now _____ for the most part. Thought and behavior are still one.

19 The preoperational stage is a period of massive growth in _____ skills and understanding the referents of words.

20 Central to the structure of cognition in this period is the differentiation of _____ and the things they stand for (referents).

21 Toward the end of the preoperational stage, the basis for logico-mathematical thinking has been laid in the use of language, but the child is still far from reaching _____ thought.

22 This latter point is often illustrated by experiments concerned with _____ .

23 A common finding is that the preoperational child will say that the taller-narrower glass contains _____ water, when nothing was added or taken away.

24 The change in height has deceived him. He missed the _____ change going on in the other dimension.

25 An operation is said to be concrete if it can be used only with concrete referents rather than _____ referents.

26 In the concrete operational stage, thinking shows many characteristics of mature logic, but it is restricted to dealing with the _____ .

27 Formal operations involve thinking in terms of the formal _____ of symbolic logic and mathematics, or in terms of principles of physics. One can deal with the _____ .

28 The framework provided by Piaget is very useful in conceptualizing the longer-term process of _____ from infancy to adulthood.

29 However, the behaviorist is more concerned with procedures for _____ cognitive structures than with _____ how cognitive structures develop.

30 Procedures are sought which are effective in _____ concepts, operations, rules, and principles.

31 The basic procedures which behaviorists have been studying for establishing classes of _____ behaviors under the control of stimulus classes should be helpful in showing the teacher how to teach concepts and operations.

32 The behaviorist would not be concerned with stages except in the sense of _____ and _____ skills required to teach more complex objectives.

33 Piaget has noted the formal _____ in structure between operations (schemas) and concepts. Both involve what is common to a set of events. When the set involves motor events, we have a _____ . When it involves stimulus events, we have a _____ .

34 Parallel distinctions are made between stimulus _____ and concepts about them, and _____ responses and the operations they may illustrate.

35 A commonality in viewpoints is the recognition of the invariant and variant components in concept instances. This distinction parallels the distinction between _____ and _____ characteristics.

36 Piaget uses the analysis of the nature of concepts and operations to _____ stages in _____ the most flexible and mobile forms of thinking.

27 propositions;
   hypothetical

28 change

29 developing;
   describing

30 teaching

31 operant

32 preskills;
   component

33 similarity;
   schema;
   concept

34 instances;
   specific

35 relevant;
   irrelevant

36 describe;
   approaching

37 design;
procedures

38a) performance

b) motivation

c) behavior

d) analysis

e) environmental;
prescriptions

39a) new;
old

b) doing;
operations

c) questions

d) goals

e) knowledge

37 The behaviorist uses this analysis to _____ and test _____ for inducing mature forms of thinking.

38 Cognitive theory is limited in its implications for teaching because:

a) there is little said on how one gets from cognition to _____;

b) noncognitive aspects of _____ tend to be ignored;

c) the teacher is not given any specifics of _____ to use as guidelines in deciding what to do or expect;

d) the focus on structure of the mind has led to a lack of _____ of conceptual contents to be taught in ways which could facilitate teaching.

e) Lastly, and most critically, cognitive theory has failed to study the _____ variables that bring about changes in cognitive structure. As a consequence, there is a lack of teaching _____ which would help foster cognitive development.

39 Positive contributions to education from Piaget's work can be summarized in five points:

a) the evidence of the ways in which _____ structures are built in an orderly fashion out of _____ structures implies a need for a careful analysis of what each child brings to the learning situation.

b) Piaget clearly recognizes that learning is _____, especially for the young child. Active responding is important to learning _____, and thinking is to a large extent built out of initially overt operations.

c) There are strong suggestions, at least by example, that the development of cognitive structures can be fostered by the teacher's _____ and probes which introduce contradictions.

d) There are implications for the _____ and design of curricula.

e) Piaget has made major contributions to the analysis of many areas of _____, noting its structurings.

discussion questions

1 What is the *convergence* discussed by the authors between Piaget's cognitive theory and behavior theory?

2 Define cognition.

3 Critique this assumption: What a man knows cannot be reduced to previously learned S-R connections since cognitive structures (the basis of thinking) always modify stimulus inputs.

4 Critique this assumption: Thinking is a determinant of action.

5 Critique this assumption: Unless we assume that cognitive structures modify stimulus inputs and add the "creative" component to behavior, there is no way to account for man's ability to deal with the new and to show novel behavior.

6 What is the basic difference in methodology between Piaget's approach to the study of cognitive processes and the behavioral approach?

7 Describe the four major stages in Piaget's theory of development, indicating a central feature of each stage.

8 Stage theories imply certain developments have to occur *before* others can. Give examples to show where and how the behavioral programer has similar concerns.

9 What does Piaget mean by a "concept" of grasping?

10 How can the concern with teaching sets of related concepts as sets be related to Piaget's descriptions of cognitive structures?

11 Specify S+, S–, and Si for the concept "relative perspective."

12 Give five shortcomings of cognitive-developmental theory as a basis for a theory of instruction.

13 Give positive contributions of Piaget's work to education.

unit 14

Implications for Education

objectives

When you complete this unit you should be able to—

1 Discuss the ways in which education can be made better.
2 Use what you have learned in this text to discuss the issue "Who can be taught?"
3 Discuss what is wrong with the concept of learning disabilities.
4 Discuss the pros and cons of special classes for some children.
5 Specify ways in which curricula can be improved, given current know how.
6 Discuss why better management systems are needed in education.
7 State the conditions under which teacher accountability is a reasonable expectation.
8 Be motivated to do something to make education better.

lesson

The overriding implication of this analysis is that *education can be better*. A rational basis for the design of curricula (programs) and instruction (teaching tasks) exists and can be used in educating intelligent people. The technology whose basic principles we have been describing offers a direct path to future progress in attacking some of the most widespread problems in education today. We will review some of these problems and the directions solutions might take.

Who Can Be Taught?

Teachers are learning to be wary of labels, but there are still many who falsely believe that some children cannot learn because they are brain-injured, retarded, disadvantaged, or disabled. The evidence from recent behavioral research clearly indicates that retarded children can be taught, disadvantaged children can be taught, and that children said to have learning disabilities *just haven't been taught*.

Let's consider this last problem in more detail since learning disabilities are the most recent fictitious explanations of teaching failure. Learning disabilities are said to exist when children of average IQ or better do not learn as well as expected. A variety of assumed neurological defects are said to be the causes of the learning failures. Parents and teachers are assured that Johnny did not learn to read, not because of a faulty teaching program, but because he is different and needs a special program. Karl's mother is assured that the reason her child is so hyperactive is that some children just come that way. If he is given the right kinds of drugs and kept out of excessively exciting situations, some improvement can be expected with age, but he'll always have the same temperament. These explanations of the "causes" of learning failures may help relieve the guilt of the parents or teachers. However, explanations of this sort do little to tell us what can be taught in the future.

The most commonly assumed cause of learning disabilities is "minimal brain damage"—that is, *possible* brain damage. It is fashionable to assume that the damage interferes with the "perception" of stimuli or with "attention." The most common learning disability is the failure to "learn" to read. While many children may in fact have some of the neurological defects that are hypothesized, in only a small percentage of the cases is there real evidence for this. More often than not, the only available evidence is the learning failure itself. The concern for the children who are not being taught or who have not learned for some reason is justifiable. However, this approach simply defines a new kind of problem child, rather than looking closely at the conditions needed to teach children and considering the possibility that many children said to have learning disabilities simply have not been taught effectively. In our experience working with large groups of disadvantaged children, the really hard-to-teach children are those who initially test in the trainable range on IQ tests (and usually have obvious physical defects). The frequency of such cases is about 1 in 100 disadvantaged children. These children can be taught with good technology. It just takes a little longer to build up the preskills that are missing. When we look in the average IQ range for children who cannot learn, we do not find *any*. Learning disabilities are a circular explanation for the failure of teaching programs.

Special Classes vs. Mainstreaming the Handicapped

The faddish trend toward special classes for handicapped children is giving way to a new fad, mainstreaming. One weakness of special classes is that they allow (train) teachers to ship out their failures, rather than learning to teach them. At first it was the retarded, then the emotionally disturbed, then the socially maladjusted (disadvantaged), and finally the learning disability. Another weakness of special classes is that they can be used as an excuse to teach children less rather than more. If the assumption is made that problem children of various types learn more slowly and they are then taught less, the prophecy will be fulfilled. They will end up being dumber. Tracking on the basis of test results has been called unconstitutional, and many other forms of special classes may also be unconstitutional. However, the decision to use special classes, and part-time special classes, should be based on what is best for the progress of the children and not fads of the time.

Special classes have a place. The more severely retarded definitely need special training procedures with persons skilled in working with them. Some kinds of severe emotional problems (such as autism) and some kinds of physical handicaps also require special classes, at least part of the time. For the most part, however, it would seem reasonable to give teachers better training, better programs, and more paraprofessional assistants in the early grades to really teach basic skills to all, and to keep the majority of children in regular classes. Some specialists should be available to assist the teacher with problems he cannot handle. Small groups of children might leave class to work with a specialist part of each day until they are at class level, and the teacher can again take over. The goal would be to return the children to their teacher as soon as possible—not to take over her problems. New students (late entries) could also be evaluated and readied for the ongoing class program by specialists.

For many problem children, especially those with deficiencies in language concepts, the key is likely to be an early identification of the children and initiation of intensive training at home and in preschools. Programs are available, along with procedures for training teachers and paraprofessionals to use them. That such efforts can be effective is proven. The only holdback is an historical resistance to the formal teaching of young children.

Behavior Problems

As demonstrated in *Teaching 1* of this series, a large number of procedures are now available that teachers can use to better motivate children in the classroom and to eliminate problem behaviors. From our classroom work with problem children and teachers, we are convinced that as many as 85 to 90 percent of the problems referred to psychologists, counselors, and social workers can be handled in the regular classroom by teachers who have been taught more positive ways of working with children.[1] Programs for the use of teacher-support personnel (psychologists, counselors, social workers) as consultants and trainers in the use of behavior technology are needed throughout education. For the more severe behavior problems, special reinforcement systems on a temporary or permanent basis can be used and should be available.[2]

Curriculum Design

The technology we have been describing offers some effective new approaches to curriculum design. We will illustrate this point by examining the area of remedial reading.

Most current approaches to remedial reading begin with an analysis of the errors made *by the student* on a test, a method that grew out of the early work of Monroe and others in the 1930s. On the basis of the errors made, the students are said to have problems such as being "word-substituters" or "word-reversers." However, a careful examination of errors made by individual readers will show that they do not make the same errors on the same word the second time they meet it, and the errors tend to pile up on certain kinds of words. Words that differ from each other *in only one way* are often confused (left-felt, rob-robe, his-this, he-the-she, on-in, not-hot, like-likes). Endings such as -ed are often confused because they can have several sounds. Irregular vowel sounds are demons. When is the vowel long and when is it short? There are many ways to write the sound "o" as in *note*, for example, *o, oa, au, oe, oh, eau, eu, eo, oo, ou, ought, ow*. A careful analysis shows that problems in reading occur where there are *problems with the English language*, that is, at those points where there are difficult discriminations to make. Analysis also shows that the poor reader is inconsistent in his reading because he is no longer even looking at the words he needs to see to read accurately. This is technically called avoidance behavior and is a function of repeated failure (punishment).

With this analysis of the problem, it is possible to design a corrective reading program that will teach *most* poor readers the decoding and attending skills they need, and provide extensive practice to overcome old habits. We can also design programs to teach kids effectively in the first place.

Engelmann and his associates designed a *Corrective Reading Program* using the kind of technology presented in this text.[3] It requires lots of reading. Unless students read out loud, there is no way the teacher can correct mistakes. The program provides direct instruction in word-attack skills and teaches irregular-word families, building them up cumulatively. After new skills are introduced and practiced with the teacher, they are used in story reading. The stories are carefully designed to give intense practice in the new skills and to use low probability sequencing so that the students have to look carefully at each word. Context guessing will not work. Gradually comprehension becomes the focus of instruction as decoding errors decrease. A point-contract system, leading to grades or other reinforcers, is used to keep a high level of motivation.

One-year results with this program show a marked reduction in reading error rates, even with increasingly more difficult stories. Gains from a year of instruction, fifty minutes a day, average close to two years on the Wide Range Achievement Test for the "run-of-the-mill" poor reader in grades four through twelve, and 1½ years for educationally handicapped children at the high school level.

Corrective reading is just one area where better curriculum design can be expected to have important social effects. There is a need for extensive curriculum work in many other areas. In the social sciences, programs are needed to teach skills for solving personal, social, and environmental problems. There is a great need for programs that provide systematic training in parenting skills. Being a parent is probably the only major role in society today for which there is no formal training. Day care centers could be tied to high schools and provide a laboratory for training in parenting skills to the benefit of young children and future parents alike.

One can foresee the eventual building of curricula that will teach stages two and three in Cronbach's three-stage-rocket analogy of education. We have made a start on stage one, *basics*, but still need much improvement there. We have an idea of how stage two, *problem-solving skills*, might be taught, and maybe just a glimmer of how stage three, *creative productiveness*, might be taught. The theoretical building blocks are available. What is needed now are new thoughtful designs to try out.

Curriculum Management and Evaluation

Behavioral technology has produced a number of systems to assist the teacher in keeping track of student progress, in determining when teaching has succeeded or failed, in providing information for *immediate* diagnostic remediation when tests are failed, and in evaluating the longer-term effects of programs. When teaching is viewed as an instructional system that should be carefully monitored to maintain quality control, new concepts of the roles of educational managers arise. In the past, the managers of education have found out that their systems have failed *after the children have already lost.* The end-of-year data, analyzed six months later, comes too late to help those children who have already lost a year. Training, monitoring, and feedback systems are available using modern behavioral technology and promise to provide teachers and educational managers with the information they need to constantly maintain good quality control in education so that the children do not lose. Individual Prescribed Instruction, Computer Assisted Instruction, Distar, and several Follow Through Models have demonstrated the effectiveness of monitoring-feedback systems. What is needed is a broader application of these models in the field. In this series, *Teaching 3: Evaluation* examines many of these issues as they relate to the classroom teacher.

Teacher Accountability

California has mandated the accountability of educators in its *Stull Act.* Other states are likely to follow. Objectives are to be set, and teachers and managers evaluated (and retained or not) on whether performance meets the objectives. Mandated teacher accountability poses no end to evaluation problems. However, the analysis we have presented leads to the conclusion that it is possible to train teachers to be effective classroom managers, and it is possible to design educational programs that will work. Given these possibilities, it is reasonable to hold teachers accountable for the learning of their students, especially in basic areas where there are common goals. However, this accountability is reasonable only when *adequate training has been provided* and where the programs selected have *demonstrated effectiveness under typical classroom conditions.* Because of the failure to meet these two conditions, efforts to establish teacher accountability at this time are likely to be resisted and will fail if imposed. However, it is possible to envisage a future where professional educators do agree to be accountable for the learning of their charges because they will know it can be done.

summary

The current technology of instruction can provide a basis for rational solutions to the problems widespread in education today. Education can be better. We need to throw away many labels used as excuses for teaching failures and look more closely at the process of instruction to be sure teaching is happening.

Educational practice has seen one series of fads after another. In the absence of effective procedures, this is to be expected. In the current push toward mainstreaming in special education, we must analyze the requirements for effective instruction of each child and stay flexible. Use special classes when they are the only way to get the job done, and get rid of them whenever possible.

Better procedures are available for the positive motivation and management of children in schools. Systematic programs for training all teachers in positive management procedures are likely to greatly benefit children and teachers alike.

Empirical and logical principles are available for designing curricula that will efficiently teach intelligent behaviors. Many basic programs using these principles have been designed or are in tryout stages. More are needed, as are programs focusing on principles critical to the solutions of personal, social, and environmental problems. One can foresee quantum jumps in the quality of instructional programs in the coming decade. Tied to new programs will be systematic monitoring and management systems that will keep the teacher informed of student progress. It will no longer be necessary to let children fail before the school system finds out about a problem.

With effective programs and adequate training, teachers can reasonably agree to be accountable for the learning of their students, just as other professions assume an accountability for their services. We must be careful, however, not to unfairly impose accountability without providing adequate training and effective programs.

self-test

1 The evidence from recent behavioral research clearly indicates that retarded children can be taught, disadvantaged children can be taught, and that children said to have learning disabilities just _____ been taught.

2 Learning disabilities are a _____ explanation for the failure of teaching programs.

1 haven't

2 circular

3 One weakness of special classes is that they _____ teachers to ship out their failures, rather than learning to teach them.

4 For many problem children, especially those with deficiencies in language concepts, the key is likely to be an _____ identification of the children and initiation of intensive training at home and in preschools.

5 A careful analysis shows that problems in reading occur where there are problems with the _____ _____ .

6 One can foresee the eventual building of curricula that will teach stages two and three in Cronbach's three-stage-rocket analogy of education. The _____ building blocks are available.

7 Behavioral technology has produced a number of systems to assist the teacher in keeping track of student _____ , in determining when teaching has succeeded or failed, in providing information for immediate diagnostic _____ when tests are failed, and in evaluating the longer-term effects of programs.

8 Given these possibilities, it is reasonable to hold teachers accountable when adequate _____ has been provided and where the programs selected have demonstrated _____ under typical classroom conditions.

NUMBER RIGHT _____

3 allow, train

4 early

5 English language

6 theoretical

7 progress;
  remediation

8 training;
  effectiveness

exercise 1 programed practice

1 A _____ basis for the design of curricula and instruction exists and can provide a _____ basis for progress in educating intelligent people.

2 The new _____ offers a direct path to future progress in attacking some of the most widespread problems in education today.

1 rational;
  rational

2 technology

3 The evidence from recent behavioral research clearly indicates that retarded children can be taught, disadvantaged children can be taught, and that children said to have learning disabilities just _____ been taught.

4 Learning disabilities are said to exist when children of _____ IQ or better do not learn as well as expected.

5 A variety of assumed _____ defects are said to be the causes of the learning failures.

6 Explanations of this sort do little to tell us what can be _____ in the future.

7 Learning disabilities are a _____ explanation for the failure of teaching programs.

8 One weakness of special classes is that they _____ teachers to ship out their failures, rather than learning to teach them.

9 Another weakness of special classes is that they can be used as an _____ to teach children less rather than more.

10 Tracking on the basis of test results has been called _____ .

11 Special classes have a place. The more _____ retarded definitely need special training procedures with persons skilled in working with them.

12 For many problem children, especially those with deficiencies in language concepts, the key is likely to be an _____ identification of the children and initiation of intensive training at home and in preschools.

13 It is probable that as many as _____ percent of the problems referred to psychologists, counselors, and social workers can be handled in the regular classroom by teachers who have been taught more positive ways of working with children.

14 A careful analysis shows that problems in reading occur where there are problems with the _____ _____ .

15 Analysis also shows that the poor reader is inconsistent in his reading because he is no longer even _____ at the words he needs to see to read accurately.

16 reading

17 families;
cumulatively

18 practice;
probability

19 point-contract

20 two

21 curriculum

22 theoretical

23 succeeded;
remediation

24 lost

25 managers;
work

26 training;
effectiveness

---

16 The Corrective Reading Program requires lots of _____ .

17 The program provides direct instruction in word-attack skills and teaches _____ of irregular words that are built up _____ .

18 Stories are carefully designed to give intense _____ in the new skills and to use low _____ sequencing so that the students have to look carefully at each word.

19 A _____ system, leading to grades or other reinforcers, is used to keep a high level of motivation.

20 Gains from a year of instruction, fifty minutes a day, average close to _____ years on the Wide Range Achievement Test.

21 There is need for extensive _____ work.

22 One can foresee the eventual building of curricula that will teach stages two and three in Cronbach's three-stage-rocket analogy of education. The _____ building blocks are available.

23 Behavioral technology has produced a number of systems to assist the teacher in keeping track of student progress, in determining when teaching has _____ or failed, in providing information for immediate diagnostic _____ when tests are failed, and in evaluating the longer-term effects of programs.

24 In the past, the managers of education have found out their systems have failed after the children have already _____ .

25 The analysis we have presented leads to the conclusion that it is possible to train teachers to be effective classroom _____ , and it is possible to design educational programs that will _____ .

26 Given these possibilities, it is reasonable to hold teachers accountable when adequate _____ has been provided and where the programs mandated or selected for use have demonstrated _____ under typical classroom conditions.

discussion questions

1 How do you know who can be taught?

2 How are most learning disabilities defined? What kind of explanation is "learning disability"?

3 What is "minimal brain damage"? How is it detected?

4 What are the educational implications of the concept "minimal brain damage"?

5 What are the potential dangers in the push toward "mainstreaming"?

6 Why do you suppose education is so subject to fads?

7 What are some of the weaknesses and dangers of special classes?

8 Just where might special classes be needed most?

9 What approach do the authors suggest for retraining teachers in more effective classroom management procedures?

10 How does the design of Engelmann's *Corrective Reading Program* differ from traditional approaches to corrective reading?

11 How do the approaches to curriculum design recommended in this book differ from traditional textbook approaches?

12 Suggest some areas in education where new curricula may be needed.

13 What are the major shortcomings of most management systems in education?

14 How might these problems be overcome?

15 Under what two conditions is it reasonable for teachers to assume accountability for the success of their students?

unit 15

Review

objectives

This review unit is designed to remind you of some of the material covered earlier in the course. It is *not* designed to teach you new material. If any terms or concepts are mentioned that you do not understand, you should go back to the original material and study it carefully. In addition, you should go back through the exercises for each unit and make sure that you know the correct answer for each item.

review

UNIT 9.   Concept Analysis in a Finite Universe (Toward a Theory of Programing)

Concept learning involves building up sets of discriminations. With knowledge of where errors occur in discriminating and skills in the logical analysis of concepts, it is possible to devise workable programs that focus on only *some* of the larger set of possible discriminations that could be taught.

The examples used to teach concepts are called positive and negative instances. Each can have three types of stimulus properties. Positive instances can have S+ and Si characteristics. Negative instances can have S– and Si characteristics. Both can also have Sc characteristics, which are those common to more than one concept within a set under analysis. Sc characteristics are the bases for forming higher-order concepts. Whether a specific characteristic is called S+ or Sc depends on the set within which the analysis takes place.

Stimulus generalization consists of treating new stimuli in the same way as some previously taught stimuli. This implies a failure to discriminate differences. Three factors control the likelihood of stimulus generalization:

1 The number of identical stimulus characteristics (Sc) shared by instances of two concepts.
2 The number and magnitude of the differences in concept characteristics between two concepts (S+/S– differences).
3 The degree of prior discrimination training with respect to the concept differences.

With knowledge of the factors controlling errors, the programer is able to design and sequence tasks to circumvent possible errors. The number of common characteristics can be reduced, the magnitude of differences can be increased, and explicit training can be provided where it is needed most.

Two logical analyses are important in programing. In the analysis of concept structure, the programer is looking for interrelated groups of concepts and independent groupings. Interrelated groupings are analyzed for hierarchical structuring, with the higher-order structures being given priority in designing teaching formats. Five concept domains (which are largely independent from each other) must be considered, from domain 1 (object concepts) to domain 5 (causal events). Each higher numbered domain uses concepts from the domains below it. To be teaching only one new concept at a time, it is important to present concepts from lower numbered domains before those from higher numbered domains.

Once related groups of concepts have been identified, a second kind of concept analysis focuses on pairs of concepts within a related set to be taught with a common format. In analyzing pairs of concepts one looks for shared characteristics (Sc) and minimal S+/S– differences. One looks for the concepts most likely to be confused with each other, that is, concepts most likely to show stimulus generalization from one to the other. Once identified, steps can be taken to minimize possible errors by modifying on the initial teaching concepts and by selecting the critical discriminations for direct teaching.

UNIT 10.   Basic Steps in Programing

First, make a preliminary statement of the program objective(s), and analyze the preliminary objective(s) for possible relations to other objectives to come later, parallel, or earlier. This provides the basis for efficient interconnecting of programs.

The basic steps in programing are:

1 Analyze the preliminary objective into sets of component terminal skills that involve common concepts and operations.
2 Restate the objective as sets of related tasks, any one of which the student can perform.
3 Analyze each of the terminal objectives (where possible) into component skills that involve related sets of concepts and operations. This process is repeated until the programer identifies components that can be taught by a common teaching format.
4 Specify the general-case task formats for each of the groupings identified in step 3.

5　Analyze the task formats for prerequisite skills.
6　Use the information derived so far to construct a program-sequence chart for terminal objectives, component skills, and prerequisite skills.
7　Within sets of terminal, component, and prerequisite tasks sharing a common task format, determine which pairs of concepts and/or operations lead to tasks that are more alike and/or which are more difficult because of their length.
8　Modify initial teaching concepts (or operations or rules) as needed to reduce shared characteristics or to simplify them.
9　Use the basic principles for teaching concepts and operations to produce and sequence tasks. (See unit 11.)
10　Evaluate the program.

UNIT 11. Sequencing Tasks in Programing

In sequencing *concepts* within related sets, the programer needs to keep these principles in mind:

1　Begin with one pair of concepts and add new members to the set one at a time, always bringing the set to criterion before going on.
2　Where concepts have many shared characteristics and few or small differences, more teaching is required or the initial teaching concepts must be modified.
3　Concepts that are easier to discriminate from each other should be taught before those more difficult to discriminate.
4　Pairs of concepts likely to be confused should be separated from each other in the program.

In sequencing *tasks* to teach specific concepts, the programer should keep these principles in mind:

1　A set of positive and negative instances is required.
2　The set should be designed so that all positive instances possess all relevant characteristics and all negative instances possess only some or none of them.
3　Irrelevant characteristics within positive and negative instances must be varied to avoid teaching misrules.

Additional programing principles should consider the values a concept characteristic can take on. When a concept characteristic can take on more than one value, it is said to have *range*. When a concept characteristic has only one value, it is said to be *fixed*. The values of S+ and S− together form a set of values that are the instances of a higher-order concept. For example, if instances of red are S+, and instances of blue, green, and so forth are S−, together the S+ and S− instances are S+ for the higher-order concept "color." The values of Si characteristics are one whole set by themselves. Irrelevant characteristics (Si) are instances of concepts that are independent of the concept being taught.

The principle of *focus* states: focus attention on critical discriminations by changing one thing at a time. Four subrules help to specify the focus principle:

1 If there is more than one essential characteristic, begin with the characteristic that will lead to the greatest reduction in alternative possibilities.
2 To teach a fixed characteristic, switch from an instance to a not-instance, changing only the fixed characteristic.
3 To teach the range of S+ or S−, present a series of instances (or not-instances) in which nothing changes but the value of S+ or S−.
4 To teach the range of irrelevant characteristics, present a series of instances or not-instances in which only the values of the irrelevant characteristics change.

The principle of *interpolation* states: in teaching a characteristic that has a range of values, sample the range with at least three instances, but do not be exhaustive. The student is taught the logical rule: "The range shown is a sample. Interpolate."

The principle of *extrapolation* states: in teaching a characteristic that has a range of values, sample the range of positive instances and then show the boundary starting the range of negative instances. The student is taught the logical rule: "Any negative instance more different than those demonstrated must also be a negative instance."

The principle of *comparison* states: facilitate the ready comparison of positive and negative instances. This can be accomplished by:

1 Changing one thing at a time, as in the focus procedures.
2 Using simultaneous rather than successive presentation.
3 Presenting carefully chosen pairs of instances and not-instances.

When the target of the programing is the teaching of operations rather than concepts, the key teaching procedures involve prompting, differential reinforcement, and fading of prompts. It is important to build sets of tasks involving related operations to be differentiated from each other and to vary irrelevant response characteristics by the way in which examples are chosen.

The choice of prompts and fades starts with "good guesses" which must then be empirically tested out. If, when a fade is introduced, errors occur that are not easily eliminated, then smaller steps in removing the fade should be considered.

Another major consideration in sequencing tasks to teach operations is the difficulty of specific tasks. Tasks may be more difficult because the response is longer or because shared characteristics lead to confusions with other tasks.

UNIT 12. Intelligence, Retardation, and Teaching

The behavior tested by intelligence tests proves on examination to consist largely of concepts and operations that can be taught. This means that intelligent behavior can be taught. It is therefore reasonable to assume that teachers can make children "smarter."

Intellectual retardation varies in severity. More severely retarded children typically have defective nervous systems for one reason or another. A variety of physiological causes for retardation have been identified. In many cases, retardation can be prevented by early action or better medical care. The majority of children labeled retarded have IQs above 50 and have no identifiable physiological or physical defects. Often they come from families where other persons are labeled retarded. These "familial" retardates are a current source of controversy. Is the basic cause heredity or environment? How much does each contribute? Phrasing the problem in this way is of little use to the teacher. The answer to the question will not tell the teacher how to teach a given child. A more appropriate question is, "How far can teachers go in improving the mental capabilities of children labeled retarded, using a given teaching procedure?" The answer must come from the analysis of experimental teaching programs. Current evidence does not show that all or most retarded children can be made normal in intelligence. Some studies suggest, however, that systematic teaching following the model outlined in this text offers some promise.

Heber found that enriched instruction in the first six years with children whose mothers were retarded produced a 30-point IQ advantage. Englemann and Becker found that children with IQs under 80 can gain more than a year in reading and math yearly when effective instruction is provided. Other findings from Follow Through, which provides for comprehensive and intensive school programs at beginning levels, indicate that disadvantaged children can be effectively taught using modern behavioral technology. It is no longer reasonable to assume that children do not learn because they are "dumb." It is necessary to examine teaching methods more carefully in order to determine why children fail. With systematic instruction, starting where the child is, building step-by-step on solid ground, and using good motivational procedures, the relation of IQ to gains made from instruction is found to decrease. Who can be taught what is best determined by actually trying to teach with the best methods available.

UNIT 13.   A Comparison of Piaget's Cognitive-Developmental Theory with Behavior Theory

The cognitive theorist wants to understand thinking and how it develops. Through the study of children at various ages, an attempt is made to describe the major features of cognitive structures as they change with age. In the work of Piaget, this approach has led to the description of a series of developmental stages that grow one into the other. In the sensorimotor stage, thinking is doing. All thinking begins as overt behavior which slowly comes to be represented by signs and symbols for actions. In the preoperational stage there is a differentiation between signifiers and the things signified. Thought and action are separated as language develops, but the child still lacks an understanding of causal processes. In the stage of concrete operations, an understanding of what-leads-to-what is achieved but is restricted to dealing with the real. Only in the stage of formal operations can the child deal with the hypothetical and perform operations upon operations.

The stages of mental development described by Piaget represent steps taken by the child in approaching the most flexible and mobile forms of mature thinking. Concepts and operations are the key components of mature forms of thinking. Piaget has noted a formal similarity in the structure of concepts and operations (schemas). Both involve what is common to a set of events (invariants), and examples of both have irrelevant characteristics (variants).

The behaviorist is concerned with the study of action. He is furthermore concerned with identifying those environmental variables (classes of stimuli) that lead to changes in behavior (social development). To find out what-leads-to-what, an experimental method is used in which independent variables are varied one at a time so that their effects can be studied. In approaching the problem of thinking, the behaviorist extrapolates from what is known about observable behavior and assumes the same processes are involved in behavior that cannot be observed. Explicit procedures have been identified for teaching concepts, operations, rules, principles, and problem-solving skills. The behavioral structures that can be built through using these procedures meet all of the requirements of flexibility and mobility characteristic of mature thought as described by Piaget.

A major difference between the cognitive-development and behavioral approaches is that the former is concerned with *describing* how cognitive structures develop while the latter is concerned with *developing* cognitive structures. However, there is a remarkable convergence in the actual concept of concepts and operations in both positions.

The weakness in the cognitive-developmental approach *as a basis for a theory of instruction* is its lack of concern with the processes and variables that can be used to induce learning. Thus, the teacher is not given the specifics needed to build cognitive structures. It should be noted, however, that instruction was (and is) of little concern to Piaget. The attempts to make Piaget's work the basis for a theory of instruction have been the responsibility of American educators. However, even without causal principles, Piaget's descriptive work does have implications for educational goals and methods. When coupled with knowledge of learning processes, Piaget's work has made important contributions to educational practice.

UNIT 14. Implications for Education

The current technology of instruction can provide a basis for rational solutions to the problems widespread in education today. Education can be better. We need to throw away many labels used as excuses for teaching failures and look more closely at the process of instruction to be sure teaching is happening.

Educational practice has seen one series of fads after another. In the absence of effective procedures, this is to be expected. In the current push toward mainstreaming in special education, we must analyze the requirements for effective instruction of each child and stay flexible. Use special classes when they are the only way to get the job done, and get rid of them whenever possible.

Better procedures are available for the positive motivation and management of children in schools. Systematic programs for training all teachers in positive management procedures are likely to greatly benefit children and teachers alike.

Empirical and logical principles are available for designing curricula that will efficiently teach intelligent behaviors. Many basic programs using these principles have been designed or are in tryout stages. More are needed, as are programs focusing on principles critical to the solutions of personal, social, and environmental problems. One can foresee quantum jumps in the quality of instructional programs in the coming decade. Tied to new programs will be systematic monitoring and management systems that will keep the teacher informed of student progress. It will no longer be necessary to let children fail before the school system finds out about a problem.

With effective programs and adequate training, teachers can reasonably agree to be accountable for the learning of their students, just as other professions assume an accountability for their services. We must be careful, however, not to unfairly impose accountability without providing adequate training and effective programs.

review exercises

UNIT 9

1 What are the three types of stimulus properties possessed by concept instances and not-instances?

2 Define Sc and give an example.

3 What determines whether a characteristic is S+ or Sc?

4 Define *stimulus generalization*.

5 Give an example of stimulus generalization.

6 How does stimulus generalization differ from the "generalization" involved in responding to "new" members of a concept class?

7 Specify three factors that influence the occurrence of stimulus generalization.

8 Give one example to illustrate each of the three factors influencing stimulus generalization.

9 What are some of the things a programer might do to reduce the probability of stimulus generalization occurring?

10 Define two types of concept analysis and give an example of each.

11 Relate matter, space, and time to the five concept domains.

12 What is a concept hierarchy?

13 Give an example of a hierarchy.

14 When concepts are ordered into hierarchies, why is it important to teach two levels at one time?

15 What are the goals for the programer in analyzing concept structure?

16 What are the goals for the programer in analyzing pairs of concepts in a related set?

17 Give examples of how the structure of concept domains influences programing (or teaching).

18 Give examples of how the structure of concept hierarchies influences programing (or teaching).

19 Suppose your concept universe involves only instances of ponies, horses, dogs, fish, and snakes. Analyze the possible S+, Sc, and Si characteristics for each of these groups of concept instances. (Hint: Start by making a hierarchy.)

20 Do a pair-by-pair analysis of the number symbols

$$4, 7, 1, \text{ and } 6$$

to determine the order of similarity (or discriminability index). Use the method of assigning weights to component parts suggested in the text.

21 Piaget has argued that the mental development proceeds from the immediate dealing with objects (sensorimotor stage), through a preoperational stage where there is much language development, through a stage of concrete operations, and on to a stage of formal operations where hypothetical and causal thinking occur. Central to this stage theory is that later stages build on earlier ones. The earlier stages are essential to the later ones. How might the five domains discussed in this unit be used as a basis for a stage theory of mental development?

UNIT 10

1 In what two areas are logical analyses of concepts used in programing?

2 What additional analysis of tasks is also important in programing?

3 Relate your answer to question 2 to the analysis of component operations as discussed in unit 5.

4 What steps should be considered before actually starting to design a program?

5 How do the terminal cognitive objectives differ from the terminal behavioral objects of a program?

6 Analyze the following terminal objectives into component skills involving related sets of concepts and operations:
   a) When asked, the student will count to any number up to 20 by ones.
   b) The student will solve any problem of the form $3 + 4 = \square$ with sums under 11 using a set of problem-solving operations (not by simple discrimination learning).
   c) The student will write a story of ten sentences or more about a field trip.

7 a) Give a general task format for counting to a number.
   b) Take another subskill found in question 6b and write a general task format for it.

8 Specify the prerequisite skills for the general formats written in question 7.

9 Draw a program sequence chart for the 6b analysis, including preskills.

10 Do a concept pair analysis of *over—under*, *on—over*, and *inside—outside*.

11 Give some examples of how initial teaching concepts might be modified to decrease shared characteristics between concepts.

12 Give four criteria for evaluating a program.

13 Explain why this is an efficient format: "This is a ball. This ball is red. What color is it?"

UNIT 11

1 State four principles or procedures that serve as guidelines in sequencing the introduction of concepts within a related set.

2 How do you determine whether concepts are easier to discriminate from each other? Give an example.

3 How do you handle pairs of concepts likely to be confused with each other in the program?

4 Give three requirements to consider in building a set of tasks to teach specific concepts.

5 Define the term *range of values* with respect to concept characteristics.

6 Define the term *fixed value* with respect to concept characteristics.

7 What does it mean to say that S+ and S– together form one whole set?

8 What does it mean to say that the values of any Si form one whole set?

9 State the focus principle.

10 State a rule for teaching a fixed characteristic.

11 State a rule for teaching a range within S+ or S–.

12 State a rule for teaching the range of irrelevant characteristics.

13 State the principle of interpolation and give an example.

14 State the principle of extrapolation and give an example.

15 What do you do to facilitate comparison of teaching examples?

16 Why do the authors reject the notion that concept learning involves "generalization" within the concept class?

17 Why is the procedure of converting instances into not-instances or new instances especially valuable to the teacher?

18 Give five requirements to be considered in selecting and sequencing tasks to teach operations.

19 How does the programer decide on what prompts to use and how to fade them in teaching operations?

20 Name two factors that determine task difficulty in teaching operations and give an example of each.

21 Take the sounds m, n, a, b, p, and c. Do a pairs analysis of the stimulus properties of the letters and suggest an order of introducing each new sound in a cumulative set based on this analysis.

22 Take the set of closed geometric figures (which includes squares, triangles, parallelograms, circles, rectangles, and ovals). Within this set (universe), design a sequence of tasks to teach the concept rectangle (vs. not-rectangles).

UNIT 12

1 Defend the statement that tests of intelligence are primarily measures of the concepts and operations that a child has been taught (or has learned on his own).

2 List three bases for saying that a child is retarded.

3 Name three levels of retardation and give the important characteristics of each.

4 Name two causes of retardation that can be treated or prevented.

5 Why do some people believe that some types of retardation may be due to heredity? Why do other people question this?

6 Why is Jensen's concern with the extent to which heredity or environment influences intelligence of little importance to the teacher?

7 How do you find out who can be taught what?

8 What kinds of changes in IQ did Engelmann observe in disadvantaged children after two years of direct teaching?

9 Describe Heber's study of children with retarded mothers. What was the outcome?

10 What kinds of gains in achievement did Engelmann and Becker find in their study of low IQ children in Follow Through?

11 What kinds of gains did Engelmann and Becker find for poor children in their Follow Through Program on the Wide Range Achievement Test?

12 Describe the E-B Follow Through scores on the Metropolitan Achievement Test in Reading.

13 What are the two conclusions that can be drawn from the data presented on the University of Kansas Follow Through Model?

14 How is IQ related to learning in the traditional classroom? How might this relationship be changed?

UNIT 13

1 What is the *convergence* discussed by the authors between Piaget's cognitive theory and behavior theory?

2 Define cognition.

3 Critique this assumption: What a man knows cannot be reduced to previously learned S - R connections since cognitive structures (the basis of thinking) always modify stimulus inputs.

4 Critique this assumption: Thinking is a determinant of action.

5 Critique this assumption: Unless we assume that cognitive structures modify stimulus inputs and add the "creative" component to behavior, there is no way to account for man's ability to deal with the new and to show novel behavior.

6 What is the basic difference in methodology between Piaget's approach to the study of cognitive processes and the behavioral approach?

7 Describe the four major stages in Piaget's theory of development, indicating a central feature of each stage.

8 Stage theories imply certain developments have to occur *before* others can. Give examples to show where and how the behavioral programer has similar concerns.

9 What does Piaget mean by a "concept" of grasping?

10 How can the concern with teaching sets of related concepts as sets be related to Piaget's descriptions of cognitive structures?

11 Specify S+, S–, and Si for the concept "relative perspective."

12 Give five shortcomings of cognitive-developmental theory as a basis for a theory of instruction.

13 Give positive contributions of Piaget's work to education.

UNIT 14

1 How do you know who can be taught?

2 How are most learning disabilities defined? What kind of explanation is "learning disability"?

3 What is "minimal brain damage"? How is it detected?

4 What are the educational implications of the concept "minimal brain damage"?

5 What are the potential dangers in the push toward "mainstreaming"?

6 Why do you suppose education is so subject to fads?

7 What are some of the weaknesses and dangers of special classes?

8 Just where might special classes be needed most?

9 What approach do the authors suggest for retraining teachers in more effective classroom management procedures?

10 How does the design of Engelmann's *Corrective Reading Program* differ from traditional approaches to corrective reading?

11 How do the approaches to curriculum design recommended in this book differ from traditional textbook approaches?

12 Suggest some areas in education where new curricula may be needed.

13 What are the major shortcomings of most management systems in education?

14 How might these problems be overcome?

15 Under what two conditions is it reasonable for teachers to assume accountability for the success of their students?

references

Unit 1

1 H. S. Broudy, "Historic Exemplars of Teaching Method." In N. L. Gage (ed.) *Handbook of Research on Teaching* (Chicago: Rand McNally, 1963).

2 L. S. Stephens, *The Teacher's Guide to Open Education* (New York: Holt, Rinehart, and Winston, 1974), p. 26.

3 Ibid., p. 19.

4 R. C. Atkinson, "Computerized Instruction and the Learning Process," *American Psychologist*, 1968, 23, pp. 225–39.

5 R. C. Atkinson, "Teaching Children to Read Using a Computer," *American Psychologist*, 1974, 29, pp. 169–78.

6 R. G. Scanlon, "Individually Prescribed Instruction." In W. C. Becker (ed.), *An Empirical Basis for Change in Education* (Chicago: Science Research Associates, 1971), pp. 502–3.

7 S. Engelmann and E. Bruner, *Distar Reading Level I* (Chicago: Science Research Associates, 1968), p. 60 (Book B).

8 W. C. Becker and S. Engelmann, *Summary Analyses of Five-Year Data on Achievement and Teaching Progress with 14,000 in 20 Projects, Technical Report 73-2* (Eugene, Oregon: University of Oregon Follow Through Project), December, 1973.

9 This discussion is parallel to one presented by Cronbach in which education is viewed as a three-stage rocket. The first stage involves training (direct instruction) in basic skills; the second stage focuses on intelligent analysis and problem solving; and the third stage on creative, self-expressive production. *See* L. J. Cronbach, "Comments on Mastery Learning and Its Implications for Curriculum Development." In E. W. Eisner (ed.), *Confronting Curriculum Reform* (Boston: Little, Brown, and Company, 1971), pp. 52–55.

Unit 4

1 K. S. Lashley, "The Mechanism of Vision: XV. Preliminary Studies of the Rat's Capacity for Detail Vision," *Journal of General Psychology*, 1938, 18, pp. 123–293.

———, "An Examination of the 'Continuity Theory' as Applied to Discrimination Learning," *Journal of General Psychology*, 1942, 26, pp. 241–65.

G. S. Reynolds, "Attention in the Pigeon," *Journal of Experimental Analysis of Behavior*, 1961, 4, pp. 203–8.

2 L. E. Moon and H. F. Harlow, "Analysis of Oddity Learning by Rhesus Monkeys," *Journal of Comparative and Physiological Psychology*, 1955, 48, pp. 188–94.

H. F. Harlow, "Learning Set and Error Factor Theory." In S. Koch (ed.), *Psychology, A Study of a Science*, vol. 1 (New York: McGraw-Hill, 1959).

3 C. B. Ferster and C. F. Hammer, Jr., "Synthesizing the Components of Arithmetic Behavior." In W. K. Honig (ed.), *Operant Behavior* (New York: Appleton-Century-Crofts, 1966), pp. 634–76.

4 Ibid.

5 S. Engelmann, *Conceptual Learning* (San Rafael, Calif.: Dimensions Publishing Co., 1969).

Unit 5

1 D. M. Baer, R. F. Peterson, and J. A. Sherman, "The Development of Imitation by Reinforcing Behavioral Similarity to a Model," *Journal of Experimental Analysis of Behavior*, 1967, 10, pp. 405–16.

2 N. Chomsky, "Verbal Behavior." In B. F. Skinner *Language*, 1959, 35, pp. 26–58.

3 D. Guess, W. Sailor, G. Ruthorford, and D. M. Baer, "An Experimental Analysis of Linguistic Development: the Productive Use of the Plural Morpheme," *Journal of Applied Behavior Analysis*, 1968, 1, pp. 297–306.

4 W. Sailor, "Reinforcement and Generalization of Productive Plural Allomorphs in Two Retarded Children," *Journal of Applied Behavior Analysis*, 1971, 4, pp. 305–310.

5 S. Twardosz and D. M. Baer, "Training Two Severely Retarded Adolescents to Ask Questions," *Journal of Applied Behavior Analysis*, 1973, 6, pp. 655–61.

6 D. M. Baer and D. Guess, "Receptive Training of Adjectival Inflections in Mental Retardates," *Journal of Applied Behavior Analysis*, 1971, 4, pp. 129–39.

7 B. Hart and T. Risley, "Establishing Use of Descriptive Adjectives in the Spontaneous Speech of Disadvantaged Preschool Children," *Journal of Applied Behavior Analysis*, 1968, 1, pp. 109–20.

Unit 6

1 R. M. Gagné, *The Conditions of Learning*, 2nd edition (New York: Holt, Rinehart and Winston, 1965).

2 D. W. Carnine, "A Comparison of Rule Teaching and Discovery Learning," Eugene, Oregon: University of Oregon, unpublished manuscript, 1974.

3 R. C. Anderson and R. W. Kulhavy, "Learning Concepts from Definition," *American Educational Research Journal*, 1973, *9*, pp. 385–90.

4 S. M. Markle and P. W. Tiemann, "Some Principles of Instructional Design at Higher Cognitive Levels." In R. Ulrich, T. Stachnik, and J. Mabry (eds.), *Control of Human Behavior*, vol. 3 (Glenview, Illinois: Scott, Foresman, 1974), pp. 312–23.

5 S. Engelmann, *Conceptual Learning* (San Rafael, Calif.: Dimensions Publishing Co., 1969).

6 Markle and Tiemann, *op. cit.*, note 4.

7 T. Jobling and L. Secrest, Unpublished study described by Markle and Tiemann, *op. cit.*, note 4.

8 S. Engelmann and D. W. Carnine, *Distar Arithmetic I* (Chicago, Illinois: Science Research Associates, 1970).

————, *Distar Arithmetic Level II* (Chicago, Illinois: Science Research Associates, 1971).

————, *Distar Arithmetic Level III* (Chicago, Illinois: Science Research Associates, 1972).

9 S. Engelmann and S. Stearns, *Distar Reading Level III, Reading to Learn* (Chicago, Illinois: Science Research Associates, 1972).

Unit 7

1 W. Kohler, *The Mentality of Apes* (New York: Harcourt Brace, 1925), p. 27.

2 H. G. Birch, "The Relation of Previous Experience to Insightful Problem Solving," *Journal of Comparative Psychology*, 1945, *38*, pp. 367–83.

3 R. M. Gagné, "Learning Hierarchies," *Educational Psychologist*, 1968, *6*, pp. 1–9.

4 L. S. Shulman, "Psychological Controversies in the Teaching of Science and Mathematics," *Science Teacher*, 1968, *35*, pp. 34–38 and 89–90.

5 J. S. Bruner, J. J. Goodnow, and G. A. Austin, *A Study of Thinking* (New York: Wiley, 1956).

6 E. M. Goetz and D. M. Baer, "Social Control of Form Diversity and the Emergence of New Forms in Children's Block-Building," *Journal of Applied Behavior Analysis*, 1973, *6*, pp. 209–17.

7 K. B. Maloney and B. L. Hopkins, "The Modification of Sentence Structure and Its Relationship to Subjective Judgments of Creativity in Writing," *Journal of Applied Behavior Analysis*, 1973, *6*, pp. 425–33.

Unit 10

1 S. Engelmann and J. Osborn, *Teacher's Guide for Distar Language Level I* (Chicago: Science Research Associates, 1969), p. 60.

2 S. Engelmann and J. Osborn, *Distar Language Level I* (Chicago: Science Research Associates, 1969); Book C, p. 150; Book A, p. 16.

3 S. Engelmann and E. Bruner, *Distar Reading Level I, Related Skills Book* (Chicago: Science Research Associates, 1968), p. 11.

4 S. Engelman and E. Bruner, *Teacher's Guide for Distar Reading I*, revised (Chicago: Science Research Associates, 1974), p. 12.

Unit 12

1 L. J. Cronbach, *Essentials of Psychological Testing* (New York: Harper and Brothers, 1949), p. 103.

2 L. M. Terman and M. A. Merrill, *Stanford-Binet Intelligence Scale Form L-M* (Boston: Houghton-Mifflin, 1960), p. 19.

3 Ibid., p. 20.

4 Ibid., p. 21.

5 Ibid., p. 25.

6 Ibid., p. 27.

7 Ibid., p. 30.

8 Ibid., p. 35.

9 E. Zigler, "Familial Mental Retardation: A Continuing Dilemma," *Science*, 1967, *155*, pp. 292–98.

10 A. R. Jensen, "The Culturally Disadvantaged and the Heredity-Environment Uncertainty." In J. Hellmuth (ed.), *Disadvantaged Child*, vol. 2 (New York: Brunner/Mazel, 1968), pp. 27–76.

11 E. W. Gordon, "Introduction." In J. Hellmuth (ed.), *Disadvantaged Child*, vol. 2 (New York: Brunner/Mazel, 1968), p. 9.

12 L. A. Dexter, "On the Politics and Sociology of Stupidity in Our Society." In H. S. Becker (ed.), *The Other Side*. (New York: Free Press, 1964), pp. 37–49.

13 J. S. Birnbrauer, "Preparing 'Uncontrollable' Retarded Children for Group Instruction." Paper read at the American Educational Research Association Convention, New York, 1967.

J. S. Birnbrauer, M. M. Wolf, J. D. Kidder, and C. E. Tague, "Classroom Behavior of Retarded Pupils with Token Reinforcement," *Journal of Experimental Child Psychology*, 1965, 2, pp. 219–35.

14 R. Heber, H. Garber, S. Harrington, C. Hoffman, and D. Falender, *Rehabilitation of Families at Risk for Mental Retardation*, Progress Report, December, 1972 (Madison, Wisc.: Rehabilitation Research and Training Center in Mental Retardation, 1972).

15 J. M. Hunt, *Intelligence and Experience* (New York: Ronald Press, 1961).

16 W. Dennis and P. Najarian, "Infant Development under Environmental Handicap," *Psychological Monographs*, 1957, 71, No. 7, pp. 60–61.

Y. Sayegh and W. Dennis, "The Effect of Supplementary Experience upon the Behavioral Development of Infants in Institutions," *Child Development*, 1965, 36, pp. 81–90.

17 W. C. Becker and S. Engelmann, *Achievement Gains of Disadvantaged Children with IQs under 80 in Follow Through. Technical Report 74-2* (Eugene, Oregon: University of Oregon Follow Through Project, October, 1974).

18 S. Engelmann, "The Effectiveness of Direct Instruction on IQ Performance and Achievement in Reading and Arithmetic." In J. Hellmuth (ed.), *Disadvantaged Child*, vol. 3 (New York: Brunner/Mazel, 1971).

19 L. Di Lorenzo and R. Salter, "An Evaluation Study of Prekindergarten Programs for Educationally Disadvantaged Children: A Follow-up and Replication Study." Paper presented at the meeting of the American Educational Research Association, February 10, 1968.

E. L. Erickson, J. McMillan, J. Bonnell, L. Hoffman, and O. D. Callahan, "Experiments in Head Start and Early Education: Curriculum Structures and Teacher Attitudes," final report, OEO contract 4150, November, 1969.

20 *Interim report on the evaluation of Follow Through: An experimental program for early education of disadvantaged children* (Washington, D. C.: HEW, Office of Education, Follow Through Evaluation Section, June, 1974).

21 W. C. Becker and S. Engelmann, *Summary Analyses of Five-Year Data on Achievement and Teaching Progress with 14,000 Children in 20 Projects. Technical Report 73-2* (Eugene, Oregon: University of Oregon Follow Through Project, December, 1973).

22 W. C. Becker and S. Engelmann, *Some Controlled Within-Site Comparisons. Technical Report 1974-1* (Eugene, Oregon: University of Oregon Follow Through Project, December, 1973).

23 Becker and Engelmann, *Technical Report 73-2*, note 21.

24 W. C. Becker, "Early Indications of Positive Outcomes." Paper delivered at the Educational Staff Seminar, George Washington University, Washington, D. C., February 14, 1974.

25 *Education as Experimentation—Evaluation of the Follow Through Planned Variation Model*, vol. 1A, *Early Effects* (Cambridge, Mass.: Abt Associates, 1974).

26 B. S. Bloom, "Time and Learning," *American Psychologist*, 1974, 29, pp. 682–88.

27 W. C. Becker, "Some Necessary Conditions for the Controlled Study of Achievement and Aptitude." In D. R. Greene (ed.), *The Aptitude-Achievement Distinction* (Monterey, Calif.: CTB McGraw-Hill, 1974).

Unit 13

1 J. Piaget, *The Origins of Intelligence in Children*, translated by Margaret Cook (New York: Int. University Press, 1952), pp. 214–15.

2 J. Piaget, *Judgment and Reasoning in the Child*, (Paterson, N.J.: Littlefield, Adams and Company, 1959), pp. 84–5.

3 D. W. Carnine, "Teaching Implications of Selecting, Sequencing, and Modifying Task Stimuli," unpublished manuscript, Eugene, Oregon: University of Oregon, 1974.

4 J. H. Flavell, *The Developmental Psychology of Jean Piaget* (Princeton, N.J.: D. Van Nostrand Company, 1963), p. 54.

5 Piaget, *The Origins of Intelligence in Children*, p. 385.

6 J. Piaget and B. Inhelder, *The Child's Conception of Space* (London: Routledge and Kegan Paul, 1956), p. 292.

7 Ibid., pp. 226–27.

8 W. D. Rohwer, P. R. Ammon, and P. Cramer, *Understanding Intellectual Development* (Hinsdale, Ill.: The Dryden Press, 1974).

9 J. M. Hunt, *Intelligence and Experience* (New York: The Ronald Press, 1961).

B. Inhelder and J. Piaget, *The Growth of Logical Thinking from Childhood to Adolescence* (New York: Basic Books, 1958).

J. Piaget, *The Construction of Reality in the Child* (New York: Basic Books, 1954).

———, *The Child's Conception of the World* (Paterson, N.J.: Littlefield, Adams, 1960).

———, *The Moral Judgment of the Child* (New York: Collier, 1962).

B. Inhelder and J. Piaget, *The Early Growth of Logic in the Child* (New York: Norton, 1964).

J. Piaget, *Plays, Dreams, and Imitation in Childhood* (New York: Norton, 1962).

———, *The Origins of Intelligence in Children* (New York: Norton, 1963).

———, *The Child's Conception of Time* (New York: Ballantine, 1971).

———, *The Child's Conception of Number* (New York: Norton, 1965).

———, *The Child's Conception of Physical Causality* (Paterson, N.J.: Littlefield, Adams, 1965).

———, *The Child's Conception of Movement and Speed* (New York: Basic Books, 1970).

———, *The Child's Conception of Space* (New York: Norton, 1967).

J. Piaget, B. Inhelder, and A. Szeminska, *The Child's Conception of Geometry* (New York: Harper and Row, 1964).

Unit 14

1 W. C. Becker, "Applications of Behavior Principles in Typical Classrooms." In *Behavior Modification, 1973,* the seventy-second yearbook of the National Society for the Study of Education (Chicago: National Society for the Study of Education, 1973).

2 H. M. Walker and N. K. Buckley, *Token Reinforcement Techniques* (Eugene, Oregon: E-B Press, 1974).

3 S. Engelmann, W. C. Becker, L. Carnine, L. Meyers, J. Becker, and G. Johnson, *The Corrective Reading Program* (Chicago: Science Research Associates, 1975).

glossary

Because this second volume on teaching builds on the first volume, we have repeated in this glossary many basic terms although their use in volume 2 is minimal.

attitude   The feelings one has about some class of stimulus events.

attention signal   Indicates who is to attend when.

aversive stimulus   A stimulus that decreases behavior when it is presented as a consequence (a punishing stimulus). A stimulus, the *contingent removal* of which increases the rate of behavior (a negative reinforcer). In common language, a painful, intensive, unpleasant stimulus.

baseline   A measured behavioral performance taken over many observations against which the effects of experimental variables can be assessed (also called "base rate" or "operant level").

behavior   Any observable and measurable act of an organism; a response.

behavior chain   A series of alternating discriminative stimuli (S^D's) and responses. S^D's in a chain function as discriminative stimuli for responses that follow them and as conditioned reinforcers for preceding responses.

cause   An antecedent event that reliably (consistently) produces an effect. If A, then B.

cognition   An unobservable internal event that refers to the act of knowing.

component operation   The links in a chain of operations; each must be under the control of a separate stimulus (class).

concept   A set of stimulus characteristics common to a group of stimulus instances and not common to other instances of a specified universe.

concept hierarchy   An ordering of concepts involving a common set of instances based on the rule that concepts higher in the hierarchy contain more instances than concepts lower in the hierarchy.

concept instances   Examples of a concept.

concept not-instances   Examples of a concept other than that being taught.

concept pair analysis   An analysis to determine the ways in which pairs are the same and the ways in which they are different, e.g., police dog and wolf have more common characteristics and fewer differences than police dog and ice cream cone.

concept structure analysis   An analysis to identify shared characteristics, e.g., polar concepts like hot-cold and wet-dry share the property of being two-member sets, such that if you know it is not one, it must be the other.

concept universe   A specified set of concepts to be discriminated from each other at the completion of a teaching program.

conditioned punisher   A formerly neutral stimulus that acquires the properties of a punishing stimulus as a result of its being presented repeatedly just before another aversive stimulus.

conditioned reinforcer   A formerly neutral stimulus that has repeatedly preceded a reinforcer and functions to strengthen or maintain a behavior on which it is contingent.

consequent stimulus   A following stimulus that controls operant behavior by increasing or decreasing its future occurrence.

contingency   A rule that governs the delivery of consequent stimuli: "If, and only if, response A occurs will reinforcer (or punisher) B be given."

contingent reinforcement   A response is specified and a reinforcing consequence is specified to occur only after the response occurs.

continuous reinforcement   Each response is reinforced.

cumulative programing   Two concepts from a related set are taught to criterion. Then new concepts are added one at a time and brought to criterion.

dependent variable   That which is caused by a causal variable. In behavior theory, behaviors are the dependent variables.

differential reinforcement   A process involving reinforcing some responses in the presence of some stimuli and not reinforcing others.

discriminative stimulus (S^D)   A preceding stimulus that sets the occasion in which a certain response is likely to lead to reinforcement. Those responses reinforced in its presence (and not reinforced in its absence) are more likely to occur when the stimulus is presented in the future.

"do it" signal   Specifies who is to respond when.

educable mentally retarded   A classification of a person having an IQ between 50 and 75, and in which there is usually no known cause for the retardation.

extinction The process whereby reinforcers are no longer presented following a response class to be weakened.

extrapolation (in programing) In teaching a characteristic that has a range of values, the range of positive values is shown, and the boundary starting the negative instances is presented. The student will learn that any negative instance more different must also be a negative instance.

fading The gradual removal of a prompt. Also, the gradual removal of components of a token system (or some special reinforcement system) to make it more like an ordinary classroom situation.

fixed value S+ or S– can take on only one value within the set defined by the sum of S– and S+.

focus (in programing) Critical discriminations are taught by changing one thing at a time.

formal operation A one-step rule such as the rules of mathematics and science, e.g., density equals weight divided by volume.

general case (in reference to teaching a concept as a general case) A general case has been taught when after teaching some members of a set, the student responds correctly to any member.

habit chain The stimulus produced in making one response is the cue for the next response. There are no alternative responses.

independent variable That which produces a change in a dependent variable; a cause. In behavior theory, stimulus events are the independent variables.

instruction A set of procedures for producing a change in behavior (learning) toward a prestated objective.

intermittent reinforcement A procedure in which only some correct responses are reinforced.

interpolation (in programing) In teaching a characteristic that has a range of values, at least three instances covering the range are presented, i.e., in teaching *blue*, the teacher shows a variety of blues from near green-blue to violet.

irrelevant characteristics Properties of concept instances and not-instances which are unrelated to their status as concept instances or not-instances.

learning disability A label for children who score average or better on an IQ test but fail to learn in some area as well as expected.

minimal brain damage A label given to explain a learning disability or hyperactive behavior. It is called minimal because it cannot be detected by the usual neurological procedures.

negative reinforcer The termination of a stimulus following a response, which has the effect of strengthening that response class.

operant behavior Involves the striated muscular system, is controlled by consequent stimuli, and is equivalent to voluntary or intelligent behavior.

operation The common effect of a set of behaviors under stimulus control.

physical prompting The teacher physically moves the student through the responses, e.g., takes hand and helps draw a letter.

profoundly mentally retarded A classification of a person who scores from 0 to 25 on an IQ test, usually has physical damage to the brain, and requires custodial care.

program A sequence of tasks.

prompt Previously learned discriminative stimulus which can be used to get a response to occur to a new stimulus. Prompts are eventually faded.

punisher (punishing stimulus) A following stimulus which weakens or decreases the future occurrence of the response class.

punishment The procedure of using a punisher.

R-direction Controls the general form of a task response and usually specifies a response class containing the response being taught.

R-prompt Controls the specific form of the task response.

range of values S+ and S– characteristics can take on more than one value within the set defined by the sum of S+ and S–.

reinforcement The procedure of using a reinforcer.

reinforcer (reinforcing stimulus) A following stimulus which strengthens or increases the future occurrence of the response class.

relevant characteristics The properties that serve to define a concept instance or not-instance.

rule chain Each step in the chain produces the stimuli needed to determine the next step. Alternative responses can be taken at each step, depending on the results of the preceding step.

S– Relevant characteristics of negative instances of a concept.

S+ Relevant characteristics of positive instances of a concept.

S-direction Stimulus which controls attending to the task stimulus, usually by specifying the higher-order class containing the task stimulus.

S-prompt Controls attending to essential aspects of the task stimulus.

Sc Stimulus characteristics common to the instances of two or more concepts, which provide the basis for forming igher-order concepts.

shaping A behavior change procedure involving differential reinforcement and a shifting criterion for reinforcement.

shifting criterion for reinforcement The criterion for reinforcement is initially set at a level that allows for reinforcement of current behavior that is closest to the target behavior. As responses closer to the target behavior are made, the criterion is again shifted. Each time the criterion is shifted, the changed criterion is a little closer to the desired target.

Si Irrelevant characteristics of positive or negative concept instances.

social reinforcer A formerly neutral stimulus that is based on the behavior of a person is presented following a response, and the response occurs more frequently in the future.

stage theory A position that holds that certain developments must occur before others can occur.

stimulus A physical object or event that an organism may respond to.

stimulus control The control of operant behavior by preceding stimuli (discriminative stimuli).

stimulus generalization Responding to a new stimulus in the same way as one was taught to respond to some other stimulus having some common characteristics with the new stimulus.

successive-pairs programing Given a set of related concepts, all possible pairs of concepts are taught as successive pairs, each pair being brought to criterion before the next pair is introduced.

task A stimulus situation that requires a response.

task directions Tell what to do in attending to a task signal or in determining the general form of the task response.

task response An instance of an operation to be performed for a given task.

task stimulus A concept instance that controls an operation.

thinking Talking to ourselves in our heads. Representations of other responses than words may also be used in thinking.

trainable mentally retarded A classification of a person having an IQ between 25 and 50 and who is usually physically handicapped. The trainable mentally retarded may be trained in useful skills, but usually do not live independently.

verbalism Being able to emit the verbal chain that is a rule without knowing the concepts and operations the rule refers to.

author index

subject index

Teaching 2 is set in ten point Palatino, a fresh, graceful typeface by Hermann Zapf, 1950. Typesetting is by Graphic Typesetting Service, Los Angeles, California.

Sponsoring Editor: Karl Schmidt
Project Editor: Carol Harris
Designer: Paula Tuerk

678/432